The Dictionary of Scottish Place Names

The Dictionary of Scottish Place Names

and the elements that go to make them up

Mike Darton

LOCHAR PUBLISHING · MOFFAT · SCOTLAND

© Mike Darton, 1990
Published by Lochar Publishing Limited
MOFFAT   DG10 9JU

British Library Cataloguing in Publication Data
    Darton, Mike
    The dictionary of Scottish place names
    1. Scotland. Place names. Etymology
    I. Title
    914.11003

ISBN 0–948403–48–9

Typeset in 11pt on 13pt Times by Dumfries ITeC
and printed in Great Britain by BPCC Wheaton's Ltd, Exeter.

Introduction

IT IS UNUSUAL for a dictionary to have an Introduction, but this dictionary requires one if for nothing else than to point out that it is more than a simple glossary of names and derivations.

Alongside such names and derivations in this book are *elements*: some are the Gaelic (or Old Norse or Old English) words from which place names in Scotland are made up in combination; others are the corrupt forms of those words as they now appear in the place names. The presence of these elements in both these forms means that to some degree it is theoretically possible to make out the meanings of some Scottish names that are not listed in this book.

But beware! Place names are notoriously subject to folk-etymology (supposed/mythological derivations) by both locals and linguistic 'experts', and subject also to assimilation – by which a name deriving from one language is recast to something that sounds similar in a different language.

And a particular problem with place names in Scotland is that names may derive from any of at least four source-languages. The most common source is, of course, Scottish Gaelic – but even here it is necessary to interject that there are or have been various forms of Scottish Gaelic.

The first form of Gaelic spoken in Scotland, and hence found in place names, was Pictish: a language related to present-day Welsh, Cornish and Breton and technically classified as Brythonic (or Brittonic). Only later did the Scots arrive from Ireland, speaking a related but very different language, today classified as Goidelic. The language the Scots spoke when they arrived, however, itself changed radically over the course of centuries. At first, for example, the Scots did not use the consonant 'p' at all in their speech: words deriving from earlier forms in which 'p' featured instead used 'k' or 'qu' – so that Welsh *pen*, 'head' is Scottish *ceann*, for instance – and for this reason Brythonic is sometimes known as P-Gaelic/P-Celtic and Goidelic as Q-Gaelic/Q-Celtic. It has always amused me that when the man destined to become patron saint of Ireland left the shores of Wales he was called Patrick, but when he arrived in Ireland he was addressed as Cothric.

Dictionary of Scottish Place Names

Since that time, 'p' has taken its rightful place in the Scottish and Irish Gaelic alphabet. (But by now, even Irish and Scottish Gaelic have some basic differences between them.)

Another major influence on place names in Scotland was Old Norse, because of the Viking raids and coastal settlements. Swedes and Danes tended more to raid England, leaving Scotland, the isles and Ireland to the Norwegians. However, relations were not always hostile and indeed many Scottish people of the middle ages – like Macbeth – had both Gaelic and Norse kinfolk. Norse words were borrowed into Gaelic, and thus appear in adapted form (some horrendously so) within place names.

Finally, place names from about that time too began to be in English. Some are early enough to have been coined when Old English was still spoken; rather more derive from Middle English (of, say, Chaucer's time), and of course most names coined today are in modern English unless there is some nationalistic excuse otherwise.

The point about this list of possible sources – and there are of course more than just the four listed above – is that place names tend to appear in groups. As you might expect, for instance, the Old Norse names tend to occur in the north, on the islands or near the coast. Likewise, English names are most common in the south. But there are patches of English names all the way up the east and even in some of the islands. Pictish names are found mostly in Grampian, Tayside and Fife Regions. So for any name that is not immediately obvious as of Scottish Gaelic derivation, some knowledge of other names in the vicinity is essential even if the meaning is apparently plain.

Not all the derivations and meanings given for place names in this dictionary are guaranteed to be correct. That is because this dictionary also goes in for speculation – informed speculation, but theoretical stuff for all that. It would be nice to have the time (and wherewithal) to spend years researching every individual place name on the map – and people have done that kind of life-work study in relation to place names elsewhere – but even after carrying out such a monster enterprise, the most scholarly of researchers may yet have to admit there are names which simply defy unravelling, and words like 'perhaps' and 'possibly' begin to creep in.

A fair proportion of all the derivations in this dictionary are thus included with less than total certainty; in such cases the degree of speculation is, however, always stated.

vi

It is also the case anyway with place names that today's derivation and meaning can all too easily become tomorrow's folk-etymology: over the past decade several place names in Scotland formerly authoritatively given both derivation and meaning have nonetheless been equally authoritatively redefined differently.

At the same time, this dictionary has no pretensions about being complete – extensive, yes, and more complete than perhaps any published to date – but not complete: not every single name on the map is included, although the dictionary is unusual in also containing mountain-, river-, loch- and headland-names. Where there is simply no inkling whatever of the precedents of a name, it is not listed at all (although potentially relevant elements may be listed separately).

Words from which place-name elements are derived are printed in *italic*.

Where such words are Old Norse (ON), Old Swedish (OSw), Old Scandinavian (OScand), Old Danish (ODan) or Old English (OE), Middle English (ME) or even Hebrew (Heb), the language is stated; if no language is stated, the word is Scottish Gaelic (Goidelic). Frequent reference is made to cognates – words of an identical derivation in other languages. Less commonly, names are described as having been back-formed – that is, a geographical feature (a mountain, say) has given its name to one or more other geographical features in the vicinity (a river or a loch, perhaps): such secondary uses of the name are then said to be back-formations, even when the feature to which the name was originally given has since been renamed (and that happens surprisingly often).

All forms of Gaelic have a peculiarity of grammar/syntax by which the initial consonants of words may alter, or 'mutate'. This is especially noticeable in some Scottish place-name elements which mutate in form to correspond with adjacent elements. The following consonants may, as initial consonants, mutate:

b-	to	*bh-*	(pronounced	'v-')
c-		*ch-*	(	'kh-')
[*d-*		*dh-*]		
f-		*fh-*	(NOT PRONOUNCED)	
g-		*gh-*	(NOT PRONOUNCED)	
m-		*mh-*	(pronounced	'v-')
p-		*ph-*	(	'f-')
t-		*th-*	(NOT PRONOUNCED)	

and anglicised versions of elements that have mutated in this way are also common, particularly beginning with 'v-'.

Within the dictionary there are also some special sections relating to the names of particular geographical features as named on the map. They are presented as separate sections because within the ordinary alphabetical sections they would occupy too disproportionate an area. The sections comprise most place-names that begin with the following elements:

abhainn	'river'
allt	'stream'
beinn	'mount[ain]'
carn	'hill'
cnoc	'mountain'
creag	'fell'
cruach	'mountain'
cruachan	'hill'
loch	'lake'
meall	'fell'
sgorr	'mountain'
sgurr	'mountain'
stob	'mountain'
strath	'valley'

but it should be noted that names of human settlements beginning with these elements are covered within the ordinary alphabetical sections (and some therefore occur in both sections).

Interest in the place names of Scotland is high, as one or two inhabitants of that fair country have recognized by publishing considerably smaller glossaries more or less accurate than each other. The number of tourists in Scotland seems to increase annually, few of them knowing more than five or six place-name elements between them, yet willing to find out. There is said to be an enormous volume on the subject due to be published, but no one can say when, nor whether it will contain merely the names of settlements and rivers (in the outstanding way that Ekwall did for England) or whether it will also include mountain names and other elements. Previous more scholarly works have been found now to contain many errors. Altogether, the appearance of this dictionary is timely and, I hope, useful.

Mike Darton
May 1990

viii

A

a' elided form of *an*: 'the', '[of] the'.

-a (also *-o*) elided form of ON å: 'river'. E.g. Lax-a [Shetland].

-a (also *-ay*) elided form of ON Ø/*oey* or OE *ey*: 'island'. E.g. Staff-a.

Abbey St Bathans [Borders] The community is named after the 12th-century abbey here, dedicated to St Columba's successor at Iona: St Baothan of Tiree.

aber- (= Brythonic Gaelic; Goidelic is *inver/inbhear* [Irish *inbhir*]) '(place) where one water meets a greater', 'mouth of the river'. Perhaps cf Latin *aper-* '(to) open', but see also *inver*.

-aber(s) elided form of (Goidelic Gaelic) *abor*: 'marsh'.

Aberchirder [Grampian] 'Mouth (*aber*, Brythonic Gaelic) of the dark (*chiar*, Goidelic Gaelic) water (*dobhar*, Brythonic Gaelic; cf Dover, etc.)'.

Abercorn [Lothian] '(River-)Mouth (*aber*, Brythonic Gaelic) with a horn (*corniog*, 'horned', Brythonic Gaelic)'.

Aberdeen [Grampian] 'Mouth (*aber*, Brythonic Gaelic) of the [River] Don'. Don is an ancient European river name, found from the Urals to the Irish Republic, that means simply 'water'. The modern city is actually now concentrated on the River Dee rather than on the slightly more northerly Don (where the original settlement is now called Old Aberdeen).

Aberdour [Fife] 'Mouth (*aber*, Brythonic Gaelic) of the water (*dobhar*, Brythonic Gaelic; cf Dover, etc.)'.

Aberfeldy [Tayside] '(River-)Mouth (*aber*, Brythonic Gaelic) of [St] Paldoc'. Paldoc was a successor to St Ninian, the Romish bishop to the Picts at the time of the Venerable Bede. (? Cf *Paldoc* with *Patrick*.) An alternative etymological ascription is not to St Paldoc but to the local water-demon *Peallaidh*. Aberfeldy is where the Urlar Burn meets the River Tay.

Aberfoyle [Central] 'Mouth (*aber*, Brythonic Gaelic) of the pool (common Celtic **phuill*; cf Welsh *pwll*)'.

Aberlady [Lothian] 'Mouth (*aber*, Brythonic Gaelic) of [? Our] Lady'. But why should an old element like *aber* be followed by an apparent Anglo-Saxon element like *lady* (Anglo-Saxon *hlaefdige* 'loaf-kneader')? Probably a corruption of something else in Gaelic – although there is a Mary's Chapel there.

9

Dictionary of Scottish Place Names

Aberlemno [Tayside] 'Mouth (*aber*, Brythonic Gaelic) of the Elm [River]'. The name of the elm tree is a common European river name (cf Ulm, Elbe, etc.), appearing in Scottish Gaelic as *leamha(i)n*.

Abernethy [Tayside] 'Mouth (*aber*, Brythonic Gaelic) of the [River] Nethy'. 'Nethy' is perhaps Goidelic Gaelic *an eitghich* 'the gullet' [cf Gk and Eng *oesophagus* and the idea that water rushes through a 'gorge']. Or it may relate historically to the Pictish King Nectan. But both of these are actually less likely than the Brythonic Gaelic river name Nedd (found as Nedd and Neath in Wales, and as Nidd in England), which probably means 'glistening'.

abhain(n) (also *aibhne, aimhne*; Irish also *aw, owen*; Brythonic Gaelic is *afon*; anglicised as *Avon*; cf Scand å) 'river'. Cf also Latin *aqua(t)-* 'water', said to be akin to Gothic *ahwa* 'river' (hence the Scand) and to Goidelic Gaelic *uisge* 'water' (anglicised to *whisky*). See separate list of river names beginning with this element.

Abington [Strathclyde] 'Village (OE *tun* 'enclosure', 'settlement') of Albin'. Albin is more likely to have been a 'noble friend' (OE *ael-wine*) than 'white' (Lat *alban-*) – but Abington is on a Roman road.

Aboyne [Grampian] 'Ford (*ath[a]*) of the cows (*bo*), white (*fhionn*)'. This large town is on the River Dee.

Abune-the-Hill [Orkney] 'Upon (Scots) the hill (Eng)'.

acair 'anchor'. Probably through ON, but cognate with Gk *agkyra* 'anchor' and Gk *aggulos*, Lat *angulus* 'angle', 'hook'; connected therefore ultimately with Indo-European root **akh-* 'sharp-pointed'.

acairseid (also *acarsaid*; ON *akkar-sæti* 'anchor-setting') 'anchorage'.

acarsaid See *acairseid*.

ach-, -ach (elided form of *achadh*, also *achar, auch-*; Irish also *augha*; connected ultimately with Indo-European root **agh(r)-* 'flat place', 'plain', as in Eng *acre* and *agriculture*) 'open space', 'field', 'place'. Cf Greek *agora*.

Acha [Coll] 'Open space (*achadh*)': the tiny village certainly is in one.

achadh 'open space', 'field', 'place'. (Primary form of *ach-*, q.v.)

A' Chailleach [Highland] 'The (*a'*) old woman (*chailleach*: literally 'anyone who might wear a cloak or habit')'.

Achanalt [Highland] 'Field (*achadh*) by the (*na*) stream (*allt*)'.

Achandunie [Highland] Possibly 'Field (*achadh*) of the (*na*) man (*duine*)'.

10

Ach' an Todhair [Highland] 'Place (*achadh*), the [one] (*an*) of manure (*todhair*)'. The word *todhar*, of which *todhair* is the genitive, can also mean 'bleaching'.

achar See *ach-*.

Acharacle [Highland] Apparently 'Ford (*ath[a]*) of Torquil (*Thorcuil*, personal name)'. This is a village on the Ardnamurchan Peninsula where there are several Scandinavian names. Torquil derives from Scandinavian *Thor-kettil* 'Thor's cauldron'.

Acharn [Highland; Tayside] 'Field (*achadh*) of the cairn (*chairn*)'.

Achentoul [Highland] 'Field (*achadh*) of the (*an*) barn (*t-sabhail*)'.

Achgarve [Highland] 'Open space (*achadh*), rough (*garbh*)'.

-achie elided form of *achadh*: 'open space', 'field', 'place'.

Achiltibuie [Highland] Possibly 'Field (*achadh*) of the stream (*allt/uillt*), yellow (*buidhe*)'. Other suggestions for the middle element are: 'Field of the yellow house (*achadh-a'-tigh-buidhe*)' and, apparently the local favourite, 'Field of the yellow[-haired] lad (*achadh-a'-gille-buidhe*).

Achilty [Highland] 'At the high [place] (*uchel* 'high'[Brythonic Gaelic] + locative)'.

achlacainn (also *achlachan*) elided form of the doublet 'ford (*ath[a]*), stony (*clachan*)'.

achlachan See *achlacainn*.

achlais 'armpit'.

Achleck [Mull] 'Field (*achadh*) of flat stones (*leac*)'. Cf **Affleck**.

A' Chleit [Highland] 'The (*a'*) rock (*chleit*, adapted form of ON *klettr*)'. A hazard to shipping 1½ miles off Kirkaig Point.

Achluachrach [Highland] 'Place (*achadh*) of rushes (*luachrach*)'. The village is on the River Spean.

Achmelvich [Highland] Possibly 'Place (*achadh*) [of the] sandbank (*melr*, ON) [in the] bay (*vík*, ON)'. It would be only when the meaning of the name had become forgotten that the bay below the village had the tautologous word 'Bay' tacked on to its name.

Achmore [Highland; Western Isles] 'Open space (*achadh*), big (*mór*)'.

Achnaba [Strathclyde] 'Field (*achadh*) of the (*na*) cow (*bà*, genitive of *bó*)'.

Achnacarnin [Highland] 'Field (*achadh*) of the (*na*) cairns (*carn*)'.

Achnacarry [Highland] 'Field (*achadh*) of the (*na*) fish-trap/weir (*caraidh*)'. Achnacarry is on the short River Arkaig between Loch Arkaig and Loch Lochy.

Achnacloich [Highland] 'Field (*achadh*) of the (*na*) stone (*clach*)'.

Achnadrish [Mull] 'Place (*achadh*) of (*na*) brambles (*dris*)'.

Achnahaird [Highland] 'Place (*achadh*) of the (*na*) height (*h-aird*)'.

Achnahannet [Highland] Probably 'Open space (*achadh*) of the (*na*) watery [place] (*h-annait*)'.

Achnaluachrach [Highland] 'Place (*achadh*) of the (*na*) rushes (*luachrach*)'.

Achnasaul [Highland] 'Place (*achadh*) of the (*na*) barn (*sabhal*)'. The tiny village is on the low-lying shores of Loch Arkaig.

Achnasheen [Highland] 'Field (*achadh*) of the (*na*) storm[s] (*sian*)'. The village is at quite a height up in the mountains, well inland, and does get some dreadful weather.

Achnashellach [Highland] 'Field (*achadh*) of the (*na*) willow (*seileach*)'. Achnashellach is in the valley of the River Carron.

Achray [Central] 'Open space (*achadh*), level (*rèidh*)'. It ought to be 'level' – it's the name of a loch in the Trossachs. But the loch probably took the name of an adjacent field.

A' Chruach [Highland; Tayside; Arran] 'The (*a'*) bold mountain (*cruach*)'.

-achy elided form of *achadh*: 'open space', 'field', 'place'.

Addiewell [Lothian] 'Adam's well'. A late name for a village that really only started in the 1860s.

adri- adaptation of *eader*: 'between'.

advie elided form of *agaidh*: 'gap', 'pass'.

Advie [Highland] 'Pass (*agaidh*)'. The village is in the deepish valley of the River Spey as it passes through the Hills of Cromdale. Cf **Aviemore**.

Affleck [Grampian] 'Field (*achadh*) of flat stones (*leac*)'.

Affric [Highland] Possibly 'Ford (*ath[a]*) of the boar (*bhraich*)'. Other suggestions for the second element include the name of a water-nymph.

agaidh 'gap', 'pass' (primary form of *advie-*, *avie-*). Cognate with Welsh *adwy* 'pass', the word is sometimes alternatively held to mean 'hill-face'.

agh 'hind', 'heifer'.

A' Ghlas-bheinn [Highland] 'The (*a'*) blue-green (*ghlas*) mountain (*bheinn*)'.

aibhne genitive form of *abhain(n)*, thus 'of the river'.

aifreann 'religious offering', 'the mass'. From Latin *offerenda*.

-aig (ON *vágr/vik*; common Germanic, hence English) 'bay/bight', thus 'shelter', 'creek'. Cf the Gaelic loaned equivalents *voe/uig*.

aighe genitive form of *agh*, thus 'of the hind', 'of the heifer'.

aighean plural form of *agh*, thus 'hinds', 'heifers'.

ail (Irish *aill*, *aul* 'cliff') 'rock(y)', 'stone', thus 'stronghold'.

aileach 'rocky', 'stony'.

ailean (also *ailein*, *-aline*) 'a green place', 'meadow', 'pasture'.

ailein See *ailean*.

Ailort [Highland] Possibly 'Rock (*ail*) fjord (Gaelic elision of ON *fjordr*)'. This is the name of the sea-loch, which then became the name of the settlement at the end of the loch. The nearby village of Inverailort seems to have been inaccurately named (q.v.).

aimhne mutated genitive form of *abhain(n)*, thus 'of the river'.

airbhe (also *eirbhe*) 'dividing wall', 'partition', 'boundary'.

aird (also *ard*; Welsh *aran*, *arddu*; cognate with Latin *arduus* 'high', 'steep' [whence English *arduous*] and Greek *ardis* 'point') 'height', 'promontory', 'crag'. As adjective: 'high'.

Aird [Dumfries & Galloway; Western Isles; Mull; etc.] 'The height'.

Aird an Troim [Lewis] Presumably 'Height (*aird*) [of] the ridge (*druim*)'.

Aird Dubh [Highland] 'Height (*aird*), dark (*dubh*)'.

Aird Mheadhonach [Harris] 'Promontory (*aird*) in the middle (*meadhonach*)'. This is the name of a large headland that juts out into the middle of an even larger enclosing bay.

Aird Riabhach [Scalpay] 'Promontory (*aird*), greyish (*riabhach*)'.

Airdrie [Strathclyde] 'High (*aird*) shieling (*ruighe*, literally 'fore-arm', thus 'shieling', 'slope', 'cattle-run')'.

13

Dictionary of Scottish Place Names

Aird Uig [Lewis] 'Promontory (*aird*) bay (*uig*; ON *vík*)'.

airidh(e) See *airigh(e)*.

airigh(e) (also *airidh[e]*) 'shieling'.

airneach 'sloe'.

Airntully [Tayside] Possibly 'Height (*aird*) of the (*na*) hillock (*tulach*)'.

aiseag 'ferry'.

aisir (also *aisridh*) 'rocky pass', 'pass between crags'.

aisridh See *aisir*.

aith elided form of ON *eith* (Eng *eyot*, *ait*) 'isthmus', especially one that becomes an island tidally – hence the slightly different English meaning.

Aith [Orkney; Shetland] 'Isthmus (*eith*, ON)'.

Aithsetter [Shetland] 'Isthmus (*eith*, ON) house (*setr*, ON)'.

aitionn 'juniper'.

-akin (ON) 'of [King] Haakon', the 13th-century king of Norway. The name means '(of) high race'.

alainn 'beautiful'.

ald elided form of *allt*: 'stream', 'burn', 'brook'.

Alexandria [Strathclyde] This town at the foot of Loch Lomond was named after the local MP (for Bonhill) in 1760, Alexander Smollett.

Alford [Grampian] Usually derived as 'ford (*ath[a]*), high (*aird*)' and said to be pronounced locally 'ahferd'. But if the 'l' is unpronounced, there are quite a few other possible Gaelic elements: cf *avie-ord* 'pass of the rounded hill' (and note that Alford is situated at the end of a pass through the Correen Hills) etc.

-aline elided form of *ailean*: 'a green place'.

-alladale 'holy (*halig*, ON) dale (*dalr*, ON)'. The meaning is this even when the elements are preceded by Strath- (*srath*, 'valley').

Allan [Central] River name, probably British and related to Aln, Alne, Ellen and Alwin; the meaning is unknown.

alligin Brythonic element thought (fairly definitively) to contain the early element *ail/all* 'rocky'. Some commentators alternatively derive the meaning 'jewel' – though they decline to explain how.

14

Alloa [Central] Either 'rocky (place)' (*aileach*) or 'rocky (*ail*) plain (*mhagh*)' – which is pretty much the same thing anyway.

Alloway [Strathclyde] Same as **Alloa**.

allt (also *uillt*) 'stream', 'burn', 'brook'. Note that in Welsh *allt* means 'hillside', 'cliff', 'wood'– virtually any kind of topographical description *except* a stream (cf Ger *wald*, Eng *weald*). The word is cognate with Latin *altus*, 'deep', and originally even in Gaelic meant 'height'. See separate list of stream names beginning with this element.

alltan diminutive of *allt*, thus 'little stream', 'streamlet'.

Alltan Dearg [Highland] 'Streamlet (*alltan*), red (*dearg*)'.

Alltan Fhearna [Highland] 'Streamlet (*alltan*) of the alder tree (*fhearna*)'.

Alltchaorunn [Highland] Possibly 'Stream (*allt*) of the rowan trees (plural of *caorann*)'.

Allt na h-Airbhe [Highland] 'Stream (*allt*) of the (*na*) boundary (*airbhe*)'. The *h-* in the name is a linguistic means of separating the two vowels. The tiny village is on a stream that divides the Cailleach peninsula, between the two Loch Brooms, in two. Cf **Altnaharra**.

Almond [Highland; Lothian] This river name is, regrettably, a corruption of *amhain[n]* 'river', the same as **Avon**.

Alness [Highland] Pre-Celtic river name, possibly related to 'Lyne', 'Lune', etc.

alt elided form of *allt*: 'stream', 'burn', 'brook'.

Altandhu [Highland] 'Little stream (diminutive of *allt*), dark (*dubh*)'.

Altnabreac [Highland] 'Stream (*allt*) of the (*na*) trout (*breac*)': it is on the Sleach Water.

Altnacealgach [Highland] 'Stream (*allt*) of the (*na*) deceiver (*cealgach*)'.

Altnaharra [Highland] 'Stream (*allt*) of the (*na*) boundary (*h-airbhe*)'. If ever there was a place suitable for a boundary, Altnaharra is it. Strath Naver, Strath Vagastie and the River Mudale (any or all of which could correspond to the 'stream'), and four ancient roads, all meet there.

Altrua [Highland] 'Stream (*allt*), red (*ruadh*)'.

Alva [Central] 'Rocky (*ail*) plain (*mhagh*)'; cf **Alloa**, of which it is only two miles north.

15

Alves [Grampian] 'Rocky (*ail*) plain (*mhagh*)'; thus the same as **Alva** – but where does the -s come from?

Am Bodach [Highland] 'The (*a-m*) old man (*bodach*)'. The second element can instead mean 'ghost'.

Am Buachaille [Strathclyde] 'The (*a-m*) herdsman (*buachaille*)'.

Am Fraoch Eilean [Inner Hebrides] 'The (*a-m*) heather[y] (*fraoch*) island (*eilean*)'.

amhach 'neck'.

A' Mharconaich [Tayside] 'The (*a'*) place of horses (derivative of *marc*)'.

A' Mhoine [Highland] 'The (*a'*) peat-bed (*mhòine*)'.

Amhuinnsuidhe [Harris] 'River (*amhainn*), level (*suidhe*)'.

Amisfield [Dumfries & Galloway] Apparently 'Amyas's field': one Amyas de Charteris was lord of the manor in early times. 'Amyas' derives from Latin *amatus* 'beloved', and the name of the village is reportedly pronounced 'aimsfield'.

Amulree [Tayside] 'Ford (*ath[a]*) of [Saint] Maelrubha'. It was Maelrubha who in AD 673 founded a monastery at Applecross, q.v.

an 'the', '[of] the'.

-an diminutive suffix; occasionally a plural suffix.

-an occasionally a corruption of (element ending in -*a[dh]*) + *na* 'of (the)' + (element later forgotten).

An Acairseid [Highland] 'The (*an*) anchorage (*acairseid*, corruption from the ON)', and no doubt a useful one too, under the Point of Ardnamurchan.

An Ard [Highland] 'The (*an*) height (*ard*)'. The village of An Ard looks down on the even smaller village of Charlestown on the shore of Loch Gairloch.

An Cabar [Highland] 'The (*an*) antler (*cabar*)'.

An Caol [Raasay] 'The (*an*) narrows (*caol*)'. The word *caol* is better known as 'kyle'.

An Ceann Geal [Highland] 'The (*an*) head (*ceann*), white (*geal*)'. On many maps this appears also as 'Whiten Head'.

An Cearcall [Tayside] 'The (*an*) circle (*cearcall*)': the mountain is relatively ring-shaped.

16

An Chailleach [Highland] 'The (*an*) old woman (*chailleach*, literally 'anyone who wears a cloak or habit')'.

An Coileachan [Highland] 'The (*an*) little cock (diminutive of *coileach*)'.

An Cruachan [Highland] 'The (*an*) little bold mountain (diminutive of *cruach*)'.

Ancrum [Borders] Probably 'The (*an*) bend (*crom*)'. The town sits within a semicircular meander of the Ale Water as it winds down to join the Teviot.

An Cuaidh [Highland] Possibly 'The (*an*) sheep-folds (plural of *cuidhe*, a corrupted form of ON *kví*).

An Dubh-aird [Highland] 'The (*an*) dark (*dubh*) height (*aird*)'.

An Dubh-sgeir [Gigha] 'The (*an*) dark (*dubh*) skerry [i.e. sharp rock] (*sgeir*, a loan-word from ON *sker*)'.

An Dùnan [Jura] 'The (*an*) little mound (diminutive of *dùn*)'. The second element can alternatively mean 'little castle'.

An Garbh-eilean [Highland] 'The (*an*) rough [water] (*garbh*) island (*eilean*)'. It lies about ½ mile off the Cape Wrath peninsula.

An Gead Loch [Highland] 'The (*an*) strip of land (*gead*), loch'.

-angie rare elided form of *innse*, dative of *innis*: 'water-meadow'.

An Grianan [Highland] 'The (*an*) sunny mound (*grianan*)'.

Angus [Tayside] Named after one of the three sons of Erc, pioneer Scottish invader from Ireland: the name means 'unique choice'.

An Iola [Strathclyde] 'The (*an*) fishing-bank (*iola*)'.

An Lairig [Highland] 'The (*an*) pass (*làirig*)'.

An Liathanach [Highland] Possibly 'The (*an*) broad (*leathan*) open space (*ach[adh]*)': it is the name of a long low mountain near Achnasheen. The second element might instead be *liath* 'grey-blue', however.

ann 'water'. Presumably related to *abhain(n)*, q.v.

annaid 'mother church'.

annait 'watery (place)'; the word is related to *ann*, above.

Annan [Dumfries & Galloway] 'The (*an*) water (*ann*)'. The town is on the River Annan close to where it meets the Solway Firth; the name could thus instead mean 'Waters (*ann-an*)'.

17

Dictionary of Scottish Place Names

Annat [Highland; Strathclyde] Both these would seem to derive from *annait* 'watery (place)' rather than *annaid* 'mother church'. Both are villages; the Highland one is on the tidal shore of Little Loch Broom and subject to flooding; the Strathclyde one is on a burn and not far from Loch Awe. Neither appears to have major ecclesiastical connections.

annet elided form of *annaid*: 'mother church'.

An Riabhachan [Highland] 'The (*an*) little brindled [one] (diminutive of *riabhach*)'.

An Sleagach [Highland] 'The (*an*) flat-stoned (*sleac*) place (*ach*)'.

An Socach [Highland; Grampian] 'The (*an*) snout (*socach*)'.

An Stac [Highland] 'The (*an*) stack [i.e. sharp pointed rock] (*stac*)'.

Anstruther [Fife] 'The (*an*) rivulet (*sruthair*)'. The mouth of the 'rivulet' forms the town's harbour, effectively dividing the town in two.

An Stùc [Highland] 'The (*an*) peak (*stùc*)'.

An Suidhe [Highland] 'The (*an*) seat (*suidhe*)': the mountain has a flat surface that is seat-like.

An Teallach [Highland] 'The (*an*) anvil (*teallach*)'.

An Torc [Highland/Tayside] 'The (*an*) boar (*torc*)'.

An Uidh [Highland] 'The (*an*) ford (*uidh*, corrupted form of ON *eith*)'.

aodann 'slope', 'mountain-face', 'hillside'.

aoidh(e) genitive plural of *uidh*, thus 'of the fords', 'of the isthmuses'.

aoineadh (also *aoinidh*) 'steep brae', 'cliff', 'moraine'.

aoinidh See *aoineadh*.

aonach 'open space', thus both 'moor' and 'market-place' – exactly as the Greek *agora*. Strangely, the word is usually used as a mountain name.

Aonach Beag [Highland] '[The] Moor (*aonach*), small (*beag*)': described thus to distinguish it from the nearby larger mountain – see below.

Aonach Eagach [Highland] '[The] Moor (*aonach*), notched (*eagach*)'. The mountain is part of the very sinuous northern boundary system of Glen Coe.

Aonach Mór [Highland] '[The] Moor (*aonach*), big (*mór*)': described thus to distinguish it from the nearby smaller mountain – see above.

18

Appin [Strathclyde] 'Abbey grounds (*apuinn*)'. The grounds are presumably those of St Maluag's foundation (cathedral) on Lismore Island across the Lynn of Lorn.

Applecross [Highland] 'Mouth (*aber*, Brythonic Gaelic) of the [River] Crossan'. The river name derives from *crossan* 'little cross', and may be associated with the monastery founded here in AD 673 by St Maelrubha.

arbhar 'corn', 'grain'.

Arbroath [Tayside] 'Mouth (*aber*, Brythonic Gaelic) of the Brothock Water'. The name of the Water derives from *brothaig* 'boiling', 'turbulent'.

Archiestown [Grampian] Village founded in around 1760 by the landowner Sir Archibald Grant.

ard (also *aird*; Welsh *aran*, *arddu*; cognate with Latin *arduus* 'high', 'steep' [whence English *arduous*] and Greek *ardis* 'point') 'height', 'promontory', 'crag'. As adjective: 'high'; also, in modern Gaelic, 'loud'.

Ardachu [Highland] Presumably 'Height (*ard*) of the (*[n]a*) dogs (*chu*)'.

Ardarroch [Highland] Presumably 'Height (*ard*) of oaks (*darach*)'.

Ardbeg [Islay] 'Promontory (*ard*), small (*beag*)'. This corresponds with an Ardmore (*ard-mór* 'big promontory') some 5 miles north-east.

Ardchattan [Strathclyde] 'Promontory (*ard*) of [St] Chattan'. Ardchattan priory, presumably dedicated to St Chattan the 6th-century founder of a monastery on Lismore, is on a headland jutting into Loch Etive.

Ardclach [Highland] 'Height (*ard*) of stone[s] (*clach*)'.

Ard-dhubh [Highland] 'Promontory (*ard*), black (*dubh*)'.

Ardentinny [Strathclyde] Possibly 'Promontory (*ard*) of the (*na*) beacon (*teine*)'. Ardentinny is an ideal place for a beacon; if a beacon was indeed lit there, it would have been visible fifteen miles up Loch Long at Arrochar, and also eight miles south at Gourock, on the Clyde. But the alternative derivation 'Promontory (*ard*) of the (*an*) fox (*t-sionnaich*)' is at least as convincing.

Ardersier [Highland] Generally derived as 'Promontory (*ard*) of the point (*ros*), west (*iar*)', but that makes little sense because although there is indeed a promontory with a point, the village of Ardersier (also called Campbelltown) is only half-way down it and it is very much on the east of the Moray Firth: there is little (except Morayshire – which is not Campbell country) that it is west *of*. Cf therefore *ard-ros-ear* 'Promontory of the point, *east*'.

Ardfern [Strathclyde] 'Promontory (*ard*) of alder tree[s] (*fearn*)'.

Ardgay [Highland] 'Height (*ard*) of the wind (*gaoith*)': the second element can alternatively mean 'of the marsh', and either meaning might be appropriate here.

Ardgoil [Strathclyde] Name devised in 1906 for an estate donated by Lord Rowallan to the city of Glasgow: 'Height (*ard*) [by Loch] Goil'.

Ardgour [Highland] Possibly 'Promontory (*ard*) of Gabran': Gabran was the name of the hero-son of King Fe(a)rgus of Ulster, the tutor of Cuchulainn. But more likely either 'Promontory (*ard*) of the goat (*gobhar*)' or 'Promontory (*ard*), sloping (Brythonic Gaelic; Welsh *gwyr* = Gower)'. The name is applied not just to the ferry station on Loch Linnhe but also to the area west of it to Loch Shiel.

Ardgowan [Strathclyde] 'Promontory (*ard*) of blacksmith[s] (*gobhainn*)'. The Clyde estuary seems an appropriate spot for blacksmiths, the old shipyards not far away . . .

Ardindrean [Highland] Presumably 'Promontory (*ard*) of the (*na*) blackthorn (*draigheann*)'.

Ardivachar [South Uist] Presumably 'Promontory (*ard*) of the (*a'*) plain (*mhachaire*)'. And indeed, there is quite a flattish lowland area between this headland and Loch Bee.

Ardlair [Grampian] Possibly 'Height (*ard*) of the mare (*làire*)'. But this may be a corruption of something else, for there is no apparent particular 'height'.

Ardmaddy [Strathclyde] 'Height (*ard*) of the fox (*madaidh*)'.

Ardmay [Strathclyde] Presumably 'High (*ard*) plain (*magh*)'.

Ardmore [Highland (2)] 'Promontory (*ard*), big (*mór*)'.

Ard na Claise Móire [Highland] 'Promontory (*ard*) of the (*na*) narrow valley (*clais*), big (*mór*)'.

Ardnacroish [Lismore Isle] 'Promontory (*ard*) of the (*na*) crossing (*croisg*)'. The harbour is station for the ferry from the island to Oban.

Ardnamurchan [Highland] Possibly 'Promontory (*ard*) of the (*na*) sea (*muir-*) otter (*chu* 'dog')'. But it is the most westerly point of mainland Scotland, on a peninsula (which is called by the same name) jutting into the sea, and the final two elements were apparently originally *muir-chol* 'sea-villainy', i.e. piracy.

20

Ardoyne [Grampian] Possibly 'Height (*ard*), green (*uaine*)', although the village of Oyne is only 1 mile south-east and this might therefore be the 'height above Oyne'.

Ardrishaig [Strathclyde] 'Promontory (*ard*), thorn(y) (*dris* 'brambles'), bay (*-aig*, corrupt form of ON *vágr*)'. A bump and an indentation on the western side of Loch Gilp.

Ardrossan [Strathclyde] 'Promontory (*ard*) of the cape (*ros*), little(*-an*)'. There is quite a sizable cape at this popular coastal resort west of Glasgow.

Ardshealach [Highland] 'Height (*ard*) [of] the willow (*seileach*)'.

Ardtornish [Highland] 'Promontory (*ard*) of Thori's (genitive of the ON personal name *Thori*) headland (elided form of ON *nes*)'. The first element was evidently added after the latter two had become simply a name. There is what may have been Thori's castle on Ardtornish Point, on the Sound of Mull. Note that Gaelic *tor* can itself mean 'castle'.

Arduaine [Strathclyde] 'Height (*ard*), green (*uaine*)'.

Ardullie [Highland] Probably 'Promontory (*ard*) of the tombs (*ulaidh*)', although the last element can alternatively mean 'treasure'.

Ardyne Point [Strathclyde] Probably 'Promontory (*ard*), marshy (*fhyne*, adapted from ON)', and the final element added later when the original meaning had been forgotten. Glen Fyne follows the Ardyne Burn northwards.

Argyll [Strathclyde/Highland] 'Coastland (*oirer*) of the Gaels (*Gaidheal*)'. At one stage, Argyll stretched from the Clyde north to Ullapool.

Aridhglas [Mull] 'Height (*aird*), blue-green (*glas*)'.

Arisaig [Highland] Apparently 'Aros [a proper name] bay (*-aig*, ON, q.v.)'. The village is at the head of a sea-loch now called Loch na Ceall ('loch of the churchyards'), presumably the 'bay' in question. But who or what was 'Aros' (whose name crops up surprisingly commonly)?

Arivruaich [Lewis] Probably 'Boundary (*airbhe*) bank (*bhruaich*)'.

Armadale [Highland; Skye] 'Arms' (i.e. branches *or* weapons) dale (ON)'. The name is usually derived from Brythonic Gaelic, however, as below – but both these places are on the Viking coast, likely ports of call, and in any case the meaning of the name is identical in both derivations.

Armadale [Lothian] 'Arms' (i.e. branches *or* weapons) dale (*dol*, Brythonic Gaelic)'. But this name was transferred here by Lord Armadale from his burgh of Armadale in Sutherland [Highland].

Arnabost [Coll] Probably 'Arni['s] (personal name, ON) settlement-steading (*bol-stathr*, ON)'.

Arnisdale [Highland] Presumably 'Arni's (personal name, ON) dale (*dálr*, ON)'.

-arra (also *-arrie, -errie*) elided forms of *airbhe*: 'dividing wall', 'partition', 'boundary'.

Arran [Inner Hebrides] 'Height (*aran*, related to *ard* but Brythonic Gaelic)'.

-arrie (also *-arra, -errie*) elided forms of *airbhe*: 'dividing wall', 'partition', 'boundary'.

Arrochar [Strathclyde] The 'Aratrum' – an ancient Scottish square measure of land taking its name from the Latin word for 'plough': 104 acres, being the area of land eight oxen could plough in a year at 13 acres each. The mountain spelled 'Ben Arrochar' on some elderly English maps alternatively derives its name from *Beinn Airigh Chiarr*: 'Mount Shieling, Dark'.

-art elided form of 1) *ard*: 'promontory', 'height'; as adjective, 'high'.
     or 2) ON *fjordr*: 'fjord', 'firth'. E.g. Knoyd-art.

Ashkirk [Borders] 'Ash church': good OE elements, as in Selkirk five miles further north.

ask elided form of *easg(a)*: 'marsh', 'swamp'. Cf *uisge* 'water'.

Asknish [Strathclyde] 'Marsh[y] (*easg*) water-meadow (*inis*)'. The village is at the end of a bay-inlet of the sea-loch Loch Fyne.

ass elided form of *eas*: 'waterfall'

Assynt [Highland] Area name thought to derive from *as-agus-int*, 'outs and ins', referring to the terrain either vertically (humps and hollows) or horizontally (headlands and recesses).

ath 'anew', 'again', 'a second . . . ', 're-'.

ath(a) 'ford'. Very occasionally, the feminine form of the word, meaning 'kiln', is also found.

Athelstaneford [Lothian] 'Athelstan's ford (OE)'. Athelstan, King of the Mercians and West Saxons took Northumbria and invaded Scotland in the first decades of the 10th century. Although he lost the battle here, in 937 he

22

finally defeated Scots, Welsh and Danes at Brunanburh. His name means 'noble stone'.

Atholl [Tayside] Possibly 'A second (*ath*) Ireland (*Fhodla*)' – but that the first element might be *ath[a]* 'ford' remains a strong possibility.

-atin elided form of *aitionn*: 'juniper'.

attow adapted form (on some maps only) of *ff[h]ada*: 'long'.

auch- variant form of *achadh*: 'open space', 'field', 'place'.

Auchenbreck [Strathclyde] Presumably 'Place (*achadh*) of the (*na*) trout (*breac*)'. The village is on a good river, not far from its confluence with the sea-loch Loch Riddon.

Auchencairn [Dumfries & Galloway] 'Place (*achadh*) of the (*na*) cairn (*carn*)'. There is a burial cairn here.

Auchencrow [Borders] 'Place (*achadh*) of the (*na*) sheep-pen (*crò*)'.

Auchendinny [Lothian] Probably 'Place (*achadh*) of the beacon (*teine*)'. The Celtic word *teine* (Irish *tine*, Welsh *tân*) literally means 'fire', and is also the second element of the name of the Celtic Mayday festival Beltane, for which fires were lit.

Auchentiber [Strathclyde] 'Place (*achadh*) of the (*na*) well (*t[i]obar*)'. The lowland area is crisscrossed by rivers.

Auchindrean [Highland] 'Place (*achadh*) of the (*na*) blackthorn (*draigheann*)'. The village is about seven miles south of Ardindrean, q.v.

Auchinleck [Strathclyde] 'Place (*achadh*) of the (*na*) flat stone (*leac*)'. The manor house is known locally as 'Place Affleck' (see **Affleck**).

Auchlany [Highland] 'Open space (*achadh*) of the enclosure (*lainne*, genitive of *lann*)'.

Auchleven [Grampian] 'Open space (*achadh*) of elm[s] (*leamhan*)'. The final element is most commonly used as a river name: the village is close to the Gadie Burn.

Auchlochan [Strathclyde] 'Place (*achadh*) of the little loch (*lochan*)'. The village is on the River Nethan.

Auchmillan [Strathclyde] 'Place (*achadh*) of the mill (*muileann*)'.

auchter- elided form of *uachdar*: 'upper (part)', 'top'.

Auchterarder [Tayside] Generally derived as 'Top (*uachdar*), high (*ard*), water (*dobhar*, Brythonic Gaelic)' but the third element seems suspicious: why Brythonic Gaelic after Goidelic?

Auchterderran [Fife] 'Top (*uachdar*) blackthorns (*draigheann*)'.

Auchtermuchty [Fife] 'Upper (*uachdar*) pig (*muc*) house (*tigh*)'. Some commentators make *muchty* one element: 'pig-rearing'.

Auchtertyre [Highland] 'Upper (*uachdar*) land (*tir*)'.

auld-, -auld (also *ault-*) elided form of *allt*: 'stream', 'burn', 'brook'.

Auldearn [Highland] 'Stream (*allt*), [River] Earn'. The river name is yet another word (*eren*) for 'water' (possibly connected with Rhine/Rhone).

Auldhouse [Strathclyde] 'Stream (*allt*) of the ghost (*fhuathais*)'.

ault- (also *auld-, -auld*) elided form of *allt*: 'stream', 'burn', 'brook'.

Aultbea [Highland] 'Stream (*allt*), birch (*beithe*)'.

Aultdearg [Highland] 'Stream (*allt*), red (*dearg*)'. The village is on the River Grudie, below Beinn Dearg.

Aultmore [Grampian] 'Stream (*allt*), big (*mór*)'. Aultmore is the name of an area between Keith and Buckie: there is a river – the Burn of Aultmore.

Aultnagoire [Highland] Probably 'Stream (*allt*) of the (*na*) goat (*gobhar*)'.

-avat in Harris and Lewis, elided form of ON genitive suffix followed by elided form of *vatn*: 'water'.

avie elided form of *agaidh*: 'gap', 'pass' (sometimes alternatively translated as 'hill-face'). This elided form corresponds much better than *agaidh* to the Welsh *adwy* 'pass'; the word may be connected with Gaelic *eadar*, 'between'.

Avielochan [Highland] 'Pass (*agaidh*), little loch (*lochan*)'. And the great A9 does indeed pass a little loch here, 4 miles north of Aviemore, q.v.

Aviemore [Highland] 'Pass (*agaidh*), big (*mór*)'. Aviemore is a popular centre in the deepish valley of the River Spey, used for many miles as the major route north and south through otherwise mountainous terrain for road and rail. To suggest that the name means 'Big hill-face' because it is a well-known ski-resort (as at least one commentator does) is wilfully to ignore the fact that Aviemore is 1) in the centre of a valley with 2) all the ski-slopes and suitable hill-faces at least three to four miles away, and 3) that the place was named well before the surrounding mountains were at all popular for tourists, let alone skiing.

avon elided form of *abhain[n]*: 'river'.

Avonbridge [Central] '[River] Avon bridge'. The Avon (*abhain[n]* 'river', with many cognates in Welsh and other Indo-European languages) forms the boundary between Central and Lothian Regions for a number of miles.

-ay (also *-a*; ON *ey*; Norw *oy*, Swed *ŏ*) 'island'.

Ayr [Strathclyde] An ancient pre-Celtic river name found also in England (Aire, Oare, Ore) and in Europe (Aar, Ahr, Ahre, Ara); it has been suggested that it might mean 'smooth-running'.

Ayton [Borders] Either 'Eye [Water] town (*tun*, OE)' or 'Island (*ieg*, OE) town (*tun*, OE)'. The river name that is the more likely derivation itself derives from OE *ea* 'river'; the second possibility suggests an island in that same river.

Abhainn

Abhainn

The following are river names that on the map are preceded by this word:

a' Bhealaich [Strathclyde] 'of the pass (*bhealaich*)'.

a' Chadh' Bhuidhe [Highland] 'of the pass (*chadha*), yellow (*buidhe*)'.

a' Choilich [Highland] Probably 'of the cock (*choileach*)'.

a' Choire [Highland] 'of the corrie (*coire*)'.

a' Gharbh Choire [Highland] 'of the rough [water] (*garbh*) corrie (*coire*)'.

a' Ghiubhais [Highland] 'of the fir tree (*ghiubhais*)'.

a' Ghlinne Bhig [Highland (2)] 'of the glen (*ghlinne*), small (*bhig*, masculine genitive of *beag*)'.

an Lòin [Highland] 'of the marsh (*lòin*)'.

an t-Srath Chuileannaich [Highland] 'of Strath Cuileannach': the river name means 'covered in holly'.

an t-Strathain [Highland] 'of Strath [Shinary] (*srathain*)'.

Beinn nan Eun [Highland] '[of] the Mountain (*beinn*) of the (*na*) bird (*eun*)'.

Bràigh-horrisdale [Highland] '[of] Upper (*bràighe*) Horrisdale': the valley name (-dale) is presumably named after some ON landowner.

Cam Linne [Strathclyde] 'Crooked (*cam*) pool (*linne*)'.

Chòsaidh [Highland] Probably 'With recesses (*chòsaidh*)', and back-formed as a river name from the name of the glen.

Chuaig [Highland] '[that flows into the sea at] Cuaig': the village name may mean 'Dog (*cù*) bay (-*aig*, corruption of ON *vágr*/Eng *bay*)'.

Crò Chlach [Highland] 'Sheep-pen (*crò*), stone (*chlach*)'.

Dalach [Strathclyde] 'Of the dale (*dalach*, adapted from ON *dalr*)'.

Dearg [Highland] 'Red-brown (*dearg*)'.

Dubh [Highland] 'Dark (*dubh*)'.

Duibhe [Tayside] 'Of the dark (*duibhe*)': the river name is probably back-formed from the name of the glen.

Ghlas [Islay] 'Blue-green (*ghlas*)'.

Mhór [Strathclyde (2)] 'Big (*mhór*)'.

na Clach Airigh [Highland] 'of the (*na*) stony (*clach*) shieling (*àirigh*)'.

na Frithe [Highland] 'of the (*na*) deer-forest (*frith*)'.

na Glasa [Highland] 'of the (*na*) blue-green colours (*glasa*, plural)'.

Rath [Highland] '[of the] circular fort (*ràth*)'.

Sithidh [Highland] Probably '[of] The fairy-hill (*sìdhein*)'.

Srath na Sealga [Highland] '[of] Strath na Sealga': the river name means 'of the huntsmen'.

Allt

Allt

The following are stream names that on the map are preceded by this word:

Ach a' Bhàthaich [Highland] 'Place (*achadh*) of the shelter (*bhàthaich*)'.

a' Chaoil-réidhe [Highland] Possibly 'of the narrow place (*chaol*), flat (*réidh*)'.

a' Chaorainn [Highland] Probably 'of the rowan trees (*chaorainn*)'.

a' Gheallaidh [Grampian] 'of the white [area] (*gheallaidh*)'.

a' Ghiubhais [Highland] 'of the fir tree (*ghiubhais*)'.

Airigh-dhamh [Highland] 'Shieling (*àirigh*) [of the] stag (*damh*)'.

a' Mhadaidh [Highland] 'of the fox (*mhadaidh*)'.

a' Mhuilinn [Highland; Tayside] 'of the mill (*mhuilinn*)'.

an Dùin [Highland] '[of] the stronghold (*dùin*)'.

an Stacain [Strathclyde] 'of the stacks [i.e. peaks] (plural of *stac*, itself a loan-word from ON *stakkr*)'.

an Tairbh [Jura] 'of the bull (*tairbh*)'.

an t-Srathain [Highland] 'of the strath (*srathain*)'.

Bail a' Mhuilinn [Tayside/Central] 'Town (*baile*) of the mill (*mhuilinn*)'.

Bhlàraidh [Highland] 'of the flat land (*bhlàraidh*)'.

Cam [Highland] 'Crooked (*cam*)'.

Cam Ban [Highland] 'Crooked (*cam*), white (*bàn*)'.

Camgharaidh [Highland] 'Crooked (*cam*) hide-out (*gharaidh*)': the stream name is probably back-formed from the name of the glen.

Choire a' Bhalachain [Highland] Possibly 'Corrie (*coire*) of the passes (*bhealachain*)'.

Cinn-locha [Strathclyde] 'Head (*ceann*) of the loch (*locha*, genitive)': the stream name takes its name from the village of Lochead overlooking the sea-loch Loch Caolisport.

Coire an Eòin [Highland] 'Corrie (*coire*) of the birds (*eòin*)'.

Coire Iain Oig [Highland] 'Corrie (*coire*) [of] Iain Oig.'

28

Coire na Saidhe Duibhe [Highland] 'Corrie (*coire*) of the (*na*) bitch (*saidhe*), black (*duibhe*, feminine genitive of *dubh*)'.

Con [Tayside] 'Of the dogs (*con*, genitive plural of *cù*)'.

Cuaich [Highland] 'Of the rounded hollow (*cuaich*)'.

Dearg [Highland] 'Red-brown (*dearg*)'.

Doe [Highland] Probably 'Dark (*dubh*)'.

Easach [Strathclyde] Probably 'Waterfall (*eas*) place (*achadh*)'.

Fearna [Strathclyde] 'Alder tree (*fearna*)'.

Fionn Ghlinne [Strathclyde] '[of the] White (*fionn*) glen (*ghlinne*)'.

Garbh [Highland] 'Rough [water] (*garbh*)'.

Garbh-airigh [Highland] 'Rough [water] (*garbh*) shieling (*àirigh*)'.

Garbh Buidhe [Tayside] 'Rough [water] (*garbh*), yellow (*buidhe*)'.

Glas Choire [Tayside] 'Blue-green (*glas*) corrie (*coire*)'.

Glas Dhoire [Highland] 'Blue-green (*glas*) clump of trees (*dhoire*)'.

Glen Loch [Tayside] '[of] Glen Loch': the valley name means 'glen of [Loch] Loch', which is not as silly a name as it sounds for the name of the loch is actually a Proto-Gaelic word meaning 'black'.

Goibhre [Highland] 'Of the goat (*goibhre*)'.

Kinglass [Strathclyde] 'Head (*ceann*), blue-green (*glas*)'.

Làire [Highland] 'Of the mare (*làire*)'.

Lon a' Chuil [Highland] 'Marsh (*lòn*) [of] the recess (*cùil*)'.

Mór [Highland; Skye; Tayside] 'Big (*mór*)'.

na Bogair [Tayside] Probably 'of the soft places (plural of *bog*)'.

na Caim [Highland] 'of the (*na*) bend (*caim*)'.

na Doire Garbhe [Highland] 'of the (*na*) clump of trees (*doire*), rough [water] (*garbh*)'.

na Gile [Strathclyde] 'of (*na*) white (*gile*, feminine genitive of *geal*)'.

na h-Eirigh [Highland] 'of the (*na*) shieling (*àirigh*)'.

na Lairige [Strathclyde] 'of the (*na*) pass (*làirig*)'.

na Lairige Moire [Highland] 'of the (*na*) pass (*làirig*), big (*mór*)'.

29

na Lùibe [Highland] 'of the (*na*) bends (*lùibe*)'.

na Muic [Highland] 'of the (*na*) pig (*muice*)'.

nan Achaidhean [Highland] Possibly 'of the (*na-n*) fields (plural of *achadh*)'.

nan Airighean [Islay] 'of the (*na-n*) shielings (*àirighean*)'.

nan Caorach [Highland] 'of the (*na-n*) sheep (*caorach*)'.

nan Ramh [Highland] 'of the (*na-n*) oar (*ramh*)'.

Odhar [Highland] 'Dun-coloured (*odhar*)'.

Riabhach [Highland] 'Brindled (*riabhach*)'.

Ruighe nan Saorach [Tayside] 'Slope (*ruighe*) of the (*na-n*) carpenter's (*saor*) place (*achadh*)'.

Sleibh [Tayside] 'Of the mountain (*sléibhe*, genitive of *sliabh*)'.

Srath a' Ghlinne [Tayside] 'Strath (*srath*) [in] the glen (*ghlinne*)'.

Tolaghan [Strathclyde] 'Little hill (diminutive of *tulach*)'; the stream ends in Loch Tulla.

Uisg an t-Sidhein [Highland] 'Water (*uisge*) of the little fairy-hill (genitive diminutive of *sìdh*)'.

B

bà genitive form of *bó*, thus 'of the cow'.

bac 'bank', 'peat-bank'; the word is an adaptation of ON *bakki*, 'back', 'ridge', 'reef', cognate with English *back*.

Bac [Lewis] 'Bank (*bac*)': the village is surrounded by others with Gaelic names – otherwise it would be tempting to derive this from ON *bakki*, 'back'.

bacaichean plural form of *bac*, thus 'banks', 'peat-banks'.

Bac Beag [Treshnish] 'Reef (*bakki*, ON), small (*beag*)': this in contrast with the nearby Bac Mór, q.v.

Bac an Eich [Highland] 'Bank (*bac*) of the horse (*eich*, genitive of *each*)'.

bachall 'staff', 'crozier'; the word derives from the Latin *baculum*, 'walking-stick'.

Backburn [Grampian (2)] Presumably 'Ridge (*baec*, OE) stream (*burna*, OE)': both villages are sited on high ground close to a stream.

Backhill [Grampian (2)] Presumably 'Ridge (*baec*, OE) hill (*hyll*, OE)', although in both cases the geography suggests the second element might instead be OE *halh*, 'corner'.

Bac Mór [Treshnish] 'Reef (*bakki*, ON), big (*mór*)': this in contrast with the nearby Bac Beag, q.v.

bad 'knoll', 'tuft', thus both 'place' (i.e. a prominent spot) and 'shrubby bush', 'clump of trees'.

Bad a' Chreamha [Highland] 'Shrubby bush (*bad*) of wild garlic (genitive of *creamh*)'.

Badachro [Highland] Possibly 'Place (*bad*) of the sheep-pen (*a' chròatha*)'.

Badandun Hill [Tayside] 'Place (*bad*) of the mound (*an dùin*), hill (Eng)': the final element was evidently added much later.

Badanloch [Highland] Presumably 'Little copse (diminutive of *bad*) loch'.

Badcall [Highland (2)] Presumably 'Clump of trees (*bad*), hazel (*call*)'.

Baddidarach [Highland] Possibly 'Clump of trees (*bad*), oak (*darach*)'.

31

Dictionary of Scottish Place Names

Badenoch [Highland] 'Liable to flood (*bàidhteanach*)': the area name originally referred more specifically to the Spey Valley than to the larger, more mountainous terrain it includes today.

Badninish [Highland] Presumably 'Place (*bad*) of the (*na*) water-meadow (*h-innis*)'.

bàgh 'bay'; this is a loan-word from the English.

Bàgh Loch an Ròin [Highland] 'Bay (*bàgh*) [of the] pool (*loch*) of the seal (*ròin*)'.

baic genitive form of *bac*, thus 'of the bank', 'of the peat-bank'.

baid genitive form of *bad*, thus 'of the knoll', 'of the tuft', 'of the place', 'of the shrubby bush', 'of the clump of trees'.

bàidhte 'drowning', 'flooded'.

bàidhteanach 'liable to flood', 'causing drowning'.

bàigh genitive form of *bàgh*, thus 'of the bay'.

baile 'homestead', thus later 'hamlet', 'town'. The etymology usually quoted for this word derives it from OFrench and ultimately Latin, but the changes of meaning necessary to make sense of this derivation defy credulity. With such a basic meaning, the word ought simply to be Gaelic. But cf also ON *bol* (present-day Sw *böle*), 'settlement', 'homestead', 'village'. The element is extremely common in Irish place names (in the form of Bally-).

Baile [Berneray] 'Settlement (*baile*)'.

Bailebeag [Highland] 'Settlement (*baile*), small (*beag*)': they don't come much smaller.

Baile Mór [Iona] 'Settlement (*baile*), big (*mór*)': the biggest, and the only, settlement on the island.

Bailiesward [Grampian] Presumably 'Bailie's [i.e. Scottish official's] (Scots) enclosed meadow (*ward*, Scots)'.

Bail Uachdraich [Uist] Presumably 'Settlement (*baile*) on the top (*uachdar-ach*)', although the land for miles around is rather low-lying.

bàine feminine genitive form of *bàn*, thus 'of the white . . .'.

baird   either 1) 'enclosed meadow' (Gaelic version of Scots *ward*);
            or 2) genitive form of *bard*, thus 'of the poet'.

32

bal   either 1)   elided form of *baile*, 'homestead', 'hamlet', 'town';
         or 2)   (also *beul*) '(river-)mouth', 'confluence'.

Balachuirn [Raasay] Probably 'Settlement (*baile*) of the cairn (*a' chuirn*)'.

Balaclava [Highland; Strathclyde] Villages named or renamed after the battle of Balaclava in 1854 (Crimean War).

Balaglas [Uist] Possibly 'Mouth (*bal*) of the stream (*a' glais*)', which would fit geographically, although it is not entirely impossible that the meaning is instead 'Settlement (*baile*), blue-green (*glas*)'.

Balbeg [Highland] Probably 'Settlement (*baile*), small (*beag*)', although the village does lie at the confluence (*bal*) of a stream into Loch Ness.

Balbeggie [Tayside] 'Settlement (*baile*), small (*beag*)'.

Balblair [Highland] 'Settlement (*baile*) of the level clearing (*blàir*, genitive of *blàr*)'.

Balchladich [Highland] Probably 'Settlement (*baile*) of the beach (*cladaich*)'.

Balchraggan [Highland] Probably 'Settlement (*baile*) [of] the rocks (*creagan*)'.

Balephuil [Tiree] Probably 'Settlement (*baile*) of the pool (*phuil*)': the village is close to the largest loch on Tiree.

Balerno [Lothian] 'Settlement (*baile*) [of] the sloe (*airneach*)'.

Balevullin [Tiree] 'Probably 'Settlement (*baile*) of the mill (*mhuilinn*)'.

Balfour [Orkney] 'Settlement (*baile*) of pasture (*phùir*, genitive of *pòr*)'.

balgair 'fox'.

balgan 'blister' – a surprising element for a place name.

Balgaveny [Grampian] Probably 'Settlement (*baile*) of the blacksmith (*gobhainn*)'.

Balgedie [Fife] Possibly 'Settlement (*baile*) of the narrow strip of land (*gead*)'.

Balgove [Grampian] Probably 'Settlement (*baile*) [of] the blacksmith (*gobha*)'.

Balgowan [Highland] 'Settlement (*baile*) of the blacksmith (*gobhainn*)'.

Balgown [Skye] 'Settlement (*baile*) of the blacksmith (*gobhainn*)'.

Balhary [Tayside] Possibly 'Settlement (*baile*) of the boundary (*h-airbhe*)': the village is right on the edge of the wide valley of the River Isla.

Baligill [Highland] Possibly 'Settlement (*baile*) [of] the ravine (*gil*)'.

Balintraid [Highland] 'Settlement (*baile*) on the shore (*an tràghad*)', overlooking the sandy Nigg Bay.

Balivanich [Benbecula] Probably 'Settlement (*baile*) of the monk (*mhanaich*)'.

balla- elided form of *baile*: 'settlement', 'homestead', 'hamlet', 'town'; modern Gaelic has reduced its meaning to merely 'wall'.

Balla [Eriskay] 'Settlement (*baile*)': the only community on the island.

Ballachulish [Highland] 'Settlement (*baile*) of the narrows (*chaolais*)'.

Ballantrae [Strathclyde] 'Settlement (*baile*) on the shore (*an traighe*)'.

Ballater [Grampian] Possibly 'Broom (*bealaidh*) land (*tìr*)': that the stress is on the first syllable makes the meaning 'settlement' (*baile*) unlikely. Another suggestion for the first element is 'pass' (*bealach*), which is geographically feasible.

Ballencrieff [Lothian] Presumably 'Settlement (*baile*) of the tree (*an craoibhe*)'

Balliemore [Strathclyde] Presumably 'Settlement (*baile*), big (*mór*)'.

Ballimore [Central] Presumably 'Settlement (*baile*), big (*mór*)'.

Ballinluig [Tayside] Presumably 'Settlement (*baile*) of the wet hollow (*an luig*, genitive of *lag*)'.

Ballintuim [Tayside] Presumably 'Settlement (*baile*) of the mound (*an tuim*, genitive of *tom*)'.

Balloch [Highland; Strathclyde] 'Pass (*bealach*)'.

Ballochan [Grampian] 'Passes (plural of *bealach*)'.

bally- elided form of *baile*: 'settlement', 'homestead', 'hamlet', 'town'.

Ballygown [Mull] 'Settlement (*baile*) of the blacksmith (*gobhainn*)'.

Balmaha [Central] Possibly 'Settlement (*baile*) on the plain (*maighe*)': the village stands on low-lying land on the shore of Loch Lomond.

Balmoral [Grampian] Said to be 'Settlement (*baile*) [in] the big (*mór*) clearing (*ial*, Brythonic Gaelic)' but such a mixture of Goidelic elements and

34

Brythonic is not at all satisfactory, especially if the stress is on the second element.

Balmore [Strathclyde] Presumably 'Settlement (*baile*), big (*mór*)': an ambitious name for a small village on the outskirts of Glasgow.

Balnabodach [Barra] 'Settlement (*baile*) of the (*na*) old man (*bodach*)': the final element can alternatively mean 'ghost'.

Balnacoil [Highland] Possibly 'Settlement (*baile*) of the (*na*) wood (*coille*)'.

Balnaguisich [Highland] Probably 'Settlement (*baile*) of the (*na*) fir trees (*giuthsaich*)'.

Balnahard [Mull] 'Settlement (*baile*) of the (*na*) height (*h-ard*)': the village stands beneath steep slopes looking out into the Atlantic.

Balnakeil [Highland] Probably 'Settlement (*baile*) of the (*na*) kyle (*caol*)', the kyle in question being the Kyle of Durness, at the end of which is Balnakeil Bay, on the shore of which stands Balnakeil.

Balnaknock [Skye] 'Settlement (*baile*) of the (*na*) rounded hill (*cnoc*)'.

Balquhidder [Central] Apparently 'Settlement (*baile*) of fodder (corrupt Gaelic form of ON *fothr* or OE *fodor*)'.

Balvaird [Highland] Possibly 'Settlement (*baile*) [of] the enclosed meadow (*bhaird*)'.

Bamff [Tayside] Name probably transferred from Banff [Grampian], q.v.

ban genitive plural form of *bean*, thus 'of the women'.

bàn 'white', 'fair' and thus 'handsome', 'beautiful'. The word is presumably cognate with Gaelic *fionn*, of identical meaning, and thus with Welsh *gwyn* (Latin *candi[dus]*), which in turn is akin – if not cognate – with English *white*.

bana plural form of *bean*, thus '[the] wives', '[the] women'.

Banavie [Highland] Presumably 'Fair (*bàn*) pass (*agaidh*)'; the second element is sometimes translated as 'hill-face', however, and that might be more suitable here.

Banchory [Grampian] Apparently 'Mountainous (*beannachar*)'.

Banff [Grampian] One commentator has suggested 'Land left fallow for a year (*bánbh*)'; others have more tentatively proposed some connection with a rare Gaelic name for Ireland, *Banba*. I could as well add that Irish *banbh*

35

means 'young pig'. None of these makes much sense as the name of an ancient seaside Royal Burgh complete with ancient castle ruins and a 1750 replacement castle. In any case the town stands on the bank of the River Deveron, a river with a name going back to pre-Celtic times. The name of the town at its estuary may well go back as far.

Bankend [Strathclyde; Dumfries & Galloway] 'Bank (ME) end (ME)', both villages being situated at the end of a ridge.

Bankfoot [Tayside] Village named in English by its founder, a Mr Wylie, in around 1815.

Bankhead [Grampian (2)] 'Bank (ME) head (ME)': the two villages, only about 14 miles apart, stand at the head of their respective ridges.

Bannockburn [Central] Apparently based on a Brythonic stream name: 'Fair (Brythonic equivalent of *bàn*) little (*-ock,* Brythonic diminutive) stream (*burn,* ME)'. The village stands on the bank of the Bannock Burn.

ban-rìgh 'queen' (literally 'woman-king').

Ban Rubha [Scarba] 'White (*bàn*) promontory (*rubha*)'

bar- elided form of *barr*: 'top', 'summit', 'height'.

Barcaldine [Strathclyde] 'Summit (*barr*) of the hazel (*calltuinn*)'.

bard   either   1)   'poet';
            or   2)   'enclosed meadow', an adaptation of the Scots word *ward*.

Bargrennan [Dumfries & Galloway] Probably 'Summit (*barr*) [of] the sunny hillock (*grianan*)'.

Barlinnie [Strathclyde] 'Summit (*barr*) of the pool (*linne*)'.

barpa in Skye and other Hebrides, 'burial-cairn', 'memorial cairn'.

barr 'top', 'summit', 'height'.

Barr [Strathclyde] 'Summit (*barr*)', although the village is actually down in the valley beneath the summit.

Barra [Western Isles] 'Of [St] Barr (personal name)'. St Barr (c.560-c.615) was the Bishop of Cork, in Ireland, where he founded a respected monastery. He never travelled out of Ireland, but his disciples took his fame to several areas of northern Scotland, and there was once a church dedicated to him (*Cille-bharra*) on this island.

B

Barrachan [Dumfries & Galloway] Presumably 'Top (*barr*) little field (diminutive of *achadh*)'.

Barran [Strathclyde] Presumably 'Little summit (diminutive of *barr*)'.

Barrapol [Tiree] Presumably 'Top (*barr*) of the pool (*a' puill*)': the village is close to the largest loch on the island.

Barravullin [Strathclyde] Presumably 'Summit (*barr*) of the mill (*a' mhuilinn*)'.

Barrhead [Strathclyde] 'Summit (*barr*) head (ME)'. The village was founded as late as in the 1770s.

Barr Liath [Strathclyde] 'Summit (*barr*), grey (*liath*)'.

Barr Mór [Lismore] 'Summit (*barr*), big (*mór*)' – all of 416 feet (127 m), but it is the highest point on the island.

Barry [Tayside] Probably 'Wood (*bearu*, OE)'.

-barton elided form of *breatainn*: 'of the Britons'.

Basta [Shetland] Possibly 'Bak's (personal name, ON) steading (*stathr*, ON)': the ON personal name is attested in Baston, Lincolnshire.

bàta 'boat'; the Gaelic is an adaptation of OE or ON.

bàtaichean plural form of *bàta*, thus 'boats'.

bàtcha genitive form of *bàthaich*, thus 'of the shelter', 'of the byre', 'of the sanctuary'.

bàthaich 'shelter', thus both 'byre' and 'sanctuary'.

Bathgate [Lothian] Apparently a Brythonic name: 'Boar (*baedd*) wood (*coed*)'; some commentators alternatively suggest 'House (*bod*)' for the first element.

-bea elided form of *beithe*: 'birch tree'.

beag (Welsh *bach*, *bychan* and mutated forms) 'small', 'little', 'lesser'.

bealach (Welsh *bwlch*) 'pass', 'gap' and also 'road'.

Bealach nam Bó [Highland] 'Pass (*bealach*) of the (*na-m*) cow (*bó*)': perhaps the most scenic, tortuous pass in the United Kingdom – sea level to 2,054 feet (626 m) in six miles (9.65 km) including a number of genuine hairpin bends. Some maps call it Bealach na Ba, and claim that this makes it the 'pass of the cattle'.

bealaidh 'broom (plant/tree)'.

bean 'woman', 'wife'.

beann genitive plural form of *beinn*, thus 'of the mountains'.

bearn 'gap'.

-beath adapted form of *beithe*: '[of a] birch tree'

Beauly [Highland] 'Beautiful (*beau*, Fr) place (*lieu*, Fr)': the name is sometimes said to have been the result of a remark made in French by Mary Queen of Scots in 1562, but in truth the derivation ought to be earlier than that date.

Beeswing [Dumfries & Galloway] Amazingly, this is the name of a racehorse who won 51 out of 64 races between 1835 and 1842, as commemorated by a pub built at that time by the horse's owner. Even more astonishingly, perhaps, other pubs were named after the same horse as far south as Northamptonshire.

beg anglicised version of *beag*: 'small', 'little', 'lesser'.

beinn 'mountain', 'peak' and thus also 'horn'. See separate list of mountain names beginning with this element.

Beinne Creagach [Ulva] Presumably 'Mountains (plural of *beinn*), craggy (*creagach*)'.

Beinneun [Highland] Presumably an elided 'Mount (*beinn*) Bird (*eun*)'.

béiste genitive form of *biast*, thus 'of the beast', 'of the monster'.

Beith [Strathclyde] Presumably 'Birch tree (*beithe*)'.

beithe 'birch tree'.

beithir 'serpent', 'wild beast', 'dragon', 'monster'.

Bellabeg [Grampian] Probably 'Settlement (*baile*), small (*beag*)'.

Bellahouston [Strathclyde] 'Settlement (*baile*) of the crucifix (*cheusadain*)'.

Bellamore [Strathclyde] 'Settlement (*baile*), big (*mór*)'.

Belleheiglash [Grampian] 'Settlement (*baile*) of the church (*h-eaglais*)'.

belloch often an elided form of *bealach*: 'pass', 'gap', 'road'.

Bellsmyre [Strathclyde] Possibly 'Settlement (*baile*) of the grime (*smúir*, genitive of *smúr*)'.

Belnacraig [Grampian] Probably 'Settlement (*baile*) of the (*na*) fell (*creag*)'; it is just possible that the fell referred to is the mountain, Creag an Eunan, about 1½ miles north, although the village sits on its own lesser height.

Belnahua [Inner Hebrides] Possibly 'Mouth (*beul*) of the (*na*) cave (*h-uamh*)'.

ben anglicised version of *beinn*: 'mountain', 'peak', 'horn'; many names of mountains on the maps, both famous and obscure (but particularly those in which the descriptive elements of the name are unknown), retain this spelling. Most are listed below. But see also *beinn*.

Benaquhallie [Grampian] Possibly 'Mountain (*beinn*) of the field (*achaidh*) of the treasure (*ulaidh*)'.

Ben Arnaboll [Highland] 'Mount (*beinn*) Arni['s] (personal name, ON) settlement (*bol*, ON; present-day Sw *böle*)'.

Ben Arthur [Strathclyde] Possibly 'Mount (*beinn*) High (*ard*) country (*tir*)'.

Benarty Hill [Fife] 'Mountain (*beinn*), high (*ard*), hill (Eng)': at 1,168 feet (356 m) it is not a particularly high mountain. The final element was evidently added after the first two had become simply a name.

Ben Aslak [Skye] Presumably 'Mount (*beinn*) Aslákr (personal name, ON)'.

Ben Attow [Highland] anglicised version of *Beinn Fhada* (remember that in Gaelic an initial Fh- is not pronounced), q.v.

Ben Avon [Grampian] 'Mountain (*beinn*) [above the River] Avon': the river name itself means simply 'river'.

Benbecula [Uist] Possibly 'Mountain (*beinn*) of the shepherd (*buachaille*)', but this is the name of an island, not a mountain – an island, moreover, that is low-lying unlike even the islands immediately north and south.

Benbuie [Dumfries & Galloway] 'Mountain (*beinn*), yellow (*buidhe*)'.

Ben Buie [Mull] 'Mount (*beinn*) Yellow (*buidhe*)'.

Ben Clach [Tayside] 'Mount (*beinn*) Stone (*clach*)'.

Ben Cleuch [Central] 'Mount (*beinn*) Ravine (*cloh*, OE)'.

Ben Cruachan [Strathclyde] 'Mount (*beinn*), Small but prominent (*cruachan*)'.

Ben Dell [Lewis] 'Mount (*beinn*) [of the village of] Dell': from the mountain the Dell River flows to Dell village. The river name comes from the ON for 'dale'.

Benderloch [Strathclyde] 'Mountain (*beinn*) between (*eadar*) lochs (*loch-*)': not a bad description for this area of upland between Loch Crerar and Loch Etive.

Ben Earb [Tayside] 'Mount (*beinn*) Roe-deer (*earb*)'.

Ben Ettow [Skye] Probably 'Mount (*beinn*), Long (*fhada*)'; see also **Ben Attow**.

Bengairn [Dumfries & Galloway] Presumably 'Mountain (*beinn*) of the cairn (*cairn*, genitive of *carn*)'.

Ben Garrisdale [Jura] 'Mount (*beinn*) [of the River] Garrisdale': the river name comes from ON for 'garden's dale'.

Ben Geary [Skye] 'Mount (*beinn*) Strip of semi-fertile land (*gearraidh*)'.

Ben Glas [Central] Probably 'Mount (*beinn*) Stream (*glas*, early Goidelic)' rather than 'Blue-green (*glas*, present-day Goidelic)': the Ben Glas Burn runs just south of the mountain and forms the Central/Strathclyde border.

Ben Griam Beg [Highland] Probably 'Mount (*beinn*) Sun (*grian*), [the] small[er] (*beag*)', with the -n becoming -m before the labial b-; the name contrasts this mountain with the neighbouring *Ben Griam Mór*.

Ben Griam Mór [Highland] Probably 'Mount (*beinn*) Sun (*grian*), [the] big[ger] (*mór*)', with the -n becoming -m before the labial m-; the name contrasts this mountain with the neighbouring *Ben Griam Beag*.

Ben Hogh [Coll] Probably 'Mount (*beinn*), High (*hoh*, OSw or OE)'.

Benholm [Grampian] 'Mountain (*beinn*) river-island (*holm*, adaptation from ON)'.

Ben Hope [Highland] Probably 'Mountain (*beinn*) Shelter (*hóp*, ON)'.

Ben Killilan [Highland] 'Mount (*beinn*) [of the village of] Killilan': the village name means 'church of [St] Fillan'. See **Killilan**.

Ben Laga [Highland] Presumably 'Mount (*beinn*) of the hollow (*lagaidh*)'.

Ben Lawers [Tayside] 'Mount (*beinn*) [of the village of] Lawers': the meaning of the village name is obscure. It is interesting that the Lawers Burn – which flows down to Loch Tay through the village of Lawers – does not rise on Ben Lawers but on the adjacent mountain.

40

Ben Lomond [Central] 'Mount (*beinn*) Beacon (from a Brythonic Gaelic source)': the loch to its west is thus named after this mountain.

Ben Lui [Central] 'Mountain (*beinn*) of the calf (*laoigh*, genitive of *laogh*)'.

Ben Luskentyre [Harris] 'Mount (*beinn*) Herbs (*lus*) headland (*ceann-tìr*)'.

Ben Macdui [Grampian] anglicised version of *Beinn Macduibh*, q.v.

Benmore [Strathclyde; Central] 'Mountain (*beinn*), big (*mór*)'.

Ben More [Highland; Mull; Central] anglicised version of *Beinn Mór*, 'Big Mountain'. See also **Beinn Mhór**.

Ben More Assynt [Highland] 'Big mountain (*beinn mór*)' in the area known as Assynt, a word that may derive from *as-agus-int*, 'outs and ins', referring to the topography.

Bennachie [Grampian] Presumably 'Mountain (*beinn*) field (*achadh*)'.

Bennan [Dumfries & Galloway] Presumably 'Little mountain (diminutive of *beinn*)', which suits it, geographically.

Ben Nevis [Highland] Possibly 'Mountain (*beinn*), Cloudy and snowy'. For a discussion on the meaning of the second element, see **Nevis**.

Ben Oss [Central] Apparently 'Mountain (*beinn*) of the elk'.

Ben Stack [Highland] 'Mount (*beinn*), Conical (*stac*, adaptation of ON *stakkr*, 'steep rock')'.

Ben Strome [Highland] 'Mount (*beinn*) [of the village of] Strome': the village name means 'point', referring to a small promontory jutting into Loch Carron.

Ben Tangaval [Barra] Presumably 'Mount (*beinn*) Tongue [of land] (*tunga*, ON) fell (*fjall*, ON)': the first element was evidently added after the remaining elements had become simply a name.

Benula [Highland] See **Beinn Fhionnlaidh**.

Benvane [Central] Anglicised version of *Beinn Bhàn*, 'White Mountain'.

Ben Vane [Strathclyde] Presumably 'Mount (*beinn*), White (*bhàn*)'.

Ben Venu [Central] Probably 'Mount (*beinn*) In the middle (*mheadhonach*)', for the mountain lies precisely between the prominent mountains Ben Lomond and Ben Ledi.

Ben Vorlich [Strathclyde] Possibly 'Mount (*beinn*), Big (*mhór*), of the flat stone (*lice*)'.

Ben Vrackie [Tayside] Presumably 'Mount (*beinn*) Of the upper part (*bràghadh*)'.

Benyellary [Dumfries & Galloway] 'Mountain (*beinn*) of the eagle (*iolaire*)'.

Ben Wyvis [Highland] 'Mount (*beinn*) of terror (*uabhais*, genitive form of *uabhas*)': the reason for the terror thus inspired is unknown.

beòil genitive form of *beul*, thus 'of the mouth'.

Bernisdale [Skye] 'Bjorni's (personal name, ON) dale (*dalr*, ON)'.

Berriedale [Skye] 'Beri['s] (personal name, ON) dale (*dalr*, ON)'.

bervie probably a Brythonic river name, meaning 'seething', 'boiling' (cf modern Welsh *berw*).

Berwick, North [Lothian] 'Barley (*bere*, OE) farmstead (*wic*, OE)': the name was almost undoubtedly transferred from the Berwick that used to be on the Scottish-English border but that now is several miles inside England.

Bettyhill [Highland] Village set up in about 1820 as an agricultural and fishing centre (and apparently to provide accommodation for workers evicted in the Clearances), named after Elizabeth, Countess of Sutherland.

beul (also *bal*) '(river-)mouth', 'confluence'.

bhaic mutated genitive form of *bac*, thus 'of the bank', 'of the peat-bank'.

bhaid mutated genitive form of *bad*, thus 'of the knoll', 'of the tuft', 'of the shrubby bush', 'of the clump of trees', or just 'of the place'.

bhàigh mutated genitive form of *bàgh*, thus 'of the bay'.

bhaile mutated genitive form of *baile*, thus 'of the settlement', 'of the homestead', 'of the hamlet', 'of the town'.

bhàin mutated masculine genitive form of *bàn*, thus 'of the white . . . '.

bhaird either 1) mutated form of Scots *ward*, 'enclosed meadow';
or 2) mutated genitive form of *bard*, thus 'of the poet'.

bhalgain mutated genitive form of *balgan*, thus 'of the blister'.

bhalgaire mutated genitive form of *balgair*, thus 'of the fox'.

bhàn mutated feminine form of *bàn*: 'white'.

bhàta mutated genitive form of *bàta*, thus 'of the boat'.

bhàthaich mutated genitive form of *bàthaich*, thus 'of the shelter', 'of the byre', 'of the sanctuary'.

bheag mutated feminine form of *beag*: 'small'.

bhealaich mutated genitive form of *bealach*, thus 'of the pass', 'of the gap'.

bhealaidh mutated genitive form of *bealaidh*, thus 'of the broom (plant/tree)'.

bhearn mutated form of *bearn*: 'gap'.

bheinn mutated form of *beinn*: 'mountain'.

bheithir mutated genitive form of *beithir*, thus 'of the serpent', 'of the wild beast', 'of the dragon', 'of the monster'.

bheil mutated genitive form of *beul*, thus 'of the (river-)mouth', 'of the confluence'.

bhig mutated masculine genitive form of *beag*, thus 'of the small . . . '.

bhiorain mutated genitive form of *bioran*, thus 'of the colt', 'of the young horse', and 'of the wild boy'.

bhlàir mutated genitive form of *blàr*, thus 'of the level clearing', 'of the plain'.

bhodaich mutated genitive form of *bodach*, thus 'of the old man', 'of the ghost'.

bhràghad mutated genitive form of *bràighe*, thus 'of the upper part'.

bhraich mutated form of *braich*: 'boar'.

bhreac mutated feminine form of *breac*: 'speckled', and 'trout'.

bhréige mutated genitive form of *breug*, thus 'of the false . . . ', 'of the misleading . . . '.

bhric mutated masculine genitive form of *breac*, thus 'of the speckled . . . ', and 'of the trout'.

bhrochain mutated genitive form of *brochan*, thus 'of the rough ground', 'of the broken stones'.

bhruic mutated genitive form of *broc*, thus 'of the badger'.

bhruthaich mutated genitive form of *bruthach*, thus 'of the slope', 'of the brae', 'of the hillside'.

43

bhuic mutated genitive form of *boc*, thus 'of the buck'.

bhuidhe mutated genitive form of *buidhe*, thus 'of the yellow . . . '.

bhuig mutated genitive form of *bog*, thus 'of the soft . . . ', and 'of the soft place'.

biast 'beast', 'monster'. Probably derived in Gaelic from ME.

bidean 'peak', 'pinnacle'.

-bie often an elided form of ON *byr*: 'community'.

Bieldside [Grampian] 'Shelter (*bield*, Scots and ME Northern dialect) side (ME)'. Presumably the sheltered side of the River Dee, on which the suburb stands.

bige feminine genitive form of *beag*, thus 'of the small . . . '.

Biggar [Strathclyde] 'Barley (*bygg*, ON) enclosed field (*garthr*, ON)'.

Biggings [Shetland] 'Buildings (*biggings*, ME)'.

Bilbster [Highland] Possibly 'Bili['s] (personal name, ON) settlement-steading (*bol-stathr*, ON)'. The personal name is attested in Bilby, Northamptonshire.

bile 'edge', 'rim', 'lip'.

Bimbister [Orkney] Possibly 'Bimme['s] (personal name, ON) settlement-steading (*bol-stathr*, ON)'. The personal name is attested in Bamber Bridge, Lancashire.

binnean 'small, peaked mountain', 'spike'.

Binnein Mór [Highland] Presumably 'Small, peaked mountain (*binnean*), big (*mór*)': for a small, peaked mountain it is certainly big, at 3,700 feet (1,128 m).

biolair 'water-cress'.

biorach 'spiny', 'sharp-pointed', thus also 'dogfish'.

bioran 'colt', 'young horse', thus 'wild, headstrong boy'.

birk- mostly 'birch', either from OE *birc* or ON *birki*.

birken- mostly OE *bircen*: 'birchen', 'of birch trees'.

Birkenshaw [Strathclyde] 'Birchen (*bircen*, OE) thicket (*scaga*, OE)'.

Birkisco [Skye] 'Birch (*birki*, ON) wood (*skógr*, ON)'.

44

Birnam [Tayside] Said to be 'Warrior (*beorn*, OE) steading (*ham*, OE)'.

Bishopbriggs [Strathclyde] 'Bishop (Eng) [of Glasgow's] fields (*rigs*, Scots)': the notion that *briggs* = 'bridge', as suggested by many commentators, does not take into account that there was no bridge here until 1790 – well after the name was established.

Blackburn [Grampian; Lothian] 'Black (ME) stream (*burn*, ME)'.

Blackford [Tayside] 'Black (ME) ford (ME)': the village stands on the Allan Water.

Blackhaugh [Borders] 'Black (ME) haugh [i.e. an area of land within the bend of a river] (ME)': the village stands on the Caddon Water.

Black Isle, the [Highland] English name given to the broad and fertile peninsula between the Beauly Firth and the Dornoch Firth, possibly because from a distance (and it is possible to look at it from a considerable distance as well as from above, by surveying from the surrounding mountains) it is generally darkish.

Blackness [Lothian] 'Black (*blaec*, OE) promontory (*naes*, OE)': name given to a small peninsula on the Firth of Forth – which once was the site of the third major port of Scotland. Now there is a small village, with a 15th-century castle later used as a prison and then as a powder magazine.

blair anglicised version of *blàr*: 'level clearing', 'plain', although this form also represents the Gaelic genitive, thus 'of the level clearing', 'of the plain'.

Blairadam [Fife] Village renamed 'Level clearing (*blàr*) of Adam (surname)' after the family of famous Scottish architects and interior designers, most famous of which was Robert Adam (1728–1792), whose father was born in this village. Its original name was Maryburgh.

Blair Atholl [Tayside] Probably 'Level clearing (*blàr*) [of] a second (*ath*) Ireland (*Fhodla*)': Fodla is an old kenning, like Erin.

Blairbeg [Strathclyde] 'Level clearing (*blàr*), small (*beag*)'.

Blairdaff [Grampian] Possibly 'Level clearing (*blàr*) of the stag (*daimh*)'.

Blair Drummond [Central] 'Level clearing (*blàr*) [of the] Drummond [family]': the family surname means 'at the ridge' and was that of the Earls of Perth (a city some 28 miles north-east).

Blairgowrie [Tayside] 'Level clearing (*blàr*) of Gabran (personal name)': Gabran was one of the three sons of Fe(a)rgus, pioneer invader from Ireland.

Blairingone [Central/Tayside] 'Level clearing (*blàr*) of the (*na-n*) blacksmiths (*gobhainn*)'.

Blairlogie [Central] 'Level clearing (*blàr*) of the hollow (*lagaidh*)'.

Blairmore [Strathclyde] 'Level clearing (*blàr*), big (*mór*)'.

Blantyre [Strathclyde] Apparently a Brythonic doublet: 'Edge (*blaen*, Brythonic Gaelic) land (*tir*, Brythonic Gaelic [identical with Goidelic])'.

blàr 'level clearing', 'plain', 'flat space'.

Blàr a' Chaorainn [Highland] 'Level clearing (*blàr*) of the rowan tree (genitive of *caorann*)'.

Blarghour [Strathclyde] Probably 'Level clearing (*blàr*) of the goat (*gobhair*)'.

Blarnalearoch [Highland] Possibly 'Level clearing (*blàr*) of the (*na*) ruined house (*làrach*)'.

Blawrainy [Dumfries & Galloway] 'Level clearing (*blàr*), ferny (*raineach*)'.

bó 'cow'; the word is evidently cognate with Greek *bous*, Latin *bov-*, English *beef*, and, ultimately, cow.

Boath [Highland] Possibly 'Herdsman's hut (*buth*, ON or *bothe*, ME, or even the Gaelic loan-word of identical meaning, *both*)'.

Boat of Garten [Highland] '[Ferry-]Boat (Eng) [across the River Spey near the confluence of the River] Garten': a bridge obviating the need for this ferry was built in 1898. The river name probably means 'tilled ground'.

boc 'buck'; the word is evidently cognate with its English translation.

Boch-ailean [Highland] Presumably 'Buck (*boc*) rocks (*ailean*)', a coastal feature between Dunbeath and Helmsdale.

bodach 'old man', 'ghost'.

Boddam [Shetland; Grampian] Probably 'Bottom [i.e. dell] (*botm*, OE or *bodom*, OSw; ON is *botn*)'.

bodha 'sea-covered rock', 'hazard to shipping'; the word derives from the ON *bothi*, 'breaker', 'roller', 'shore-wave'.

bog 'soft', 'damp', thus also 'soft place', 'marshland'. The English word *bog* is thought to have been loaned from Gaelic.

Bogbrae [Grampian] Presumably 'Marsh (*bog*) slope (*brae*, Scots)'.

46

B

Bogend [Strathclyde] Presumably 'Marsh (*bog*) end (Eng)'.

Bogh a' Chuirn [Jura] 'Bay (*bàgh*) of the cairn (genitive of *carn*)'.

boghal 'danger'; the word is cognate with English/Scots *bogle*.

Bogie [Grampian] Probably 'Boggy (*bogeadh*)'; it is a river name that may in fact be back-formed from the name of the valley, Strath Bogie.

Bogmoor [Grampian] Presumably 'Marsh (*bog*) moor (Eng)': the village stands in the very fertile area of the Spey estuary.

Bogton [Grampian] Presumably 'Marsh (*bog*) community (*toun*, ME)'.

Bohenie [Highland] Possibly 'Hut (*both*) on the steep brae (*aoinidh*)'.

Bohuntine [Highland] Possibly 'Hut (*both*) of the beacon[-keeper] (*an teine*)'.

bòideach ' beautiful' (modern Gaelic).

Boisdale [Uist] Possibly 'Boia's (personal name, OE/ON) dale (OE/ON)'; the personal name is attested in several English place names.

bol 'settlement' (ON; cf present-day Swedish *böle*); the element is often combined with ON *stathr* in the form of *bol-stathr*, 'settlement-steading'.

-bole elided form of *boghail*, genitive of *boghal*, thus 'of danger', 'dangerous'.

Bonaly [Lothian] Apparently 'Hut (*both*) of the (*na*) rocks (*h-aile*)'.

Bonawe [Strathclyde] 'Mouth (*bun*) of the river (*abha[inn]*)': the ironic thing is that the river is now called the River Awe. This is where the river flows into Loch Etive.

Bo'ness [Central] A contraction of *Borrowstounness*, that is: 'Burgh's (ME) town (ME) ness [i.e. promontory] (ME)'. The town has long been a Royal Burgh. A decade ago the derivation was said to be 'Beornweardes (personal name, OE) town ness'. Who knows what the next decade will bring. Incidentally, 'Beornwearde' means 'bear-keeper'.

Bonjedward [Border] Probably 'Mouth (*bun*) [of the River] Jed, enclosed meadow (*ward*, Scots)'; the fact that the name refers to the meadow, on slightly more solid ground, explains why the village is actually half a mile from the actual confluence of the Jed with the Teviot, which is a distinctly marshier prospect. The meaning of the river name Jed is obscure . . . but see **Jedburgh.**

Bonkle [Strathclyde] Possibly 'Confluence (*bun*) ridge (*cùl*)': just below the village is a meeting of major streams.

bonn 'base', 'foot'. Probably cognate with *bun*: 'root', thus '(river-)mouth'.

bonny 'fair', 'good', 'nice', 'handsome'; the word derives through ME from OFr and ultimately from Latin *bonus*, 'good'.

Bonnybridge [Highland] '[River] Bonny bridge (Eng)': the meaning of the river name is thought to be 'fair', 'handsome' (see *bonny*).

Bonnyrigg [Lothian] 'Bannock[-shaped] (Scots) ridge (Scots)': the town is situated on a flat oatmeal-cake-shaped ridge.

Borgie Bridge [Highland] '[River] Borgie bridge (Eng)': the river name is probably ON, meaning 'fort-river'.

Borgue [Highland] Probably 'Fort (*borg*, ON)'.

Borgue [Dumfries & Galloway] Possibly 'Security (*borg*, OE)': the village is quite remote. The only actual stronghold (*borg*, ON or *burh*, OE) in the area is a 16th-century castle, too late to influence the name. However, the even smaller community at the end of the peninsula seaward is consequently called *Borness*.

Borness [Dumfries & Galloway] '[Village of] Borgue ness [i.e. peninsula] (OE/ON)'. For the possible meanings of Borgue, see above. Ironically, the peninsula on which Borness stands is now called Borness Point.

borrach 'rough hill-grass'.

Borrodale [Highland] 'Fort (*borg*, ON) dale (*dalr*, ON)'; the local pronunciation is, amazingly, 'ba-roddle'.

Borthwick Water [Borders] The meaning of *Borthwick* is said to be 'Home farmstead', the second element then evidently (*wic*, OE). The name of the Borthwick Water is thus obviously derived from a 'home farmstead' somewhere on its banks, presumably at Borthwickbrae (*brae*, 'hillside', Scots), for Borthwickshiel (*shiel*, 'sheltering slope', Scots) is at least 1 mile up the hill to the north. But both these final elements are very much later than the original OE name anyway . . . It is just possible that all these names are in fact transferred from Mary Queen of Scots' Borthwick Castle, on the banks of the Heriot Water some 30 miles north, now no longer named or even marked on many maps. If so, the initial element is far more likely to be OE *burh*, 'castle'.

-bost elided form of ON *bol-stathr*: 'settlement-steading'.

both (also *bothan*) 'hut', 'cabin', 'turf lean-to'; the word is an adaptation of ON *buth* or OE *bothl* (and is cognate with English *bothy* and *booth*).

B

Bothwell [Strathclyde] Probably '[St] Bathan's (personal name) well (ME)': St Bathan was an abbot of Bangor in the mid-600s.

Bousd [Coll] Possibly 'Bui's (personal name, ON) house (*setr*, ON)': the personal name is attested in a Norfolk place name.

bower- often 'cottage', from OE *bur*.

Bowden [Borders] Probably '[Village dedicated to St] Bathan (personal name)': St Bathan was an abbot of Bangor in the mid-600s.

Bowhill [Borders] Presumably 'Curved (*boga*, OE) hill (*hyll*, OE)': this is an accurate geographical description of the location.

Brabster [Highland] Possibly 'Broad (*breithr*, ON) settlement-steading (*bol-stathr*, ON)', although the first element might alternatively be a personal name, such as Bragi['s].

Bracadale [Skye] Possibly 'Bracca['s] (personal name, ON) dale (*dalr*, ON)'.

bradan 'salmon'.

brae 'hillside', 'slope', 'top end', 'hill with a valley beneath'; the word is a Scots and Northern English (ME) dialect word, probably cognate with English *brow*.

Brae [Shetland; Highland (2)] 'Hillside (*brae*, Scots)'.

Braehead [Orkney; Strathclyde (2); Tayside; Dumfries & Galloway] 'Hillside (*brae*, Scots) head (Eng)'.

Braemar [Grampian] 'Top end (*brae*, Scots) [of the area called] Mar': the derivation of the area name is unknown. Mar Lodge, 4 miles west, is modern.

Braemore [Highland] 'Hillside (*brae*, Scots), big (*mór*)', and indeed the road south from Ullapool seems to rise steeply over several miles to reach Braemore Junction at the top, near by the famous Corrieshalloch Gorge.

Brae of Achnahaird [Highland] 'Hillside (*brae*, Scots) of (Eng) the place (*achadh*) of the (*na*) height (*h-aird*)'; the first two elements were evidently added much later, and presumably by non-Gaelic-speakers.

Braeriach See **Braigh Riabhach**.

Braeside [Strathclyde] 'Slope (*brae*, Scots) side (Eng)': the suburb lies along the A78 and the railway as they both skirt a ridge on the Greenock-Gourock peninsula.

Braes of Balquhidder [Central] 'Hillsides (*braes*, Scots) of [the village of] Balquhidder': the village name apparently means 'settlement of fodder'.

Braes of the Carse [Tayside] 'Hillsides (*braes*, Scots) of the [lowland area known as the] Carse [of Gowrie]'. See **Carse of Gowrie**.

bràghad (also *bràighaid*, *bràighe*) 'neck', thus also 'top end', 'upper slope'.

Braidwood [Strathclyde] Probably 'Broad (*braid*, Scots) wood (Eng)'.

brèagha 'beautiful' (modern Gaelic).

bràighaid (also *bràighe*) 'top end', 'upper slope'; the word derives in effect from Gaelic *bràghad*, 'neck', but also represents a more Gaelic adaptation of the Scots (ME) word *brae*.

Bràigh-nam-bàgh [Harris] 'Hillside (*bràighe*) of the (*na-m*) bay (*bàgh*)'.

Braigh Riabhach [Grampian] 'Upper slope (*bràighe*), brindled (*riabhach*)'.

Braigh Sròn Ghorm [Tayside] 'Upper slope (*bràighe*) point (*sròn*), grey-blue (*ghorm*)'.

Branault [Highland] Possibly 'Salmon (*bradan*) stream (*allt*)'.

Branxholme [Borders] Probably 'Branoc's (personal name, OE) land mostly surrounded by a stream (*holm*, OE adaptation of ON *holmr*)': the village lies on the bank of the River Teviot.

Breabag [Highland] 'Top (*bràighe*), small (*beag*)'.

breac 'speckled', 'mottled', and thus, as a noun, 'trout'.

Breadalbane [Grampian/Tayside/Central] 'Top end (*bràghad*) [of] Albyn': Albyn is an ancient name for Scotland.

Breakachy [Highland] 'Speckled (*breac*) field (*achadh*)': the name is unusual in placing the adjective before the noun – just like English.

Brechin [Tayside] '[Of] Brecon (personal name)'. The personal name is common to Celtic mythologies, and is found in place names all over Britain (Brecon, Brechin, Wrekin, etc.). In Scottish Gaelic legend the name can also be spelled Brychan; it may mean something like 'holy' or 'high' and is related to the British river and tribal name *Brigant-*. The name may well have been taken by tribal leaders – Brychan is said to have been an Irish prince – cf the forename Brian, when not of Norman then of Celtic derivation, as in Brian Boru, the earliest known exemplar.

bréige genitive form of *breug*, thus 'of a deception', and so 'false', 'misleading'.

50

Brettabister [Shetland] Probably 'Britons' (*bretta*, ON/OE) settlement-steading (*bol-stathr*)', although there was also a personal name Bretta, either of identical meaning or a version of 'Bert'.

breug 'deception', 'falsification'.

breugach 'false', 'deceptive', 'misleading', 'substitute', 'pseudo-'.

breun 'foul'.

-bride elided form of the name of [St] Bridget/Bridie; for the derivation and further information, see below, and **Kilbride**.

Brideswell [Grampian] Usually supposed to be '[St] Bridie's (personal name) well (ME)', but the name really only commemorates the fact that the well was regarded as holy before Christian times, and was thus attributed to Bridie, or Brigit, the Celtic goddess of fire, daughter of the sun god, whose worship the church had to overcome. See **Kilbride**.

bridge of . . . usually connotes a settlement at the bridge, and is followed by the river name. See river names independently.

Bridgeton [Strathclyde] Name of an estate bought by John Orr in 1731 representing land near to a bridge over the River Clyde.

Brig o' Turk [Central] Romanticised form of 'Bridge over [the River] Turk', only the river is more commonly called the Finglas Water. The river name Turk means 'boar' but is a name commonly given to rivers that are particularly deep and may become subterranean.

Broadford [Skye] 'Broad (Eng) ford (Eng)': the village is of relatively late foundation and stands on the Abhainn Suardal. The name is probably a translation of the original (very late 18th-century) Gaelic.

broc 'badger'; the word is cognate with *breac*, 'speckled', because of the badger's very visible variegation in colour. The OE cognate was *brocc*.

brochan 'porridge', and thus 'rough ground', 'broken stones'.

Brodick [Arran] 'Broad (*breithr*, ON) bay (*vík*, ON)': ironically, the bay on which the town now stands is called Brodick Bay. The Gaelic name for the town is Invercloy.

Brora [Highland] Apparently '[The] Bridge's (*bru'r*, ON) river (å, ON)'; for centuries until the 1800s, the bridge at Brora was the only one in the duchy of Sutherland.

brothach 'boiling', 'turbulent'.

Brough [Shetland (3)] Probably 'Fort (*burh*, OE)' or the ON equivalent.

broughton either
1) 'brook (*broc*, OE) community (*tun*, OE)';
2) 'fort (*burh*, OE) community (*tun*, OE)
or 3) 'hill (*beorg*, OE) community (*tun*, OE)'.

-brox usually 'badger's' either from Goidelic *bruic(h)* or OE *brocc*.

Broxburn [Lothian (2)] Probably 'Badger's (*brocc-s*, OE) stream (*burna*, OE)', although the first element could be a personal name of identical etymology; badgers are not known for frequenting streams, it must be said. In any case, both elements are OE. An earlier name for this region was Easter Strathbrock.

bruach 'bank', 'brim', 'brink', 'edge'.

Brue [Lewis] Possibly 'Bridge (*bru*, ON)'.

Bruernish [Barra] Possibly 'Bridge's (*bru'r*, ON) cape (*nes*, ON)': it is possible that the only way on to the peninsula at the head of which the village stands was via a bridge. Ironically, the peninsula is now called Bruernish Point.

bruic genitive form of *broc*, thus 'of the badger'.

Bruichladdich [Islay] Possibly 'Edge (*bruach*) of the shore (*chladaich*)', which would fit, geographically.

Brunton [Fife] Possibly 'Stream (*burna*, OE) community (*tun*, OE)'.

bruthach 'hillside', 'slope'; the word is in effect a doublet of *brae*.

-bsta often an elided form of ON *bol-stathr*: 'settlement-steading'.

-bster often an elided form of ON *bol-stathr*: 'settlement-steading'.

buachaill 'herdsman', 'shepherd'; the word is cognate with Greek *boukolios*, cf English 'bucolic', the root meaning being 'beef farmer', although in practice the Scottish farmer tended after the late 18th century to be sheep-oriented.

Buachaille Etive Beag/Mór [Highland] The 'Etive Shepherds', 'big (*mór*)' and 'small (*beag*)', are two high mountains that contribute to the southerly heights over Glen Coe. Behind them, Glen Etive leads to Loch Etive – but the meaning of *etive* is unknown.

buaile 'cattle-pen'; the word contains the element *bó*, 'cow'.

buailtean 'place of cattle-pens', 'cow-enclosures'.

B

Bualnaluib [Highland] Probably 'Cattle-pen (*buaile*) of the (*na*) bend (*lùib*, genitive of *lùb*)': the community is situated in the bend of a stream.

Buccleuch [Borders] Probably 'Buck['s] (*bucc*, OE) ravine (*cloh*, OE)': the name is pronounced 'ba-Klew'. And yet the legend is that an isolated tower gave the name to the estate. What rubbish, eh? The Duke of Buccleuch employs the piper who plays at Gretna Green, some 30 miles directly further south. And more power to his pibroch.

buchan an old word, used as a surname, of which the true meaning may be 'calf' (diminutive of *bó*), 'little hut' (*bothan*), 'little buck' (diminutive of *boc*), or something else entirely.

Buckhaven [Fife} Probably 'Buck (*bok*, OScand) haven (OScand)'.

Buckholm [Borders] 'Buck (*bok*, OScand) river-island (*holm*, OScand)': the village stands on the bank of the Gala Water.

Buckie [Grampian] Probably 'Of bucks (*bocaidh*)'.

Bucksburn [Grampian] 'Buck's (*bucc-s*, OE) stream (*burna*, OE)'.

buic genitive form of *boc*, thus 'of the buck'.

buidhe 'yellow'.

Buidhe Bheinn [Highland] 'Yellow (*buidhe*) mountain (*bheinn*)'.

buidheanaich 'yellow place'.

buie elided form of *buidhe*: 'yellow'.

buige genitive form of *bog*, thus 'of the soft . . . ', and 'of the marsh'.

builg 'rise', 'hillock'.

bùirich 'roaring', 'thundering'.

Buldoo [Highland] Possibly 'Rise (*builg*), dark (*dubh*)'; it is less likely that a cattle-pen (*buaile*) or a hamlet (*baile*) should be dark.

Bulg [Tayside] Probably '[The] Rise (*builg*)'.

bun (literally, 'root') 'river-mouth'.

Bunacaimb [Highland] Probably 'River-mouth (*bun*) of the bend (*a' caime*)': the nearby stream takes a Z-bend shortly before reaching the sea just in front of the village.

Bunarkaig [Highland] 'River-mouth (*bun*) of Arkaig': at this village the water flowing from Loch Arkaig meets the Great Glen at Loch Lochy. The meaning of *arkaig* is unknown.

Bunavoneadar [Harris] Presumably 'River-mouth (*bun*) of the river (*abhainn*) between (*eadar*)': this careful description may refer to the river's flowing between the two mountains Uisgnaval Mór and Clisham.

Bunchrew [Highland] 'River-mouth (*bun*) of the tree (*chraoibhe*)'.

Bundalloch [Highland] Presumably 'River-mouth (*bun*) of the field (*dalach*, genitive of *dail*)'.

Bunessan [Mull] 'River-mouth (*bun*) of the waterfalls (*easan*, genitive plural of *eas*)'.

Bunloinn Forest [Highland] 'Mouth (*bun*) of [the River] Loyne forest (Eng)': the river name probably means 'marshy'.

Bunnahabhainn [Islay] 'River-mouth (*bun*) of the (*na*) river (*h-abhainn*)'.

Burdiehouse [Lothian] Said to be 'Bordeaux house', and even more fancifully to have something to do with Mary Queen of Scots' retinue. Make of that what you will.

Burg [Mull] Probably 'Hill (*beorg*, OE)' rather than 'Fort (*burh*, OE)'.

Burghead [Grampian] Possibly '[Pictish] Broch (adaptation of OE/ON) head (Eng)': there are ancient ramparts and structures in and close to the village.

burn 'stream'; although considered a classic Scottish word, it derives in fact from OE *burna* and has Germanic cognates.

Burnfoot [Borders (2)] 'Stream (*burn*, ME) foot (ME)'.

Burnhaven [Grampian] Village established in around 1840 as a haven (harbour) at the mouth of a burn (stream) by one George Mudie.

Burnhead [Dumfries & Galloway] 'Stream (*burn*, ME) head (ME)'.

Burnmouth [Borders] 'Stream (*burn*, ME) mouth (ME)'.

Burn of Cambus [Central] Presumably 'Stream (*burn*, ME) of (Eng) the river-bend (*camas*)': the village stands where a stream joins the Annet Burn as it negotiates a curve. The first two elements of the name were evidently added later.

Burnside [Shetland; Strathclyde; Fife; Lothian] 'Stream (*burn*, ME) side (ME)'.

Burntdales [Grampian] Possibly 'Burnt (ME) portions (ME equivalent of Eng *deals*)'.

Burntisland [Fife] Said to be 'Burnet's (personal name, ME) land (ME)', although there are several other possible personal names (like Brand). Anyway, despite folk-etymological rumours to the contrary, there is no island to have been involved in a conflagration and no record of any fire.

Burrafirth [Shetland] Presumably 'Fort (*borg*, ON) *fjord* (*fjordr*, ON)': the village thus takes its name from the firth, which is now called Burra Firth.

Burravoe [Shetland (2)] Presumably 'Fort (*borg*, ON) bay (*vágr*, ON)': the villages are, respectively, on Busta Voe (Mainland) and Burra Voe (Yell).

Busby [Strathclyde (2)] Possibly 'Butr's (personal name, ON) community (*byr*, ON)'.

Busta [Shetland] Possibly 'Butr's (personal name, ON) steading (*stathr*, ON)', or some other personal name.

Beinn

Beinn

The following are mountain names that on the map are preceded by this word:

a' Bheithir [Highland] 'of the monster (*bheithir*)'.

a' Bhoth [Lewis] 'of the turf hut (*bhoth*)'.

a' Bhragaidh [Highland] 'of the upper part (*bhràghad*)'.

a' Bhuird [Grampian] Apparently 'of the poet (genitive of *bard*)', but the final element might instead refer to an 'enclosed meadow (*ward*, Scots)' although that is less likely for a mountain name.

a' Chaisil [Highland] 'of the stone fort (genitive of *caiseal*)'.

a' Chaisteil [Highland] 'of the castle (genitive of *caisteal*)'.

a' Chaolais [Harris] 'of the narrows (*chaolais*)': south of the mountain is the narrows separating Harris from Scalpay.

a' Chaorainn [Highland; Grampian] 'of the rowan tree (genitive of *caorann*)'.

a' Chapuill [Highland] 'of the horse (genitive of *capall*)'.

a' Charnain [Pabbay] 'of the little cairn (genitive of *carnan*)'.

a' Chearcaill [Skye] 'in a circle (*chearcaill*)'.

a' Chlachain [Highland] 'of the stone building (genitive of *clachan*)'.

a' Chlachair Highland] 'of the stone-cutter (genitive of *clachar*)'.

a' Chlaidheimh [Highland] 'of the sword (genitive of *claidheamh*)'.

a' Chreachain [Tayside] 'of the windswept summit (genitive of *creachann*)'.

a' Chroin [Central] Possibly 'of the sheep-pens (*chròithean*)'.

a' Chuirn [Highland] 'of the cairn (genitive of *carn*)'.

a' Ghlo [Tayside] 'of the mist (genitive of *glo*)'.

Aird da Loch [Highland] 'Height (*aird*) of two (*dà*) lochs': the large Lochs Glencoul and Glendhu run one each side.

Airigh Charr [Highland] 'Shieling (*àirigh*), rocky (*charr*)'.

Alligin [Highland] The name is thought to contain the element *ail*: 'rock';

some commentators alternatively derive a meaning 'jewel' – though they decline to explain how.

a' Mhanaich [Strathclyde] 'of the monk (genitive of *manach*)'.

an Eòin [Highland (2)] 'of the bird (genitive of *eun*)'.

an Lochain [Strathclyde] 'of the little loch (genitive of *lochan*)'. Surprisingly, this mountain is only 5 miles north-east of Beinn Lochain (without the 'an').

an Oir [Jura] 'of gold (genitive of *or*)'.

an t-Sneachda [Highland] 'of the snow (*sneachda*)'.

an Tuirc [Strathclyde] 'of the boar (genitive of *torc*)'.

a' Sgà [Skye] Possibly 'of the shelter (*sgàth*)'.

Bhalgairean [Strathclyde] Probably 'Of the foxes (*bhalgair-*)'.

Bhàn [Highland (2); Islay] 'White (*bhàn*)'.

Bharrain [Arran] Presumably 'Of the summits (genitive plural of *barr*)'.

Bheag [Highland; Strathclyde] 'Small (*bheag*)'.

Bhràghad [Skye] 'Of the upper part (*bhràghad*, genitive of *bràighe*)'.

Bhreac [Skye (3); Soay; Highland (5); Tayside (2); Strathclyde (7); Central (2); Colonsay; Jura (2); Islay; Arran] 'Speckled (*bhreac*)'.

Bhreac-liath [Strathclyde] 'Speckled (*bhreac*) grey (*liath*)'.

Bhreac Mhór [Highland] 'Speckled (*bhreac*), big (*mhór*)'.

Bhuidhe [Highland (2); Mull; Strathclyde] 'Yellow (*bhuidhe*)'.

Bhuidhe Mhór [Highland] 'Yellow (*bhuidhe*), big (*mhór*)'.

Chapull [Strathclyde] 'Of the horse (*chapuill*, genitive of *capall*)'.

Charnach Bheag [Skye] Presumably '[Of the] Little cairn (*charnach*), small (*bheag*)'.

Cheathaich [Central] 'Misty (*cheathaich*)'.

Choin [Central] 'Of the dog (*choin*, genitive of *cù*)'.

Chreagach [Skye; Mull] 'Craggy (*chreagach*)'.

Chreagach Mhór [Mull] 'Craggy (*chreagach*), big (*mhór*)'.

Damh [Highland] 'Stag (*damh*)'.

Dictionary of Scottish Place Names

Dearg [Highland (3); Tayside; Strathclyde; Central] 'Red (*dearg*)'.

Dearg Bad Chailleach [Highland] 'Red (*dearg*), clump of trees (*bad*) of the old woman (*chaillich*)'. This name seems a jumble of ideas and probably combines two quite distinct appellations.

Dearg Mhór [Highland] 'Red (*dearg*), big (*mhór*)'.

Dhubh [Harris] 'Black (*dhubh*)'.

Domhnaill [Highland] 'Of Donald (genitive of *Domhnall*)'.

Donn [Strathclyde] 'Brown (*donn*)'.

Dorain [Tayside] Probably 'Of the otter (genitive of *doran*)', but there is a remote possibility that it might instead be 'Of the exile (genitive of *dòran*)'.

Dubhchraig [Central] 'Black (*dubh*) crag (*chreag*)'.

Dubh [Islay] 'Black (*dubh*)'.

Each [Central] 'Horse (*each*)'.

Edra [Skye] Possibly '[In] Between (*eadar*)': the mountain is the middle of three in a not very distinguished line.

Eich [Strathclyde] 'Of the horse (genitive of *each*)'.

Eighe [Highland] Possibly 'Wailing (*eigheach*)'.

Eilideach [Highland] Probably 'Of hinds (*eilideach*)'.

Eunaich [Strathclyde] Presumably 'Of birds (*eun-*)'.

Fhada [Highland] 'Long (*fhada*)'. On older maps the name of this mountain may appear anglicised as *Ben Attow* (remember an initial Fh- is not pronounced in Gaelic).

Fhionnlaidh [Highland] Possibly 'Of the fair (*fhionn*) land between a fork (*laidhre*)': the mountain lies between the converging arms of Benula Forest. 'Benula' is itself an anglicisation of 'Beinn Fhionnlaidh'. Fionnlaidh may be the derivation of the surname Finlay, although the second element of that is usually quoted as *laoch*, 'hero'.

Fhionnlaidh [Strathclyde] Possibly 'Of the fair (*fhionn*) land between a fork (*laidhre*)': the mountain lies between the converging arms of Glen Creran and Glen Ure. Fionnlaidh may be the derivation of the surname Finlay, although the second element of that is usually quoted as *laoch*, 'hero'.

Gharbh [Highland] 'Rough [water] (*gharbh*)'.

58

Ghlas [Strathclyde (3)] Probably in all cases 'Blue-green (*ghlas*)' rather than 'Of the stream (*ghlais*)', although either is (again in all cases) topographically possible.

Ghobhlach [Highland] 'Forked (*ghobhlach*)'.

Iaruinn [Highland] 'Of iron (genitive of *iarann*)'.

Làir [Highland] 'Of the mare (*làire*)'.

Liath Bheag [Highland] 'Grey (*liath*), small (*bheag*)'.

Liath Mhór [Highland] 'Grey (*liath*), big (*mhór*)'.

Liath Mhór a' Ghiubhais Lì [Highland] 'Grey (*liath*), big (*mhór*), of the fir tree (*ghiubhais*) in quantity (*lì*)'.

Lochain [Strathclyde; Arran] 'Of the little loch (genitive of *lochan*)'.

Loinne [Highland] Probably '[Overlooking the River] Loyne': the name of the river presumably means 'marshy'. North of the mountain is Bunloinn Forest (q.v.).

Macduibh [Grampian] 'Of [someone called] MacDuff': the personal name means 'son of the black-haired'. The name is sometimes anglicised to Macdui.

Maol Chaluim [Highland] Possibly '[The] Bare summit (*maol*) of [St] Columba (genitive of *Calman*)': the final element could alternatively mean 'of the dove'.

Mhanach [Tayside] 'Of the monk (*mhanaich*)'.

Mheadhoin [Highland (2)] 'Middle (genitive of *meadhon*)'.

Mheadhonach [Lewis; Strathclyde] 'In the middle (*mheadhonach*)'.

Mholach [Tayside] Possibly 'Massive (*mol-*)'.

Mhór [Uist; Lewis; Highland; Mull; Strathclyde (2); Central] 'Big (*mhór*)'.

na Caillich [Skye; Highland] 'of the (*na*) old woman (*caillich*)': the final element can alternatively mean 'hag' or 'nun'.

na Cille [Highland] 'of the (*na*) church (*cille*)'.

na Crò [Skye] 'of the (*na*) sheep-pen (*crò*)'.

na Croise [Mull] 'of the (*na*) crosses (*croise*)'.

na Drise [Mull] 'of the (*na*) brambles (*drise*)'.

na Greine [Skye] 'of the (*na*) sun (*gréine*)'.

59

Dictionary of Scottish Place Names

na h-Uamha [Highland] 'of the (*na*) caves (*h-uamha*)'.

na Lice [Strathclyde] 'of the (*na*) flat stone (genitive of *leac*)'.

nam Bad Mór [Highland] 'of the (*na-m*) clump of trees (*bad*), big (*mór*)'.

nam Bó [Highland] 'of the (*na-m*) cow (*bó*)'.

nan Cabar [Highland] 'of the (*na-n*) antler (*cabar*)'.

nan Caorach [Highland] 'of the (*na-n*) sheep (*caorach*)'.

nan Carn [Skye] 'of the (*na-n*) cairn (*carn*)'.

nan Cuithean [Skye] 'of the (*na-n*) narrow little glen (diminutive of *cuithe*)'.

nan Eun [Highland] 'of the (*na-n*) bird (*eun*)'.

nan Losgann [Highland] 'of the (*na-n*) frog (*losgann*)'.

nan Lus [Strathclyde] 'of the (*na-n*) herbs (*luss*)'.

nan Ramh [Highland] 'of the (*na-n*) oar (*ràmh*)'.

na Seamraig [Skye] 'of the (*na*) shamrock (genitive of *seamrag*)'.

na Seilg [Highland] 'of the (*na*) hunt (*sealg*)'.

na Sròine [Strathclyde] 'of the (*na*) points (genitive plural of *sròn*)'.

Odhar [Strathclyde] 'Dun-coloured (*odhar*)'.

Odhar Bheag [Highland] 'Dun-coloured (*odhar*), small (*bheag*)'.

Odhar Mhór [Highland] 'Dun-coloured (*odhar*), big (*mhór*)'.

Raah [Taransay] Possibly 'Roe-deer (*raa*, ON)'.

Ràtha [Highland] Probably '[of the village of] Reay', which is about 2 miles north; both names are forms of *ràth*: 'circular fort'.

Rifa-gil [Highland] Probably 'Cleft (*rifa*, ON) water-course (*gil*, ON)'; the mountain overlooks the village of Rhifail, which would seem to be the same name.

Ruadh [Highland; Strathclyde (2)] 'Red-brown (*ruadh*)'.

Sgeireach [Highland] Probably 'Rocky (*sgeireach*)', although this word should technically be used only in coastal contexts.

Sgreamhaidh [Highland] Possibly 'Dusty (*sgreamh-*)'.

Spionnaidh [Highland] 'Thorny (*spionnaidh*)'.

Suidhe [Strathclyde] 'Seat-like ledge (*suidhe*)'.

Tarsuinn [Highland (2); Arran] 'Athwart (*tarsuinn*)': the name is meant to suggest a mountain at right-angles to some other feature of the landscape.

Teallach [Highland] 'Anvil (*teallach*)'.

Tulaichean [Central] Probably 'Of the hillocks (*tulaich-*)'.

Udlamain [Tayside] 'Gloomy (*udlamain*)'.

Uidhe [Highland] 'Isthmus (*uidh*)'.

Uird [Central] 'Round hill (genitive of *ord*)'.

C

cabar 'horn', 'antler'.

cabhail '(fishing) creel', 'pot'.

cabhsair 'causeway': regrettably, the Gaelic is a corruption of the English.

Cabrach [Grampian] 'Stony (*cabrach*)'.

cachaileith 'field gate', 'hurdle'.

Cadder [Strathclyde] Possibly 'Stronghold (*cadair*, early form of Brythonic Gaelic *caer*, modern Gaelic *cathair*)': the suburb is close to the Antonine wall.

cadha 'steep place', 'pass'.

Caddonfoot [Borders] 'Caddon [Water's] foot (Eng)': the village lies where the Caddon Water flows into the River Tweed. The river name may derive from the Brythonic word for 'fox'.

caer 'stronghold', 'fort': the word derives from an earlier form *cadair* (now *cathair*) that was applied also to significant mountains (as in Cader Idris in Wales): the root meaning is 'seat', and the word is cognate with the Greek *cathedra*, 'throne', and the English *chair*.

Caerlaverock [Dumfries & Galloway] 'Fort (*cathair*) [in] the elm trees (*leamhreaich*)'.

caibeal 'chapel': an obvious derivative from Latin *capella*.

cailleach fascinating word: it derives ultimately from the Latin *palliata*, 'cloaked [woman]', thus either a nun or an elderly woman who smothered herself in dun-coloured weeds (and generally therefore considered an old hag); but the word was borrowed from Latin at a time when Gaelic had no equivalent for the letter 'p', and used the 'k' sound instead (cf Welsh *pen* and Gaelic *ceann*)'.

Cailleach Head [Highland] '[The] Old hag (*cailleach*) headland (Eng)': this is the headland between the sea-entrances to Loch Broom and Little Loch Broom; for the etymological ramifications of the first element, see above.

caillich genitive form of *cailleach*, thus 'of the nun', 'of the old hag'.

caime genitive form of *cam*, thus 'of the crooked . . . '.

caiplich 'place of horses': the word is a derivative of *capall*, 'horse'.

cairn anglicisation of Gaelic *carn*, 'heap of stones', 'memorial stones', 'humped hill', although in fact the anglicisation also represents the genitive Gaelic form, thus 'of a cairn'.

Cairnbaan [Strathclyde] Possibly '[The] Cairn (*carn*), white (*bàn*)': ancient monuments litter the area.

Cairndow [Strathclyde] Presumably '[The] Cairn (*carn*), dark (*dubh*)'.

Cairngorm [Highland] 'Humped mountain (*carn*), blue (*gorm*)'.

Cairnharrow [Dumfries & Galloway] 'Humped mountain (*carn*) of the [pagan] temple (*hearga*, OE): the ancient monument known as Cairn Holy lies on its southern slopes.

Cairn Ryan [Dumfries & Galloway] 'Cairn [on Loch] Ryan': the village was in fact renamed after the loch on which it stands. The loch name may mean simply 'water'. The village was originally called Macherie (*machar*, 'the sandy plain').

caise genitive form of *cas*, thus 'of the steep . . .'.

caiseal 'stronghold', 'fort': the word derives from Latin *castellum*, from which the English later derived 'castle'.

caisteal 'castle': the word is of later derivation from the Latin *castellum*.

Caisteal Liath [Highland] '[The] Castle (*caisteal*), grey (*liath*)': this name is often used as an alternative to *Suilven*, although it technically refers only to one of the two peaks of that mountain.

caith- in the north, 'cat' (ON *köttr*), either as a tribal name or as a geographically descriptive term for the terrain.

Caithness [Highland] 'Cat (*köttr*, ON) ness (*nes*, ON)': the animal name may represent the name of the dominant tribe of the area (cf Orkney, just across the Pentland Firth) or instead reflect some geographical feature of the coastline.

cala (also *caladh*) 'harbour'.

Calder [Highland; Strathclyde; Lothian] River name transferred to communities on the shore: most commentators plump for 'Hard (*caled*, Brythonic Gaelic) water (*dobhar*, Brythonic Gaelic)'. The latter element is undoubtedly 'water', but for the first element some commentators alternatively suggest the Gaelic element *callaidh*, 'rapid'; most attractive of all is the possibility of the Brythonic equivalent of modern Welsh *celydd*, 'wooded shelter' (see **Caledonia**).

Dictionary of Scottish Place Names

Caledonia Roman (Latin) name for the Highlands of Scotland, often now used for the whole of the country. Found in the writings of both Lucan and Tacitus, the name is nevertheless first evidenced in Greek histories, spelled with an initial K- and with a long second syllable; it is presumably derived from the name given the region by its contemporary inhabitants, who were Brythonic Celts. The name may thus mean no more than Celt(onia), place of Celts – cf Galatia (with a long second syllable), place of Celts in Asia Minor – possibly with a second element approximating to *dùn*, 'stronghold' (which in Latin became *-dunum* in many place names): cf the reversal of this idea in *Dunkeld*. The race name 'Celts' is thought to mean, appropriately, '[people of] the mountains'. Alternatively, the initial element may correspond to the Brythonic equivalent of the modern Welsh *celydd*, 'wooded shelter', which would also be apt – or, less aptly, may be either of the first two water-elements proposed under **Calder**.

Calgary [Mull] 'Kali['s] (personal name, ON) enclosure (*garthr*, ON)'.

call (also *calltuinn, coll*) 'hazel'.

Callander [Central] Probably 'Hard (*caled*, Brythonic Gaelic) water (*dobhar*, Brythonic Gaelic)'.

Callanish [Lewis] Possibly 'Calf's (*calfa*, OE) ness (*naes*, OE)' or the ON equivalents. The first element may simultaneously be a personal nickname.

calltuinn (also *call, coll*) 'hazel'.

calman   either 1) 'dove';
            or 2) [St] Columba (a name that means 'dove' in Latin).

Calvay [Uist] Presumably 'Calf (*kalfr*, ON) island (*ey*, ON)', although the first element could be a personal nickname of the same meaning.

cam 'crooked', 'bending', 'winding', 'distorted'.

Cama [Highland] 'Winding (*cam*)': the name of a winding loch.

Cama' Choire [Tayside] 'Winding (*cam*) corrie (*choire*)': the corrie follows the Edendon Water.

camas 'bay', 'bend in the coastline', 'bend in a waterway': the word is an extension in form and meaning of *cam*, 'bending', and is also related to the Welsh *cwm*, 'valley' (a different sort of geographical bending), English *combe*. (Cf the eccentricity of shape implied in 'cam[shaft]' and 'camber'.)

Camas a' Mhoil [Lewis] 'Bay (*camas*) of the shingle beach (*mhoil*, genitive of *mol*)'.

64

Camas Ceardaich [Strathclyde] 'Bay (*camas*) of the smithy (genitive of *ceardach*)'.

Camas Coille [Highland] 'Bay (*camas*) of the wood (*coille*)'.

Camas Eilean Ghlais [Highland] 'Bay (*camas*) of Eilean Ghlais': the island name means 'blue-green island'.

Camas Gorm [Highland] 'Bay (*camas*), blue (*gorm*)'.

Camasnacroise [Strathclyde] 'Bay (*camas*) of the (*na*) cross (*croise*)': the bay was the site of the ferry across to Lismore, an island with considerable religious connections from the latter half of the 6th century.

Camasunary [Skye] 'Bay (*camas*) of the white (*fhionn*) shieling (*àirigh*)'.

cambus extended form of *camas*: 'bay', 'bend in the coastline', 'bend in a waterway'.

Cambus [Central] 'Bend [in the Forth estuary] (*camas*)'.

Cambusavie [Highland] 'Bend (*camas*) [in the] pass (*agaidh*)'.

Cambusbarron [Central] 'Bend (*camas*) in the little crest (diminutive of *barr*)': the 'little crest' is now known as Gillies Hill.

Cambuscurrie Bay [Highland] 'Bay (*camas*) of the marshes (*curraich*), bay (Eng)'; the final element was evidently added later, after the first two elements had become simply a name.

Cambuskenneth [Central] 'Bend [in the River Forth] (*camas*) [associated with St] Caioneach (personal name)': St Caioneach was Irish, was a friend of St Columba of Iona, and apart from being the founder of the abbey here is associated with several churches in the west of Scotland. The name is indeed the origin of the present-day forename 'Kenneth', although in Roman Catholic literature the saint is referred to as 'Canice': it means 'fair'.

Cambuslang [Strathclyde] 'Bay (*camas*) of the ship (*luinge*)'.

Cambusmore [Highland] 'Bay (*camas*), big (*mór*)'.

Cambus o' May [Grampian] 'Bend [in the River Dee] (*camas*) on the plain (*a' m[h]aigh*)'.

Cam Chreag [Tayside] 'Crooked (*cam*) crag (*chreag*)'.

Cameron Burn [Fife] '[Clan] Cameron stream (*burna*, OE)': the clan name derives from a nickname, *cama srón*, 'hooked nose'.

Cammachmore [Grampian] Possibly 'Crooked (*cam*) open space (*achadh*), big (*mór*)'.

Campbelltown [Highland] Village renamed in 1623 some 50 years after the Campbells of Cawdor acquired the land. To the Post Office, however, the name has never changed from its former name, Ardersier (q.v.).

Campbeltown [Strathclyde] Town renamed after the contemporary head of the Clan Campbell, the Earl of Argyll, in 1667: Campbell, the family name of the Dukes of Argyll, means 'crooked [river-]mouth'. At that time the town had been called Lochhead, although even earlier it was known as Kilkerran.

camus adapted version of *camas*: 'bay', 'bend in the coastline', 'bend in a waterway'.

Camusnagaul [Fort William, Highland] 'Bay (*camas*) of (*na*) Caol': Caol ('narrows') is the name of the area in which Loch Linnhe narrows mightily to become the River Lochy and the Caledonian Canal.

canach 'cotton grass'.

Canisbay [Highland] Possibly 'Cana's (personal name, ON or OE) community (*byr*, ON)': many commentators prefer to suggest the religious title 'canon' for the first element, although the ON second element rather militates against that.

Canisp [Highland] Said to mean '[The] White mountain', although the elements involved are obscure.

Canonbie [Dumfries & Galloway] 'Canon[s'] (ME) village (*by*, OE)': the community was the site of a well-known priory that was finally demolished by the English in 1542.

caochan 'streamlet'.

Caochan Lub [Tayside] 'Streamlet (*caochan*), meandering (*lùb*)'.

caol (also *caolas*) 'kyle', 'narrows', 'strait'.

Caol [Highland] 'Narrows (*caol*)': the name applies to an area in which Loch Linnhe narrows mightily to become the River Lochy and the Caledonian Canal.

Caolas [Tiree] 'Narrows (*caolas*)'.

Caolas Bàn [Coll] '[The] Narrows (*caolas*), white (*bàn*)'.

Caolas Beag [Highland] '[The] Narrows (*caolas*), small (*beag*)'.

Caolas Mór [Highland] '[The] Narrows (*caolas*), big (*mór*)': the narrows are between the mainland and the Crowlin Islands.

C

Caol Gleann [Strathclyde] '[The] Kyle (*caol*) glen (*gleann*)': the River Ruel runs through the glen to the Kyles of Bute.

Caolis [Vatersay] 'Narrows (*caolas*)': the village overlooks the Sound of Vatersay.

Caol Lairig [Highland] 'Narrows (*caol*) pass (*lairig*)': the pass follows a tributary of the River Roy.

Caol Raineach [Highland] 'Narrows (*caol*), ferny (*raineach*)'.

caora 'sheep'.

caorach genitive form of *caora*, thus 'of sheep'.

caorann 'rowan tree', 'mountain ash'.

capall 'horse', 'mare': the word is cognate with the Late Latin *caballus*, related to English *cavalry*.

-caple elided form of *capuill*, genitive of *capall*, thus 'of the horse'.

capuill genitive form of *capall*, thus 'of the horse'.

car 'bend'.

carach 'bending', 'winding', 'sinuous'.

caraidh 'weir', 'fish-pond', 'fish-trap'.

Carbost [Highland (2)] Probably 'Brushwood in marshland (*ciarr*, ON) settlement-steading (*bol-stathr*, ON)', although the first element may alternatively be the ON personal name Kári. Note that ON *ciarr* became the surname Kerr, often pronounced 'car'.

card- (also *carden*, *-cardine*) Brythonic Gaelic *cardden*: 'wooded', therefore 'copse', 'thicket'. The meaning implies cultivation and the word is cognate with English *garden*, *earth*, *yard* and *court*.

Cardenden [Fife] Hybrid name: 'Wooded (*cardden*, Brythonic Gaelic) valley (*denu*, OE)'.

-cardine elided form of Brythonic Gaelic *cardden*: 'wooded', therefore 'copse', 'thicket'. The meaning implies cultivation and the word is cognate with English *garden*, *earth*, *yard* and *court*.

-cardoch elided form of *ceardach*: 'smithy', 'forge', 'iron-foundry'.

Cardross [Strathclyde] 'Wooded (*cardden*, Brythonic Gaelic) promontory (*rhos*, Brythonic Gaelic)'.

Carishader [Lewis] Presumably 'Kári's (personal name, ON) house (*setr*, ON)'.

67

Carloway [Lewis] Presumably 'Karli['s] (personal name, ON) bay (*vágr*, ON)': the bay on which the village stands is now ironically called Loch Carloway.

Carluke [Strathclyde] Possibly 'Fort (*caer*, Brythonic Gaelic) on the marsh (*lwch*, Brythonic Gaelic)', except that although the area is exceptionally fertile, there is little evidence now of any marshland.

carn 'cairn', 'heap of stones', 'humped mountain': the genitive form is *cairn* ('of the cairn'), and it is perhaps surprisingly in this form that English has adopted the word. See separate list of hill and mountain names beginning with *carn*.

Carn [Mull] 'Humped mountain (*carn*)': actually it's more a hill, at only 812 feet (247 m) in height.

Carnach [Harris; Highland (2)] Presumably 'Place of cairns (*carn-ach*)'.

Carnan [Mingulay] 'Little humped mountain (diminutive of *carn*)': little indeed, at 896 feet (273 m) in height.

Carnan Eoin [Colonsay] 'Little humped mountain (diminutive of *carn*) of the birds (*eòin*, genitive plural of *eun*)'.

Carnan Mór [Tiree] 'Little humped mountain (diminutive of *carn*), big (*mór*)', presumably so called to distinguish it from an even smaller *carnan* close by.

Carn-gorm [Highland] 'Cairn (*carn*), blue-grey (*gorm*)'.

Carnie [Grampian] Presumably 'Cairn (*carn*)'.

-carnoch either 1) elided form of *cearnach*: 'square', 'four-sided';
or 2) plural of *carn*, thus 'cairns'.

Carnock [Fife] Probably 'Little cairn (diminutive of *carn*)'.

Carnousie [Grampian] Presumably 'Cairn (*carn*) of the fir trees (*ghiuthsaich*)'.

Carnoustie [Tayside] Possibly 'Rock (*carraig*) of the (*na*) fir tree (*ghiuthais*), house (*tigh*)'. The first element is said not to be *carn*: 'cairn'.

Carnwath [Strathclyde] Apparently an Old Scandinavian name: possibly 'Kærandi['s] (personal name, OScand) ford (*vath*, OScand)'.

carr either 1) Proto-Gaelic 'rock' of which *carraig*, 'crag' (Welsh *careg*), is the diminutive;
or 2) elided form of *càthair*: 'rough ground', 'moss'.

carraig 'rock (especially a prominent one)', 'steep mountain': the word is cognate with Welsh *careg*, English *crag* – all the more surprising, then, that it also represents a diminutive of an original *carr* (cognate with ON *sker*, English *skerry*) and that the alternative form of diminutive should produce *carn*, 'cairn'.

Carraig Bhàn [Islay] 'Crag (*carraig*), white (*bhàn*)'.

Carraig Dubh [Islay] 'Crag (*carraig*), black (*dubh*)'.

Carraig Fhada [Islay] 'Crag (*carraig*), long (*fhada*)'.

Carrick [Strathclyde; Dumfries & Galloway] '[Prominent] Rock (*carraig*)'.

Carrington [Lothian] The land here was acquired in 1613 by William Ramsey who in 1633 was created Lord Carrington and Earl of Dalhousie. The property was then in 1661 purchased by Sir Archibald Primrose, whose successor, Viscount Primrose, gave the name Primrose to the village – a name it is still sometimes called by.

Carron [Highland; Grampian; Central] Possibly 'Of the cairn (genitive of *carn*)'

Carr Rocks [Fife] 'Boulder (*carr*, proto-Goidelic) rocks (Eng)': the dangerous rocks lie 3 miles off the ancient town of Crail (q.v.), whose name also includes the element *carr*. The rocks are signalled by the North Carr lighthouse.

-carry elided form of *caraidh*: 'weir', 'fish-pond', 'fish-trap'.

Carscreuch [Dumfries & Galloway] Possibly 'Water-meadows (*carse*) boundary (*crìoch*)'.

carse 'alluvial land by a river', 'water-meadows': the word is probably cognate with the Welsh *cors*, 'bog'.

Carsegowan [Dumfries & Galloway] Presumably 'Alluvial riverside land [on the shores of the Cree estuary] of the blacksmith (*gobhainn*)'.

Carse of Gowrie [Tayside] 'Alluvial riverside land [on the shores of the Tay estuary] in the area ascribed to Gabran': Gabran was the son of Fe(a)rgus, one of the pioneering Celtic invaders from Ireland.

cas 'steep'.

Cas [Strathclyde] 'Steep (*cas*)'.

Castlebay [Barra] '[Kiessiemul] Castle bay (Eng)'.

Castlecraig [Highland; Borders] Probably 'Castle (Brythonic Gaelic), fortified (*cearrog*, Brythonic Gaelic)'.

69

Castle Douglas [Dumfries & Galloway] 'Castle [that is the seat of the Clan] Douglas'; the clan name means 'black stream' (Brythonic Gaelic). The original Douglas of the name was Sir William, who bought the village in 1789 having made his fortune through trade with Virginia. Previously, the town had first been known as Causewayend, then Carlingwark.

Castle Semple [Strathclyde] 'Castle [built by and for the] Sempill [family]': the first Lord Sempill was killed at Flodden Field in 1513. The surname is Norman French *simple*, i.e. 'open', 'honest'.

Catfirth [Shetland] 'Cat fjord (ON)': the first element may represent a personal name or a tribal name.

cath 'battle'; the word is probably cognate with English *beat*, evident also in the word *battle*.

cathair 'stronghold', 'fort': the word derives from an earlier form *cadair* that was applied also to significant mountains (as in Cader Idris in Wales): the root meaning is 'seat', and the word is cognate with the Greek *cathedra*, 'throne', and the English *chair*.

Cathcart [Strathclyde] Brythonic Gaelic name that probably means 'Woods (cf Welsh *coed*) [on the River] Cart', although the first element may instead mean 'fort' (cf *cathair*). The river name is thought to mean 'cleanser'.

Cauldcleuch Head [Borders] 'Cold (ME) ravine (*cloch*, ME) head[land] (Eng)'.

Caversta [Lewis] Possibly 'Cafhere's (personal name, OE) steading (*stathr*, ON)'.

Cawdor [Highland] Adapted river name transferred to a community on the shore: 'Hard (*caled*, Brythonic Gaelic) water (*dobhar*, Brythonic Gaelic)'; some commentators alternatively suggest the Gaelic element *callaidh*, 'rapid', for the first element. See **Calder**.

cealgach 'deceiver', 'swindler', 'cheat'.

ceall genitive plural of *cill*, thus 'of churches', 'of churchyards'.

ceann 'head'; cognate with the Germanic English word *chin*, but also with Welsh *pen* 'head'. In the guise of Ken- the word is a popular place-name element. The dative/locative form of the word is *cinn* which, in the guise of Kin-, is an equally popular place-name element: 'at the head of . . .'.

Ceannacroc Forest [Highland] Presumably 'Head (*ceann*) of the (*na*) antler (*cròc*), forest (Eng)'.

Ceann na Beinne [Skye] 'Head (*ceann*) of the (*na*) mountains (*beinne*)'.

Ceann-na-Cleithe [Harris] 'Head (*ceann*) of the (*na*) cliffs (*cleithe*, adapted form of ON *klettr*)'.

ceap 'block', 'stump'; the word is derived from the Latin *cippus*.

ceapach 'arable land', 'tillage plot'.

cearc 'hen'.

cearcall 'circle', 'hoop'; the word is derived from Latin *circulum*.

cearc-fhraoich 'grouse' (literally, 'hen-of-the-heather').

ceard 'smith', 'craftsman'.

ceardach 'smithy', 'forge', 'craftsman's workshop', 'iron-foundry'.

cearnach 'square', 'four-sided'.

ceathach 'mist'.

ceathaich 'misty'.

ceathairne originally 'band of peasants', then 'reivers', 'robbers', 'highway-bandits'; the English word *cateran* (which is a singular) derives from the medieval Gaelic through medieval Latin.

ceathramh 'quarter'; the word is cognate with its English translation.

Ceathramh Garbh [Highland] 'Quarter (*ceathramh*) [of] rough [water] (*garbh*)'.

Ceol na Mara [Highland] Presumably '[The] Music (*ceol*) of the (*na*) sea (*mara*, genitive of *muir*)': the tiny community lies on the shore of a bay within the sea-loch Loch Sunart.

chaim mutated form of the genitive of *cam*, thus 'of the crooked . . .'.

chairn mutated form of the genitive of *carn*, thus 'of a cairn', 'of a humped hill'.

chais mutated form of the genitive of *cas*, thus 'of the steep . . .'.

chaolais mutated form of the genitive of *caolas*, thus 'of a kyle', 'of the narrows', 'of the strait'.

chaolas mutated form of *caolas*: 'kyle', 'narrows', 'strait'.

Charlestown [Fife] Village founded around 1765 by Charles Bruce, Earl of Elgin, to accommodate colliery and limekiln workers on his estate.

71

Charlestown of Aberlour [Grampian] Town refounded as a model village in around 1812 by Charles Grant. Its previous name had been Skirdustan, 'parish (*sgìre*) of [St] Drostan', a local saint, abbot and founder of monasteries during the very early 7th century. It is now commonly called just Aberlour, formerly the name of its surrounding district.

chearcall mutated form of *cearcall*: 'circle', 'hoop'.

cheathaich mutated form of *ceathaich*: 'misty'.

Chesters [Borders] Probably '[Roman] Encampments (*ceasters*, OE)': the village is only 4 miles from Dere Street, a major Roman road. Yet the same word was also used to describe prehistoric hill-forts.

Chesthill [Tayside] 'Plateau (*seasduil*)'.

cheusadan 'crucifix', 'rood'.

chiar 'dark'.

chille mutated form of *cille*, thus 'of the church', 'of the churchyard'.

-chillis elided form of *chaolais*: '[of] the kyle', '[of] the narrows'.

chipper adapted form of *tiobar*: 'well', 'spring'.

chlach mutated form of *clach*: 'stone', 'rock', 'boulder'.

chlachan mutated form of *clachan*: 'place of stones', 'stony place', 'house made of stones', 'churchyard', 'burial-ground', 'hamlet with a church'.

chlachar mutated form of *clachar*: 'stone-cutter'.

chladaich mutated form of the genitive of *cladach*, thus 'of the shore', 'of the beach'.

chlair mutated form of the genitive of *clàr*, thus 'of the level area', 'of the crossing-place with planks'.

chlamain mutated form of the genitive of *claman*, thus 'of the buzzard'.

chlarsair mutated form of the genitive of *clarsar*, thus 'of the harpist'.

chleirich mutated form of *cléireach*: 'priest', 'minister'.

Chno Dearg [Highland] Possibly 'Nut (*chnó*), red-brown (*dearg*)', the name of a tall mountain, 3,433 feet (1,046 m) high.

choimhead mutated form of *coimhead*: 'level', 'parallel', 'equal'.

choin mutated form of the genitive of *cù*, thus 'of the dog'

chòin[n]ich mutated form of the genitive of *còinneach*, thus 'of moss', 'of the moss'.

C

choinneachan 'lamentation'.

choire mutated form of *coire*: 'corrie', 'cirque', 'chine', 'sea-gulf'.

chon mutated form of the genitive plural of *cù*, thus 'of dogs', 'of the dogs'.

chraisg mutated form of the genitive of *crasg*, thus 'of the crossing'.

chroisg mutated dialectal variant of the genitive of *crasg*, thus 'of the crossing'.

chròtha mutated form of the genitive of *crò*, thus 'of the sheep-fold'.

chruidh mutated form of the genitive of *crodh*, thus 'of the cattle'.

chruim mutated genitive form of *crom*, thus 'of the crooked . . . '.

chuilc mutated form of *cuilc*: 'reed'.

chuile mutated form of the genitive of *cùl*, thus 'of the back', 'of the ridge'.

chuilinn mutated form of the genitive of *cuileann*, thus 'of holly'.

-chulish elided form of *chaolais*, thus 'of the kyle', 'of the narrows'.

chumhainn mutated genitive form of *cumhann*, thus 'of the narrows', 'of the strait'.

ciarr 'brushwood', 'brushwood in marshland' (ON). The word is the origin of the surname Kerr (which was once more often pronounced 'car').

cìche genitive form of *cìoch*, thus 'of the breast', 'of the nipple'.

cill (also *cille*) 'church', 'churchyard', 'graveyard', 'hermit's cell', 'retreat'. The word derives from the Latin *cella*, of which the root meaning is 'to hide'; the English cognate is *cell*, closely related to con*ceal*. In the guise of Kil-, the word is a popular place-name element, particularly followed by a saint's name.

cìoch 'breast', 'nipple'; probably cognate with 'pap' (which has Latin and Sanskrit cognates, among others).

Cioch Mhór [Highland] '[The] Breast (*cìoch*), big (*mhór*)'.

clach 'stone', 'rock', 'boulder'. The word is in effect an extension in form and meaning of *leac*, 'flat stone', 'flagstone', 'slab', cognate with Welsh *llech*, and possibly akin to Greek *lith-*.

Clachaig [Strathclyde] Probably 'Stony (*clach-*) river-bend (*-aig*, corrupt form of ON *vágr*, 'bay')'; Clachaig is in Glen Lean.

clachan 'place of stones', thus either 'a stony place' or 'a house made of stones' (especially a hermit's cell or a church), and following the latter, thus also 'churchyard', 'burial-ground', and even 'hamlet with a church'.

Clachan [Strathclyde (5); Highland] Generally, 'stone house (*clachan*)', whether a church or private dwelling – but see further definitions under *clachan*.

Clachan-a-Luib [Uist] 'Stone house[s] (*clachan*) on the (*na*) bend (*lùib*, genitive of *lùb*)'. The 'bend' is probably that in the major road there.

clachar 'stone-cutter'.

Clach Bheinn [Strathclyde] 'Stone (*clach*) mountain (*bheinn*)'.

Clachbreck [Strathclyde] Presumably 'Stone (*clach*), speckled (*breac*)'.

Clach Leathad [Highland] 'Stone (*clach*) slope (*leathad*)'.

Clachnaharry [Highland] Presumably 'Stone (*clach*) of the (*na*) boundary (*h-airbhe*)': the boundary stone probably marked parish limits, for the spot is not on county or clan borders.

Clackmannan [Central] Apparently 'Stone (*clach*) [of] Manau': the ancient Stone of Manau (or Manu) lies next to the Tolbooth in the town and is thought to relate to an area perhaps once called Manau near the head of the Firth of Forth.

cladach 'shore', 'beach'.

Claddach Kirkibost [Uist] 'Beach (*cladach*) [of] the church [*kirkja*, ON] settlement-steading (*bol-stathr*, ON)'; the initial element was evidently added later.

cladh 'burial-ground', 'cemetery'.

Cladich [Strathclyde] Probably 'Beach (*cladach*)': the village is not far from the shoreline of Loch Awe, where the Cladich River meets the loch.

Claggain Bay [Islay] Probably 'Hummocky hill (*claigeann*) bay (Eng)': the bay is overlooked by Beinn Bheigier (1,609 feet/490 m), the highest point on the island, from where the Claggain River flows down to the sea – but even closer is the small but humped Cnoc Mór, 354 feet (108 m) high.

Claggan [Highland] Probably 'Hummocky hill (*claigeann*)'.

claidheamh 'sword', 'lance': the word is the first element of the Scots *claymore*, once the national broadsword; but the final -mh proves also that it is another guise of the word *glaive* used several times as a historical word for 'sword' by Sir Walter Scott, and ultimately cognate with the Latin *gladius*, 'sword' and Greek *glyphein*, 'to carve'.

C

Claigan [Skye] Probably 'Hummocky hill (*claigeann*)'.

claigeann either 1) 'skull', 'head', and thus 'hummocky hill';
or 2) 'field within an otherwise residential area'.

clais 'furrow', and thus 'narrow valley'.

claman variant of *clamhan*: 'buzzard', 'kite'.

clamhan 'buzzard', 'kite'.

Clappers [Borders] Probably 'Stepping-stones (dialectal ME)' although another possible meaning is 'Bridges'; the village lies on a tributary of the Whiteadder Water.

clàr literally 'plank' (OIr *claar*, Welsh *claur*; see also *cléireach*), and thus 'level area', 'plain', but also 'marshy place where the means of crossing was over planks laid down'.

clarsar 'harpist', 'harper'.

Cleadale [Eigg] Probably 'Cliff (*klettr*, ON) dale (ON)': the community huddles under steep slopes overlooking the Bay of Laig.

Cleat [Barra] Probably 'Cliff (*klettr*, ON)'.

cléireach 'priest', 'minister', 'pastor'; the word derives from the Latin *clericus*, 'cleric', 'clergyman', which in turn derives from the Greek *klerikos*, 'issued with a piece of wood' – cf *clàr* above. The piece of wood issued to Greeks was that used to draw lots – the priesthood was thus regarded as the 'chips' to be issued to the lay people for them to profit by. Cf also the idea of the *pontifex*, the bridge-builder, the plank for people to walk across, the original version of the title of Pontiff.

Cleish [Tayside] Possibly 'Narrow valley (*clais*)' – there is a river running east-west through the community – but it is hard then to reconcile the name with the nearby Cleish Hills . . .

cleit 'cliff', 'rock-face'; the Gaelic is an adaptation of the ON *klettr*.

-clet, *clett* 'cliff', 'rock-face' (ON *klettr*).

Clett Ard [Harris] 'Cliff (*cleit*), high (*ard*)'.

Clettraval [Uist] Presumably 'Rock-face (*klettr*, ON) fell (*fjall*, ON)'.

-cleuch, *-cleugh* 'ravine' (OE *cloh*, modern Eng *clough*, as in the surname).

Cleughbrae [Dumfries & Galloway] 'Ravine (*cloh*, OE) hillside (*brai*, ME)'.

75

Clifton [Central] Village named after the owners of the local lead mines in the late 1600s.

clò 'tweed' (modern Gaelic).

cloch dialectal variant of *clach*: 'stone', 'rock'.

clochan dialectal variant of *clachan*: 'place of stone', thus 'stony place' but also 'building of stone' (that might be a church, manor or fortified premises) and thus 'churchyard', and even 'hamlet with a church'.

Clochan [Grampian] 'Place of stone (*clachan*)': for the ramifications of this definition, see *clochan*.

cloiche genitive form of *clach*, thus 'of stone', 'of the rock'.

Clousta [Shetland] Possibly 'Ravine (*klof*, ON) steading (*stathr*, ON)', although the first element may be a personal name instead.

Clouston [Orkney] Possibly 'Ravine's (*cloh*-s, OE) community (*tun*, OE)', although the first element may be a personal name instead.

cluain 'green flat area', 'pastureland', 'isolated meadow'.

cluas 'ear', thus also 'handle', and even 'spit [of land]'.

Cluas Deas [Highland] 'Spit (*cluas*), southern (*deas*)'.

Clunes [Highland] Apparently 'Pasture (*cluain*) resting-place'.

Clyde [Strathclyde] Brythonic Gaelic river name that probably means 'cleanser' (cognate with Latin *cluo* 'to wash', OE *hluttor* 'clean') – unless it is identical with the Welsh water name Clwyd (found also in the Irish for Dublin: Baile Atha Cliath) meaning 'wicket-gate', 'hurdle'. Another Scottish form is Cluden, in Dumfries & Galloway.

Clydebank [Strathclyde] '[River] Clyde['s] bank (Eng)'. The development of the area began only in 1871 with the founding of the shipyards that quickly became world-famous.

cnàimh 'bone'.

cnàmha genitive form of *cnàimh*, thus 'of bone', 'of the bone'.

cnap 'small hill'; the word is an adaptation of the ON *knappr*, of which the OE cognate was *cnaepp*, 'hill-top'.

cnoc 'rounded hill'; the element is very popular in place names, found also in various guises (such as Cannock and Knock). See separate list of mountain and hill names beginning with this element.

76

C

Cnocan Conachreag [Highland] Possibly 'Rounded hills (plural of *cnoc*), mossy (*còinneachraich*)'.

cnuic genitive form of *cnoc*, thus 'of the rounded hill'.

-coat (also *-coats*) 'house(s)', 'cottage(s)' (ME *cote[s]*).

Coatbridge [Strathclyde] 'Cottages (*cotts*, Eng 1676) bridge (Eng)'. The bridge was not built until around 1800, after which time the town developed as a mining community.

Cockpen [Borders] Apparently 'Red (*coch*, Brythonic Gaelic) head (*pen*, Brythonic Gaelic)'.

còig 'five'; the word is cognate with its English translation.

Coigach [Highland] An area name relating to territory north and west of Ullapool: it may mean '[The] Five (*còig*) open spaces (*achaidh*)'.

Coignafearn Forest [Highland] Possibly 'Five (*còig*) [of] the (*na*) alder tree[s] (*fearn*), forest (Eng)'.

coileach 'cock'.

Coillaig [Strathclyde] 'Wood (*coille*) bay (*-aig*, corrupt form of ON *vágr*)': the village is at the head of an inlet off Loch Awe.

coille 'wood', 'forest' – a strange word because the -ll- seems to be an attempt at a sound between l and d : the Welsh equivalent is *coed*, and commentators are unable to say whether the root meaning therefore is 'trees' or 'shelter/concealment'. The result is that most refer to modern Welsh *celydd* as a sort of mid-form, defining it as 'wooded shelter'. In parts of Ireland and Scotland the word has become the surname Kelly.

Coiltie [Highland] River name: 'Wooded (*coilltean*)'; the river runs from Balmacan Forest to Loch Ness at Urquhart Bay.

coimhead 'level', 'parallel', 'equal'.

còinneach 'moss'.

còinneachan 'mossy place'.

còin[n]ich genitive form of *còinneach*, thus 'of moss', 'of the moss'.

coirce 'oats'.

coire 'corrie', 'cirque', 'chine', 'sea-gulf'; but also 'whirlpool'.

coireach '[place] of corries'.

Coire an Fhamhair [Highland] 'Corrie (*coire*) of the (*na*) giant (genitive of *famhar*)'.

Coire Cas [Highland] 'Corrie (*coire*), steep (*cas*)' – the major slope for skiing in the Cairngorms.

Coire na Beinne [Highland] 'Corrie (*coire*) of the (*na*) mountains (*beinne*)'.

Coire na Poite [Highland] 'Corrie (*coire*) of the (*na*) pot (genitive of *pot*)'.

Coire Odhar [Highland; Tayside] 'Corrie (*coire*), dun-coloured (*odhar*)'.

coitcheann 'common pastureland', 'green'.

Colaboll [Highland] Possibly 'Koli['s] (personal name, ON) community (*bol*, ON)'.

Colbost [Skye] Probably 'Koli['s] (personal name, ON) settlement-steading (*bol-stathr*, ON)'.

Coldbackie [Highland] Possibly 'Cold (*kaldr*, ON) hillside (*bakki*, ON)': the village lies on a fairly steep north-facing slope. Alternatively, the second element might be ON *bekkr*, 'brook': a small stream enters Tongue Bay just north of the village.

Coldstream [Borders] The name is English – and in former centuries people would have known all about the temperature of the stream here because it was not until 1766 that a bridge was built (by Smeaton) over the rather deep ford through the River Tweed.

Colinsburgh [Fife] Village founded and named by Colin Lindsay, 3rd Earl of Balcarres, in 1705.

Colintraive [Strathclyde] Corruption of 'Narrows (*caol*) of the (*a-n*) swimming (*t-snàimh*)', for it was close to here that cattle drovers used to drive their beasts to wade and swim across the eastern Kyles of Bute from that island.

coll (also *call*, *calltuinn*) 'hazel tree'.

Colonsay [Inner Hebrides] Probably '[St] Columba's (personal name) island (*ey*, ON)'. Some commentators have suggested the popular OScand name Kolbein as at least a possible alternative for the personal name.

Colvister [Shetland] Possibly 'Kolfr's (personal name, ON) house (*setr*, ON)'.

comar 'confluence', 'junction of waters'.

Comers [Grampian] Possibly 'Confluence (*comar-s*)': at least two streams join in the village.

comraich 'sanctuary'.

Comrie [Tayside] 'Confluence (*comar*)': in or near Comrie both the River Lednock and the Water of Ruchill join the River Earn.

con genitive plural form of *cù*, thus 'of dogs', 'of the dogs'.

Conisby [Islay] '[The] King's (*konungs*, OScand) settlement (*byr*, ON)'.

Conival [Highland] Said to mean '[The] Enchanted fell', although the first element is obscure; the second appears to be ON *fjall*.

Conningsburgh [Shetland] '[The] King's (*konungs*, OScand) stronghold (*burh*, OE)'.

Coolin Hills See **Cuillin Hills**.

Cora Linn [Strathclyde] 'Marshy area (*currach*), pool (*linn*)'.

corr 'crane', 'heron'.

corran 'spit', 'low pointed promontory', 'pier' (literally, 'sickle').

Corran [Highland (2)] 'Low pointed promontory (*corran*)'. The more famous southerly example is the site of a ferry across Loch Linnhe to Glenrigh Forest (towards Fort William) from Ardgour, Kingairloch and Morvern.

corrie (also *corry*) adapted (anglicised) form of *coire*: 'corrie', 'cirque', 'chine', 'sea-gulf', and also 'whirlpool'.

Corrie [Arran] 'Corrie (*coire*)': the village lies at the foot of Goat Fell, the highest mountain on Arran.

Corriemony [Highland] Possibly 'Corrie (*coire*) of peat (*mòna*, genitive of *mòine*)'; the site has been inhabited for thousands of years.

Corrieshalloch [Highland] 'Corrie (*coire*) of the willow[s] (*seilich*, genitive of *seileach*)'. The willows weep over the fast-flowing Abhainn Droma as it descends through the Gorge to Loch Broom.

Corrievreckan [Strathclyde] 'Whirlpool (*coire*) of Brecon (personal name)'. The personal name is common to Celtic mythologies, and is found in place names all over Britain (Brecon, Brechin, Wrekin, etc.). In Scottish Gaelic legend the hero Brecon perished in Corrievreckan with all his fifty ships.

Dictionary of Scottish Place Names

Corrour [Highland] 'Corrie (*coire*), grey (*odhar*)'.

Corry [Skye] 'Sea-gulf (*coire*)': the village lies on the shore of the large Broadford Bay.

còs 'nook', 'recess'.

Costa [Orkney] Possibly 'Kupsi's (personal name, ON) steading (*stathr*, ON)', although there is another possible ON candidate for the personal name, Kostr.

Cottown [Grampian (3)] This is one of the series with Milton ('mill-farm'), Kirkton ('church-farm'), Hatton ('hall-farm'), Hilton ('upper-farm') and Netherton ('lower-farm') as taken from medieval English. Cottown is the 'cottage-farm' where the cottar, or labourer, lived.

coul adapted form of *cùl*: 'back', 'ridge'.

Coull [Grampian] Probably 'Ridge (*cùl*)', although the village lies rather at the foot of a pass up into the mountains.

Coupar Angus [Tayside] Possibly '[The] Common[land] (*comhpairt*) [in the area called] Angus [as opposed to Cupar in Fife]'. The common was pastureland held for their common use by the local villagers. The area name represents the name of one of the three sons of Erc, pioneer Scottish invader from Ireland.

Coulter [Strathclyde] 'Back (*cùl*) country (*tìr*)', and indeed the surrounding land is extremely full of backs, i.e. hills and ridges. Coulter lies on the Culter Water, below Culter Fell.

Cove [Highland; Strathclyde; Grampian] 'Haven (*cobh*)': the root meaning of the word is more 'shelter' than 'harbour', a curve of the coastline being generally the only reason for the name.

Covesea [Grampian] Village established by Sir William Cumming in about 1810; he chose the name merely for its attractive associations.

Cowal [Strathclyde] The name of an area between Loch Fyne and the Clyde estuary, it is a corruption of Comgall, the name of one of the sons of Fe(a)rgus, a pioneer Scottish invader from Ireland. See also **Gowrie**.

Cowdenbeath [Fife] Possibly 'Wooded (*coilltean*) [with] birch (*beithe*)'. Nice name for what is essentially a coalfield town – but the first element remains shrouded in conjecture.

Cowie [Central] Possibly 'Cattle-pen (*cuidhe*, adaptation of an ON word)'; the village is in a fertile area in the estuary of the River Forth.

80

coy- elided form of *cuidhe*: 'cattle-pen'.

Craggan [Highland] 'Rocks (plural of *creag*)'.

craig adapted form of *creag*: 'fell', 'cliff', 'crag', 'rock'.

Craig [Highland; Grampian; Dumfries & Galloway] 'Fell (*creag*)': all three communities lie beneath appropriate rocky heights.

Craigellachie [Grampian] 'Fell (*creag*) of the rocks (*eileach*)'.

Craigendoran [Strathclyde] 'Fell (*creag*) of the (*a-n*) otter (*dobhran*)': the final element is actually a diminutive of *dobhar*, 'water'. The village lies on the shore of the Clyde just south of Helensburgh.

Craigentinny [Lothian] 'Rock (*creag*) of the (*a-n*) fox (*t-sionnaich*)'.

Craigie [Strathclyde; Grampian] 'Rock (*creag*)'.

Craig nan Caisean [Tayside] Presumably 'Crag (*creag*) of the (*na-n*) steep slopes (plural of *cas*)'.

Craigneuk [Strathclyde (2)] Apparently 'Fell (*creag*) nook (ME Northern dialect)'.

Craigrothie [Fife] Presumably 'Fell (*creag*) of the old fortification (*ràth*)': to the north-west there is a suitably ancient tower, but to the south are the better-known remains of what was once the magnificent Struthers Castle.

Craigruie [Central] Probably 'Fell (*creag*) of the cattle-run (*ruighe*)'.

Craigton [Tayside (2); Grampian] 'Fell (*creag*) farmstead (*tun*, OE)'.

Craigtown [Highland] 'Fell (*creag*) farmstead (*tun*, OE)'.

Craik [Borders] 'Fell (*creag*)'; the community is a centre for hikers and climbers in the middle of Craik Forest. A Roman road leads from there straight over Craik Cross Hill (and into Dumfries & Galloway) to a Roman fort by the White Esk River.

Crail [Fife] Ancient town with a name more ancient than most: 'Boulder (*carr*, proto-Goidelic) rock (*ail*, proto-Goidelic)'. The dangerous Carr Rocks (q.v.) lie 3 miles out to sea.

craisg genitive form of *crasg*, thus 'of a crossing'.

Cramond [Lothian] 'Fort (*caer*, Brythonic Gaelic) [on] the [River] Almond': Cramond church now stands on the site of a Roman fort. The river name, incidentally, is an awful corruption of *amhainn*, 'river'.

crann 'tree'.

Cranna [Grampian] Probably 'At the tree (locative of *crann*)'.

Crannoch [Grampian] Probably 'Trees (plural of *crann*)'.

Cranshaws [Borders] Possibly 'Cranes (*cran-s*, OE) land by a river (*halh*, OE, 'haugh-s')'. The village stands on the Whiteadder Water.

craobh 'tree', especially one with branches.

crasg (also *crosg*) 'crossing', that is, a place to cross (via a bridge, a ferry, or whatever).

crask adapted form of *crasg*: 'crossing'.

Craskins [Grampian] Possibly 'Crossing (*crasg*) water-meadow (*innis*)'.

Crask of Aigas [Highland] 'Crossing (*crasg*) of (Eng) [the island of] Aigas', on which stood Eilean Aigas House, once a refuge of Lord Lovat, later the country seat of Sir Robert Peel.

creachann 'windswept summit', 'bare hill-top'.

creag 'fell', 'crag', 'cliff', 'rock'. The word is in fact a diminutive of a proto-Goidelic word now found only in place names, *carr*; cognate is Welsh *careg*, English *crag*. Another diminutive of *carr* is *carn*, 'cairn'. In the guise of Craig and Carrick, the word is a popular place-name element. See also separate list of mountain and hill names beginning with *creag*.

creagan either the diminutive or the plural of (the already diminutive) *creag*, thus either 'little fell', 'little rock' or 'fells', 'crags', 'rocks'.

Creagan [Strathclyde] 'Little crag (*creagan*)': the village lies on the steep slopes of Beinn Churalain (1,792 feet/546 m), overlooking Loch Creran.

Creagan a' Chaise [Highland/Grampian] Presumably 'Little crag (*creagan*), the steep (genitive of *cas*)'.

Creagan an Eich [Strathclyde] 'Rocks (*creagan*) of the (*na-n*) horse (*eich*, genitive of *each*)'. A TV booster towers above Loch Fyne from the slopes of this 1,070-ft (326-m) mountain.

Creagan Glas [Highland] 'Little crag (*creagan*), blue-green (*glas*)'.

Creagan Mór [Highland] 'Little crag (*creagan*), big[ger] (*mór*)'.

creamh 'wild garlic'.

Creetown [Dumfries & Galloway] Village renamed by the local laird in 1785: Cree is the name of the river on which the community stands, and probably means 'fresh', 'pure' (as the rivers Cray in England and Crai in

Wales). The village's name had previously been Ferrytown of Cree – equally English.

Creggans [Strathclyde] Presumably 'Rocks (*creagan*)'.

creige genitive form of *creag*, thus 'of a fell', 'of a rock', 'of a cliff'.

Crianlarich [Central] Possibly '[The] Aspen tree (*critheann*) of the ruined house (*làraich*)'.

crìche genitive form of *crìoch*, thus 'of the boundary', 'of the region'.

Crieff [Tayside] 'At the tree (dative/locative of *craobh*)'.

crìoch 'boundary', 'region', 'destination'.

critheann 'aspen tree'.

crò 'sheep-pen', 'fold'.

cròc 'antler', 'horn'; the word is cognate with the Latin *cervus*, 'horned beast', 'stag'.

cròcach 'branching', 'forked' (but literally, 'horned').

crodh 'cattle'.

Croe [Highland; Strathclyde] River name that is likely to have been back-formed in both cases from the name of the glen through which the river runs: probably 'the glen of the sheep-pen (*cròtha*)'.

Crofts [Grampian (2); Highland] 'Crofts (ME)', although in ME the real meaning was 'enclosed field' and only later became 'dwelling within an enclosed area'.

Croggan [Mull] Presumably '[The] Little fell (*creagan*)': the village lies on fair slopes overlooking the huge inlet Loch Spelve and its narrow entrance Port nan Crullach.

croich 'gallows', 'gibbet': the word is cognate with the Latin *crux*, 'cross' (as a means of execution).

crois 'cross' (as a shape or religious symbol): the word is cognate with its English translation.

croisg variant genitive form of *crasg*, thus 'of the crossing', 'of the place to cross over'.

croit 'croft': the word is an adaptation of the ME *croft*, 'enclosed field'.

Croit Bheinn [Highland (2)] 'Croft (*croit*) mountain (*bheinn*)'.

cròithean genitive plural form of *crò*, thus 'of the sheep-pens'.

crom (Welsh *crwm*) 'crooked', 'with a bend'. There is an OE cognate, *crumb*, also found in place names (such as Cromwell). Cf also Eng *curve*.

Cromalt Hills [Highland] 'Crooked (*crom*) stream (*allt*) hills (Eng)'.

Cromarty [Highland] Probably 'Crooked (*crom*) promontory (*ard*)': an apt description for the site of the town with its two headlands near the tip of the Black Isle.

Cromdale [Highland] 'Crooked (*crom*) dale (*dail*)': the River Spey begins to meander rather significantly here, in the shadow of the Hills of Cromdale lying to the east, which form the Highland/Grampian Regions border.

Cromlet [Tayside] Possibly 'Crooked (*crom*) slope (*leathad*)'.

Crom Loch [Highland] 'Crooked (*crom*) loch'.

Cromra [Highland] Possibly 'Crooked (*crom*) road (*rathad*)': even the modern two-lane road is not particularly straight as it follows Strath Mashie. But the second element might instead be 'fort (*ràth*)'.

Crook of Devon [Tayside] 'Acute angle (*crok*, ME) of [the River] Devon': the river, which is the Tayside/Central Regions border, suddenly turns from flowing south-east to flowing west-south-west here. The river name means 'black river'.

Crosby [Strathclyde] 'Crosses (*krossa*, ON) settlement (*byr*, ON)': that the area was especially religious is demonstrated by the nearby towns of Monkton and Prestwick ('priest-farm'). All the same, it is just possible that the first element is instead a personal name, such as ON Krókr.

Crossapol [Tiree] Possibly 'Crosses (*krossa*, ON) pool (*pol*, OScand)'.

Crossbost [Lewis] Presumably 'Cross (*kross*, ON) settlement-steading (*bol-stathr*, ON)', although it is just possible that the first element may be a personal name.

Crossford [Strathclyde; Fife] 'Cross (Eng) [at a] ford (Eng)': the more southerly example was a ford across the River Clyde. In both these cases the 'cross' may in fact be a 'crossroads'.

Crosskirk [Highland] 'Cross (*kross*, ON) church (*kirkja*, ON)'; the tiny village lies in a strongly ON area.

Crossroads [Tayside] 'Crossroads (Eng)': at both ends of the village the road forks in two – so the village is the crossroads.

cròtha genitive form of *crò*, thus 'of the sheep-pen'.

cruach 'bold hill', 'prominent stack', 'conspicuous height' (literally 'heap', 'pile'). See separate list of mountain and hill names beginning with the element.

cruachan diminutive or plural form of *cruach*, thus either 'small but prominent mountain', 'conspicuous hillock', thus also 'hip', 'haunch', or 'prominent stacks', 'conspicuous heights'. See separate list of mountain and hill names beginning with *cruachan*.

Cruachan [Central] 'Small but prominent mountain (*cruachan*)'.

Cruban Beag [Highland] Possibly 'Little hoof (diminutive of *crúb*), small[er] (*beag*)'; the nearby lodge is called Crubenmore [sic].

cruidh genitive form of *crodh*, thus 'of cattle'.

cruim(e) genitive form of *crom*, thus 'of the crooked . . . '.

cruinn 'round', but also 'accurate'.

Cruinn a' Bheinn [Central] Presumably 'Round (*cruinn*), the mountain (*bheinn*)'.

Cruinn Bheinn [Central] 'Round (*cruinn*) mountain (*bheinn*)'.

cù 'dog'; the genitive forms (singular *coin*, plural *con*) prove that the word is cognate with the Latin *canis*, English *hound*.

cuach 'scooped-out hollow', 'cup-shaped hollow', 'rounded dell'.

cuaich genitive form of *cuach*, thus 'of the cup-shaped hollow'.

Cuaig [Highland] Possibly 'Dog (*cù*) bay (*-aig*, corruption of ON *vágr*/Eng *bay*)'. Both the river reaching the shore through the village, and the promontory in front of the village, take the village's name.

cuan 'seaside', 'harbour'.

Cuan Ferry [Strathclyde] 'Harbour (*cuan*) ferry (Eng)': the ferry plies between the islands of Seil and Luing; the added implication of sea-going traffic inherent in the word is technically correct in that the islanders of Seil have long regarded themselves as surrounded by the Atlantic Ocean.

-cudbright elided form of the personal name of [St] Cuthbert, Prior of Lindisfarne in the 7th century.

cuidhe 'byre', 'cattle-pen', 'animal enclosure'; the word is an adaptation of the ON *kví*, said to derive in parallel to the OE *cu-eg*, 'cow-island', that has resulted in Quy, Cambridgeshire.

cùil 'recess', 'nook'.

cuilc 'reed'; probably cognate with the Greek *kalamos*, 'reed', especially one used for writing – cf English *quill*.

cuileann (Welsh *celyn*) 'holly'; another cognate is OE *holen* from which our present word *holly* derives. The root meaning is 'prickly'.

cuilinn genitive form of *cuileann*, thus 'of holly'.

Cuillin Hills [Skye] These formidable crags and peaks are supposedly named after the hero-giant Cuchullin or Cuchulainn, a Hercules-figure of Celtic legend. The nephew of King Conchobar of Ulster, whose life in battle he once saved, his lifelong enemies were the rulers of Connaught. After an eventful life in which he stole the magic cauldron of Mider, king of the underworld, and travelled to a magical island and married its queen, he was finally slain by the king of Leinster. On old maps, the name is sometimes spelled Coolin. The true derivation is unknown.

cuinge variant genitive form of *cumhann*, thus 'of the narrows', 'of the strait'.

cuithe 'pit', 'shaft', thus also 'narrow glen'; the word derives from the Latin *puteus*, '[something] excavated out' (from which the French derive their *puits*, 'well'). The change from p- to c- was because the loan of the word was effected at a time when Goidelic had an alphabet altogether without p (cf Welsh *pen*, Goidelic *ceann*).

cùl 'back', 'ridge'; this is probably cognate with Latin *collis*, 'hill' and elements in English words such as *col*umn and *cul*minate, not to mention *hill* itself.

Cul Beag [Highland] 'Ridge (*cùl*), small[er] (*beag*)'; the mountain stands 4 miles south of Cul Mór, the 'big[ger] ridge'.

Cùl Doirlinn [Highland] 'Ridge (*cùl*) of the tidal isthmus (*dòirlinn*)'.

Culdrain [Grampian] Probably 'Ridge (*cùl*), blackthorn (*draigheann*)'.

Culduie [Highland] Possibly 'Ridge (*cùl*), dark (*dubh*)'.

Cul Mór [Highland] 'Ridge (*cùl*), big[ger] (*mór*)'; the mountain stands 4 miles north of Cul Beag, the 'small[er] ridge'.

Culnacraig [Highland] Presumably 'Ridge (*cùl*) of the (*na*) cliff (*creige*)': the village sits on a ledge along the steep slopes of Ben Mór Coigach above the sea.

Culnaknock [Skye] Presumably 'Ridge (*cùl*) of the (*na*) rounded hill (*cnuic*)': there is such a hill at the foot of the nearby headland.

Culross [Fife] Said to be a Brythonic name: 'Holly (*celyn*, Brythonic Gaelic) moorland (*rhos*, Brythonic Gaelic)', but both elements could as easily be Goidelic: 'Ridge (*cùl*) of the promontory (*rois*)', and the low ridge on which the town stands does end in a sandy headland.

Culswick [Shetland] Probably 'Cula's (personal name, OE) farm (*wic*, OE)'; the elements might instead be the ON equivalents, but the meaning of the second would then be 'bay' – and the settlement is not on a bay – and the personal name is relatively common in OE.

Culter [Grampian] Probably 'Back (*cùl*) country (*tìr*)'.

Cumbernauld [Strathclyde] 'Confluence (*comar*) of the (*na-n*) stream[s] (*allt*)'.

Cumbrae islands [Bute] 'Brythonic Gaels' (*Cymri*, Brythonic Gaelic) islands (*aer*, OScand) islands (Eng)'.

cumhann 'narrows', 'strait'.

Cuminestown [Grampian] Model village planned in around 1760 by Joseph Cumine of Auchry.

Cummingstown [Grampian] Village built in around 1810 by Sir William Cumming, the landowner, to accommodate local fisherfolk. See also **Covesea**.

Cunnister [Shetland] Probably 'King's (*konungs*, OScand) steading (*stathr*, ON)'.

Cupar [Fife] Possibly '[The] Common[land] (*comhpairt*)', that is, pastureland held in common by local villagers. Some commentators would prefer an older derivation.

currach 'marshy area', 'bogland'.

Currie [Lothian] 'In the marshy area (dative/locative of *currach*)'.

Carn

Carn

The following are hill names that on the map are preceded by this word:

a' Bhiorain [Highland] 'of the colt (genitive of *bioran*)'.

a' Bhodaich [Highland] 'of the ghost (genitive of *bodach*)'; the second element can alternatively mean 'the old man'.

a' Chaochain [Highland] 'of the streamlet (genitive of *caochan*)'.

a' Chlamain [Tayside] 'of the buzzard (genitive of *claman*)'.

a' Choin Deirg [Highland] 'of the dog (*choin*, genitive of *cù*), red-brown (*deirge*)'.

a' Choire Mhóir [Highland] 'of the corrie (*choire*), big (*mhóir*)'.

a' Chrasgie [Highland] 'of the crossing (*chrasg*)'.

a' Chuilinn [Highland] 'of the holly (genitive of *cuileann*)'.

a' Ghaill [Canna] 'of the stranger (genitive of *gall*)'.

a' Gheòidh [Grampian/Tayside] 'of the goose (genitive of *gèadh*)'

a' Ghlinne [Highland] 'of the glen (*ghlinne*)', the glen being Glen Docherty; from the summit can be seen one of the best views in Scotland, straight down the glen and on down the length of Loch Maree.

a' Mhaim [Grampian] 'of the mountain pass (*mhàim*, genitive of *màm*)'.

an Daimh [Tayside] 'of the stag (genitive of *damh*)'.

an Righ [Tayside] 'of the king (*rìgh*)'.

an t-sabhail [Grampian] 'of the barn (genitive of *sabhal*)'.

an t-suidhe [Grampian] 'of the level shelf (*suidhe*)'.

an Tuirc [Grampian] 'of the wild boar (genitive of *torc*)'.

Bàn [Highland (3)] 'White (*bàn*)'.

Bàn Mór [Highland] 'White (*bàn*), big (*mór*)': the nearest other Carn Bàn is about 15 miles west-north-west.

Beag [Highland] 'Small (*beag*)'.

Bhac [Grampian/Tayside] '[The] Peat-bank (*bhac*, adapted form of ON *bakki*)'.

88

Breac Beag [Highland] 'Speckled (*breac*), small (*beag*)'.

Breugach [Strathclyde] 'False (*breugach*)'.

Cas nan Gabhar [Highland] 'Steep (*cas*), of the (*na-n*) goat (*gabhar*)'.

Chòis [Tayside] 'Of the nook (genitive of *còs*)'.

Daimh [Grampian] 'Of the stag (genitive of *damh*)'.

Dearg [Highland (4); Highland/Tayside; Strathclyde] 'Red-brown (*dearg*)'.

Dearg Mór [Highland] 'Red-brown (*dearg*), big (*mór*)': there are no fewer than three other Carn Deargs within 30 miles for this to be bigger than.

Eas [Grampian] '[The] Waterfall (*eas*)'.

Easgann Bàna [Highland] 'Of the swamp (genitive of *easg*), white (*bàna*)'.

Eige [Highland] Apparently 'File (*eige*)'.

Eilrig [Highland] Possibly 'Of the deer-trap (genitive of *eileirg*)': there are several passes near this carn suitable for trapping deer.

Garbh [Highland] 'Rough [water] (*garbh*)'.

Glas-choire [Highland] 'Blue-green (*glas*) corrie (*choire*)'.

Gorm [Highland (3); Tayside] 'Blue (*gorm*)'.

Leac [Highland] '[The] Flat stone (*leac*)'.

Liath [Grampian (2)] 'Grey (*liath*)'.

Loch nan Amhaichean [Highland] '[of] Loch nan Amhaichean', half-way down its slopes; the loch name means 'of the necks'.

Loch nan Dearcag [Highland] '[of] Loch nan Dearcag', about 1 mile beneath its summit; the loch name means 'of the berry'.

Mairg [Tayside] Probably 'Of the borderland (genitive of *marg*)'; much less likely to be 'Sorrow (*mairg*)'.

Mór [Highland (3); Mull] 'Big (*mór*)'.

na Cailliche [Grampian] 'of the (*na*) cloaked woman [i.e. nun or old hag] (*caillich*, genitive of *cailleach*)'.

na Caim [Highland/Tayside] 'of the (*na*) bend (genitive of *cam*)': the contours of the mountain are indeed curvaceous, but the regional boundary also veers wildly at the summit.

na Cloiche Móire [Highland] 'of the (*na*) stone (*cloiche*, genitive of *clach*), big (*móire*, genitive of *mór*)'.

na Cóinnich [Highland] Possibly 'of the (*na*) mossy places (*còinneaich*)'.

na Drochaide [Grampian] 'of the (*na*) bridges (*drochaide*)'.

na Dubh Choille [Highland] 'of the (*na*) dark (*dubh*) wood (*coille*)'.

na Feannaige [Grampian] 'of the (*na*) crows (*feannaige*)'.

na h-Easgainn [Highland] 'of the (*na*) swamp (*easgainn*)'.

na Lòine [Highland] 'of the (*na*) morass (genitive of *lòn*)'.

nam Bad [Highland] 'of the (*na-m*) clump of trees (*bad*)'.

nam Buailtean [Highland] 'of the (*na-m*) cattle-enclosures (*buailtean*)'.

nan Iomairean [Highland] 'of the (*na-n*) ridges (plural of *iomaire*)'.

nan Sgeir [Highland] 'of the (*na-n*) skerry (*sgeir*, adaptation of ON *sker*)': skerry at the sea-entrance to Loch Broom.

na Saobhaidh [Highland] 'of the (*na*) fox-earth (*saobhaidh*)'.

na Sean-lùibe [Highland] 'of the (*na*) old (*sean*) bends (*lùibe*)'.

Phris Mhóir [Highland] 'Of the thicket (genitive of *preas*), big (*mhóir*)'.

Ruigh Chorrach [Highland] Possibly 'Slope (*ruighe*), heron (*chorr*) place (*achadh*)'.

Salachaidh [Highland] 'Foul (*salach*)'.

Cnoc

Cnoc

The following are mountain names that on the map are preceded by this word:

a' Choire [Highland] 'of the corrie (*choire*)'.

a' Ghiubhais [Highland (2)] 'of the fir tree (genitive of *giubhas*)'.

a' Mhadaidh [Strathclyde] 'of the fox (genitive of *madadh*)'.

an dà Chinn [Mull] 'of two (*dà*) heads (*chinn*, genitive of *ceann*)'.

an Earranaiche [Highland] Presumably 'of the land-portion (*earran*) open space (*achadh*)'.

an Eireannaich [Highland] Possibly 'of the land-portion (*earran*) open space (*achadh*)'.

an Fhuarain Bhàin [Highland] 'of the spring (genitive of *fuaran*), white (genitive of *bàn*)'.

an Liath-bhaid Mhóir [Highland] 'of the grey (*liath*) clump of trees (genitive of *bad*), big (genitive of *mór*)'.

Badaireach na Gaoithe [Highland] Probably 'Sheltered place of trees (*bad-aireach*) in the (*na*) marshes (plural of *gaoth*)': the land immediately west is indeed very marshy.

Breac [Highland] 'Speckled (*breac*)'.

Ceann nam Bad [Highland] 'Head (*ceann*) of the (*na-m*) clump of trees (*bad*)'.

Ceislein [Highland] Possibly 'Of the castle (*caisleáin*)'.

Coinnich [Strathclyde] Probably 'Of the dog (genitive of *cù*)'.

Coire na Feàrna [Highland] Presumably 'Corrie (*coire*) of the (*na*) alder tree (*fearna*)'.

Craggie [Highland] 'Of the crag[s] (*creige*)'.

Creagach [Strathclyde] 'Craggy (*creagach*)'.

Donn [Strathclyde] 'Brown (*donn*)'.

Leamhnachd [Highland] Presumably 'Elm (*leamhan*) place (*achadh*)'.

Loch Mhadadh [Highland] '[of] Loch Mhadadh': the loch name means 'fox'.

91

Meadhonach [Highland] 'In the middle (*meadhonach*)': the mountain is quite correctly the middle of a trio of ascending height.

Mór [Strathclyde] 'Big (*mór*)'.

Mór na Claigin [Islay] 'Big (*mór*), of the (*na*) hummocky hill (*claigeann*)': the hummocky hill in question may be nearby Beinn Bheigier, the highest point on the island, from which the Claggain River runs down to Claggain Bay.

Moy [Strathclyde] 'On the plain (*moigh*, dative/locative of *magh*)'.

Muighe-blàraidh [Highland] 'Of the plain (genitive of *magh*) with the cleared space (*blàr-*)'.

na Carraige [Strathclyde] 'of the (*na*) rocks (*carraige*)'.

na Glas Choille [Highland] 'of the (*na*) blue-green (*glas*) wood (*coille*)'.

na h-Airighe [Strathclyde] 'of the (*na*) shieling *(h-àirigh)*'.

na Maoile [Highland] 'of the (*na*) bare summit (genitive of *maol*)'.

na Meine [Strathclyde] Possibly 'of the (*na*) ore (*mèinne*)'.

nan Craobh [Strathclyde] 'of the (*na-n*) tree (*craobh*)'.

nan Cùilean [Highland] Probably 'of the (*na-n*) little recess (diminutive of *cùl*)'.

nan Tri-clach [Highland] 'of the (*na-n*) three (*tri*) stones (*clach*)'.

Odhar [Strathclyde] 'Dun-coloured (*odhar*)'.

Preas a' Mhadaidh [Highland] 'Thicket (*preas*) of the fox (genitive of *madadh*)'.

Reamhar [Strathclyde] 'Thick (*reamhar*)'.

Creag

Creag

The following are fell/rock names that on the map are preceded by this word:

a' Chaorainn [Highland] 'of the rowan tree (genitive of *caorann*)'.

a' Chlachain [Highland] 'of the place of stones (genitive of *clachan*)'; whether the name derives from a stony place or from a stone building is not known.

a' Choinneachan [Highland] 'of lamentation (*choinneachan*)': the fell overlooks the glen in which Montrose fought his last battle – Carbisdale – in 1650.

a' Lain [Skye] Possibly 'of the enclosure (*lainne*, genitive of *lann*)'.

an Lòin [Highland] 'of the morass (genitive of *lòn*)'.

an Dail Bheag [Grampian] 'of the dale (*dail*), small (*bheag*)'.

an Eunan [Grampian] 'of the little bird (diminutive of *eun*)'.

an t-Sithein [Tayside] 'of the little fairy hill (diminutive of *sìdh*)'.

a' Phuill [Strathclyde] 'of the pool (genitive of *poll*)'; the final element can alternatively mean 'mud', which may be more appropriate to this headland on the shore of the tidal Loch Fyne.

Beinn nan Eun [Tayside] '[of] Beinn nan Eun': the mountain name means 'mountain of the bird'.

Bhàn [Highland; Gigha] 'White (*bhàn*)'.

Dhubh [Highland (2); Tayside] 'Black (*dhubh*)'.

Gharbh [Central] 'Rough [water] (*gharbh*)'.

Leacach [Tayside] 'Stony-sloped (*leacach*)'.

Liath [Highland; Tayside] 'Grey (*liath*)'.

Loisgte [Highland] 'Of the burned ground (*loisgte*, genitive of *losg*)'.

Mholach [Strathclyde] Possibly '[The] Summit (*mullach*)'.

Mhór [Highland (2); Tayside/Central; Strathclyde (2); Central] 'Big (*mhór*)'.

na h-Iolaire [Highland (3)] 'of the (*na*) eagle (*h-iolaire*)'.

93

nam Bodach [Highland] 'of the (*na-m*) ghost (*bodach*)'.

nam Fiadh [Highland] 'of the (*na-m*) deer (*fiadh*)'.

nan Gabhar [Grampian] 'of the (*na-n*) goat (*gabhar*)'.

nan Gall [Grampian] 'of the (*na-n*) stranger (*gall*)'.

Riabhach na Greighe [Highland] Probably 'Grey-brown (*riabhach*), of the (*na*) crags (*creige*)'.

Veann [Grampian] Probably 'Of the mountains (*bheann*, genitive plural of *beinn*)'.

Cruach

Cruach

The following are mountain names that on the map are preceded by this word:

a' Bhuic [Strathclyde] 'of the buck (genitive of *boc*)'.

an Eachlaich [Strathclyde] Possibly 'of the horsemen (*eachla-*)'.

an Locha [Strathclyde] 'of the loch (genitive of *loch*)': Loch a' Chaorainn is situated close to the top of the mountain.

an Lochain [Strathclyde] 'of the little loch (genitive of *lochan*)'.

an Uillt Fheàrna [Jura] 'of the stream (*uillt*, variant of *allt*) [of the] alder tree (*fearna*)'.

a' Phubuill [Strathclyde] Possibly 'of the people (genitive of *pobal*)' but also possibly 'of the tents (genitive of *pebyll*)'.

Chuilceachan [Strathclyde] 'Of the reed (*chuilce*) places (*achan*)'.

Lagain [Strathclyde] 'of the little hollow (genitive of *lagan*)'.

Lusach [Strathclyde] 'Herb (*luss*) place (*achadh*)': the mountain overshadows the stream that runs beneath it to flow to the sea at Kilmichael of Inverlussa; that stream presumably takes its name from the mountain.

Maolachy [Strathclyde] Presumably 'Bare slope (*maol*) open space (*achadh*)'.

Mhic Fhionnlaidh [Strathclyde] Either 'Of the son (genitive of *mac*) of Finlay (personal name)' or 'Of [a man called] MacKinley (personal name)': either way, the derivation is the same – Finlay means 'fair [-haired] hero'.

Mhór [Strathclyde] 'Big (*mhór*)'.

nam Fiadh [Strathclyde (2)] 'of the (*na-m*) deer (*fiadh*)'.

nan Caorach [Strathclyde] 'of the (*na-n*) sheep (*caorach*)'.

nan Capull [Strathclyde (3)] Presumably 'of the (*na-n*) horse (*capall*)'.

nan Cuilean [Strathclyde] Presumably 'of the (*na-n*) holly (*cuileann*)'.

nan Gabhar [Strathclyde] 'of the (*na-n*) goat (*gabhar*)'.

nan Tarbh [Strathclyde] 'of the (*na-n*) bull (*tarbh*)'.

Scarba [Inner Hebrides] '[of the island of] Scarba': the name of the island means 'sharp island', from ON.

Cruachan

Cruachan

The following are hill names that on the map are preceded by this word:

Beinn a' Chearcaill [Skye] '[of] Beinn a' Chearcaill', some 6 miles east-north-east.

Druim na Croise [Mull] '[of] The ridge (*druim*) of the (*na*) crosses (*croise*)'.

Min [Mull] Presumably 'Smooth (*mín*)'.

Odhar [Mull] 'Dun-coloured (*odhar*)'.

D

dà 'two': evidently cognate with most Indo-European languages.

daal elided form of ON *dalr*: 'dale'.

dabhach (also *dabhoch*) 'a great measure', thus both a large vessel or container, and a large area of land (192 Scots acres). See **Davoch**.

dail 'field', 'haugh [i.e. a piece of land within the bend of a river]'; the word is an adaptation of the Brythonic Gaelic *dol*, 'meadow', influenced by the ON *dalr*/OE *dael*, 'dale'.

Dailly [Strathclyde] 'Haugh (*dail*)': the village lies within a large bend of the Water of Girvan (which is why it is a 'haugh'; see *dal-*).

daimh genitive of *damh*, thus 'of the stag'.

dal-   elided form of   1)   Brythonic Gaelic dol: 'meadow';
        or   2)   Gaelic loan-word dail: 'field', 'haugh [a piece of land within the bend of a river]'.

dalach genitive of *dail*, thus 'of the field', 'of the haugh'.

Dalbeattie [Dumfries & Galloway] 'Haugh (*dail*) of the birches (*beitheach*)': the town is enclosed by a bend in the Urr Water.

Dalbeg [Lewis] 'Field (*dail*), small (*beag*)': this to distinguish the village from Dalmore (q.v.) ½ mile south-west.

Dalblair [Strathclyde] 'Haugh (*dail*) of the plain (*blàir*)'.

-dale   elided form of   1)   ON *dalr*: 'dale';
        or   2)   OE *dael*: 'dale'.

Dale [Shetland] 'Dale (*dalr*, ON)'.

Dalelia [Highland] Probably 'Haugh (*dail*) of the fish-trap (*eileach*)': this accords well with the nearby location of Dalnabreac (q.v.) and its angling associations, although again 'dale' would make more sense than 'haugh'.

Dalginross [Tayside] 'Haugh (*dail*) at the head (*cinn*) of the headland (*rois*)': the proximity of the headland itself is denoted by the location of the village of Ross, ½ mile east.

Dalhousie [Borders] 'Field (*dail*) of the corner (*a' h-oisinn*)'; the village lies in a valley with a distinct dog-leg, and 'dale' would once more make better sense than 'field'.

Daliburgh [Uist] Presumably 'Dale (OE) fort (*burh*, OE).

Dalinlongart Hill [Strathclyde] 'Field (*dail*) of the ship (*an luing*), height (*ard*), hill (Eng)': the hill overlooks Holy Loch, where there are plenty of ships. The final element was evidently added much later: it may actually not be tautological if '-longart' instead derives from ON *lang-fjordr*, 'long fjord', but this is less likely.

Dalkeith [Lothian] 'Meadow (*dol*, Brythonic Gaelic) [of the] wood (*coed*, Brythonic Gaelic)'.

Dall [Tayside] Probably 'Dale (OE)': the village is in a wide valley on the shore of Loch Tummel.

Dallas [Grampian] Probably 'Meadow (*dol*, Brythonic Gaelic) resting-place (from a Brythonic Gaelic source)': the area has several other Brythonic names (e.g. Pluscarden).

Dalleagles [Strathclyde] Presumably 'Haugh (*dail*) of the church (*eaglais*)'.

-dalloch adapted form of *dalach*, genitive of *dail*, thus 'of the field', 'of the haugh'.

Dalmally [Strathclyde] Possibly 'Field (*dail*) of the bare summit (*maoile*, genitive of *maol*)'.

Dalmarnock [Strathclyde] Presumably 'Field (*dail*) of my (*mo*) Ernon (personal name)': this would parallel the apparent derivation of Kilmarnock – but there is no saint with a name like either 'Marnock' or 'Ernon' with Scottish connections, even assuming that a saint's name is in question here, as it should be in Kilmarnock.

Dalmore [Highland; Lewis] 'Field (*dail*), big (*mór*)'.

Dalmuir [Strathclyde] 'Field (*dail*), big (*mór*)' – an unusual corruption of the second element.

Dalnabreck [Highland] Presumably 'Haugh (*dail*) of the (*na*) trout (*breaca*)', although 'dale' would appear to be more apt than 'haugh' for this village above the shore of Loch Shiel.

Dalnacardoch [Tayside] Possibly 'Haugh (*dail*) of the (*na*) smithy (*ceardach*)': this would be a good place for a forge, where two old roads crossed – one General Wade's and the other now the A9.

Dalnamein [Tayside] Possibly 'Field (*dail*) of (*na*) ore (*mèinne*)'.

Dalnaspidal [Tayside] 'Haugh (*dail*) of the hostelry/hospice (corrupt form in fact of [place of ho]spital[ity])', and a good place for it, too, at the end of the Pass of Drumochter.

Dalqueich [Tayside] 'Haugh (*dail*) [on the River] Queich': the village is in a bend of the river, of which the name may mean 'of the hollow'.

Dalreavoch [Highland] Probably 'Haugh (*dail*), brindled (*riabhach*)': the village is located within a bend of the River Brora.

Dalry [Strathclyde; Dumfries & Galloway] Probably both 'Field (*dail*) of heather (*fhraoich*)' – but the Dumfries town was associated briefly with King James IV, and may just therefore be 'Field of the king (*righ*)'.

Dalwhinnie [Highland] Said to be 'Haugh (*dail*) of the champion (from a Gaelic source)'.

damh 'stag'.

damph corrupt form of *damh*: 'stag'.

daoine plural form of *duine*, thus 'men'.

darach 'oak tree': in early Celtic times in what is now England the oak tree was practically sacred; the word is thus related not only to *doire*, 'grove' (originally a grove of oak trees in which worship was ritualised: cf 'tree') but also to *druid* (who performed the sometimes gory ritual: cf 'dryad').

Darnick [Borders] Apparently 'Secret (*derne*, OE) settlement (*wic*, OE)'.

Darra [Grampian] Possibly 'Grove (*doire*)'.

-darroch adapted form of *darach*: 'oak tree' (q.v.).

daugh elided form of *dabhoch*, an area totalling 192 Scots acres.

Dava [Highland] Probably 'Of the stag (*daimh*)'.

Davoch [Grampian] A *dabhach* (or *dabhoch*) was an area totalling 192 Scots acres, or four *ceathramh* (quarters). See also **Kirriemuir**.

dead 'tooth'; the word is evidently cognate with Latin *dent-*, Eng *tooth*.

Deadh Choimhead [Strathclyde] Possibly 'Teeth (*deadh*), parallel (*chóimhead*)'.

dearcag 'berry', possibly because many berries are red – see *dearg* – but the word is occasionally also translated 'bilberry' and bilberries are classically blue-black (but closely related to cranberries which are red).

dearg 'red-brown', 'red', 'brown' – the point is that ultimately this describes the colour of trees, for the word is again related to *darach* '[the sacred] oak tree'.

deas 'south'.

Dee [Grampian] The river name would seem to represent the Gaelic equivalent of Latin *dea*, 'goddess', 'divine [female]', the feminine of *deus*, 'god', a word also related to the English word *day*. An original Gaelic form *Deva* has been suggested.

Deer [Grampian] 'Grove (*doire*)'.

Deerness [Orkney] 'Deer (*djur*, ON) ness (*nes*, ON)'.

Dell [Lewis] Probably 'Dale (OE)' – the English 'dell' is after all the same word.

Delnadamph [Grampian] Presumably 'Field (*dail*) of the (*na*) stag (*daimh*)'.

den elided form of OE *denu*: 'valley' (modern form: 'dene').

Denhead [Grampian; Fife] 'Valley (*denu*, OE) head (OE)'.

Denholm [Borders] Presumably 'Valley (*denu*, OE) island (*holm*, OE loan-word from OScand)': the village is on the River Teviot.

Denny [Central] Presumably 'Valley (*denu*, OE)': three rivers pass through the sprawling conurbation.

Dennystoun [Strathclyde] Town named after the shipbuilder William Denny in 1853.

derg elided form of *dearg*: 'red-brown', 'red', 'brown' (q.v.).

derry adapted form of *doire*: 'grove'.

Deveron [Grampian] Probably 'Black (*dubh*) water (ancient pre-Celtic river name found also in Earn and Findh-orn)'.

Devon [Central; Fife; Tayside] 'Black (*dubh*) river (*abhainn*)'.

Devonside [Central] '[River] Devon['s] side (Eng)': for the meaning of the river name, see above.

dhu, dhubh mutated forms of *dubh*: 'black', sometimes deriving from the Brythonic Gaelic equivalent.

dhui mutated form of *duibh(e)*, genitive of *dubh*: 'black'.

diallaid (also *diollaid*) 'saddle'.

dig 'moat'; evidently cognate with English *ditch*, something *dug*.

Dingwall [Highland] 'Parliament (*thing*, ON) open space (*völlr*, ON)'. The site of the annual *stad-mot* or 'estate-meet' (later corrupted in Welsh to *eisteddfod*) at which laws were promulgated, outlaws banned, and crimes paid for in cash or kind to the victims. And of course the scene afterwards for much merry-making and amorous dalliance.

-dinny elided form of *teine*: 'fire', and thus 'beacon'.

dìollaid (also *dìallaid*) 'saddle'.

Dipple [Strathclyde] Possibly 'Black (*dubh*) pool (*poll*)': if this is the case, it would accord well with its situation beneath the village of Dowhill, q.v.

dìseart 'seclusion', '[hermit's] retreat'; evidently cognate with Latin *desertum*, 'set apart'.

dìthreabh 'wilderness', 'desert'.

dobhar Gaelic adaptation of a Brythonic element (represented in modern Welsh by *dwyfr* and in England by *-dover*) meaning simply 'water'.

dobhran 'otter', because it lives in water (*dobhar*, q.v.). Cf 'otter' and 'water'.

doch elided form of *dabhach*, or *dabhoch*, a measure in area of 192 Scots acres.

doirbh 'grim', 'dour', 'gloomy'.

doire 'grove', 'clump of trees' – but originally a grove of sacred oak trees: see *darach*.

Doire Bhuidhe [Arran] 'Grove (*doire*), yellow (*bhuidhe*)'.

dòirlinn 'causeway covered at high tide', 'tidal isthmus'.

Doll [Highland] 'Valley (*dalr*, ON)': the ON is more likely than Brythonic Gaelic *dol*, 'meadow', in this area.

Dollar [Central] 'Field (*dol*, Brythonic Gaelic), arable (*ar*, Brythonic Gaelic)'.

domhain 'deep'.

donn 'brown'; evidently cognate with English *dun* and *tan*.

doon occasionally, elided form of *dùn*: 'castle', 'fortified premises', 'pile', 'heap', 'mound'.

dorain elided form of *dobhrain*, genitive of *dobhran*, thus 'of the otter'.

dòrain genitive form of *dòran*, thus 'of the exile', 'of the stranger'.

doran elided form of *dobhran*, diminutive of *dobhar*, thus 'little water' or 'otter'.

101

dòran 'exile', 'stranger'; the word is technically a diminutive.

dorcha 'dark' – possibly with the darkness of the forest, for the word is another that is related to *dearg* 'red-brown [tree colour]' and *darach* '[the sacred] oak tree'. It is also cognate with English *dark*.

Dores [Highland] Possibly 'Dark (*dubh*) shrubland (*ras*)': the description would be appropriate to the locality.

dornach 'with pebbles', 'pebbly': apparently some sort of a diminutive of a word (*dorn*) that means 'fist'.

Dornie [Highland] 'Pebbly (*dornach*)': there is a shingle beach here where Loch Long empties into the junction of Loch Duish and Loch Alsh

Dornoch [Highland] 'Pebbly (*dornach*)': all the same, much of the beach is sandy at the end of the Dornoch Firth.

Dornock [Dumfries & Galloway] Probably 'Pebbly (*dornach*)': the village is surrounded by ancient towers and a stone circle, and is close to the shore of the Solway Firth.

douglas a Brythonic Gaelic double element: 'black (*du*, Brythonic Gaelic) stream (*glas*, Brythonic Gaelic)'.

Douglas [Strathclyde] The town is named after the river on which it stands (now called the Douglas Water): the name means 'Black (*du*, Brythonic Gaelic) stream (*glas*, Brythonic Gaelic)'.

Douglas and Angus [Tayside] This district of the city of Dundee has two ancient names, though only one so ancient as to be Brythonic. Douglas is 'Black (*du*, Brythonic Gaelic) stream (*glas*, Brythonic Gaelic)', and is thus named after the stream on which it stands; Angus is named after one of three brothers who were pioneer Scottish invaders from Ireland: the name means 'unique choice'.

Douglastown [Tayside] Village founded by William Douglas of Brigton, a corn and flax miller, in the early 1790s.

Douglas Water [Strathclyde] The village is named after the river near which it stands: the name means 'Black (*du*, Brythonic Gaelic) stream (*glas*, Brythonic Gaelic)'. It would seem likely that Douglas Water as a community is younger than the town of Douglas some 5 miles south-west, because of the addition of the tautologous 'Water' to both the name of the river and the village.

D

doun   either 1)   generally, an elided form of *dùn*: 'castle', 'fortified
premises', 'pile', 'heap', and thus 'mound';
or 2)   adapted form of OE *dun*: 'a down', 'hill'.

Dounby [Orkney] Probably 'Hill (OE *dun*, 'a down') village (*by*, OE
loan-word from OScand)'. But if the name is entirely OScand, the first
element may be a personal name.

Doune [Central] Probably 'Castle (*dùn*)': Doune Castle dates from the early
1400s, but there were probably fortifications there even before then.

Douneside [Grampian] Possibly 'Hill (*dun*, OE) side (Eng)': the tiny
village is indeed on the side of a hill (and in an area of some OE names).

Dounie [Highland] Probably 'Mound (*dùn*)': the village stands on a slight
rise each side of a stream about to flow down into the River Carron.

-dour elided form of *dobhar*: 'water'.

dove elided form of *dubh*: 'black', 'dark'.

dow elided form of *dubh*: 'black', 'dark'.

Dowhill [Strathclyde] Probably 'Black (*dubh*) hill (Eng)': if this is the case,
it would accord well with its situation above Dipple, q.v.

draigheann (also *droigheann*) 'blackthorn'.

-drain elided form of *draigheann*: 'blackthorn'.

-drean elided form of *draigheann*: 'blackthorn'.

Dreghorn [Strathclyde] The suburb is possibly named after the river it
stands on (now called the Annick Water): 'Red (*dearg*) water (*eron*, an
ancient river name found also in Earn, Findh-orn and Dev-eron, the last two
also citing colours; see also *darach*)'.

Drem [Lothian] 'Ridge (*druim*)': actually more a harder strip of land than
the surrounding rather low-lying fertile area.

drim elided form of *druim*: 'ridge'.

drish adapted form of *dris*: 'bramble', 'blackberry', 'thorns'.

drochit elided form of *drochaid*: 'bridge': actually cognate with English
draught, being something 'drawn' between two sides.

Droma [Highland] 'Of the ridge (*druima*, genitive of *druim*)'.

droigheann (also *draigheann*) 'blackthorn'.

103

Droman [Highland] Probably 'At the ridge (*drumein*, dative/locative of *druim*)'.

Dron [Tayside] Probably 'Hump (*dronn*)'.

Drongan [Strathclyde] Possibly 'Hump (*dronn*) head (*ceann*)'.

druid 'thrush'; the word is evidently cognate with Latin *turdus*, 'thrush'.

druim 'back' – both the back of the human body and the geographical back, that is, a 'ridge'.

Druimavuic [Strathclyde] 'Ridge (*druim*) of the pig (*a' mhuice*)'.

Druimdrishaig [Strathclyde] 'Ridge (*druim*), bramble (*dris*), bay (*-aig*, corrupt form of ON *vágr*)'.

Druim Fada [Highland] 'Ridge (*druim*), long (*fada*)'.

Druim Fiaclach [Highland] 'Ridge (*druim*), toothed (*fiacleach*)'.

Druim Gleann Laoigh [Highland] 'Ridge (*druim*) of Glen Loy': the glen name means 'of the calf' – the river name associated with the glen is likely to be back-formed.

Druimindarroch [Highland] Presumably 'Ridge (*druim*) of the oak tree (*an daraich*)'.

Druim na Dubh Ghlaic [Shuna] 'Ridge (*druim*) of the (*na*) black (*dubh*) hollow (*ghlaice*, genitive of *glac*)'.

drum elided form of *druim*: 'ridge'.

Drum [Tayside] 'Ridge (*druim*)'.

Drumbeg [Highland] 'Ridge (*druim*), small (*beag*)'.

Drumbuie [Highland] 'Ridge (*druim*), yellow (*buidhe*)'.

Drumchapel [Strathclyde] 'Ridge (*druim*) of the horse (*chapuill*)'.

Drumchardine [Highland] Possibly 'Ridge (*druim*) [of] the thicket (*cardden*, Brythonic Gaelic)'.

Drumclog [Strathclyde] Possibly 'Ridge (*druim*) of the stone (*cloiche*)'.

Drumelzier [Borders] Originally in the 6th century named Dunmedler ('Mound of [?] Merlin'; cf the Welsh mystique surrounding the name Carmarthen), the village's name has through the centuries been assimilated to later Gaelic forms.

Drumfearn [Skye] 'Ridge (*druim*) [of] the alder tree (*fearn*)'.

D

Drumin [Grampian] Presumably 'At the ridge (*drumein*, dative/locative of *druim*)'.

Drumlanrig [Dumfries & Galloway] 'Ridge (*druim*) [of] the glade (*llanerch*, Brythonic Gaelic)'.

Drummond [Tayside] 'At the ridge (*drumein*, dative/locative of *druim*)'. This is the origin also of the surname.

Drummore [Dumfries & Galloway] 'Ridge (*druim*), big (*mór*)'.

Drumnadrochit [Highland] 'Ridge (*druim*) of the (*na*) bridge (*drochaid*)': the bridge is over the River Enrick, about to join Urquhart Bay (part of Loch Ness); and the precipitous nature of the car-park behind the Loch Ness Museum at Drumnadrochit proves at least to drivers how much of a ridge there is there too.

Drumochter [Highland/Tayside] 'Ridge (*druim*) of the upper part (*uachdair*)': and indeed the line of the ridge is the highest part of the pass on the A9 between Glen Truim ('The glen of [the river of] the ridge') and Glen Garry.

Drumphail [Dumfries & Galloway] Possibly 'Ridge (*druim*) of the pool (*phuill*)'.

Drumrash [Dumfries & Galloway] Possibly 'Ridge (*druim*) of the promontory (*rois*)' in that the village lies on the shore of Loch Ken, and despite the fact that *rois* can also mean 'of the wood'. But that second element might alternatively be 'of the heath (*rais*)'.

Drumsheugh [Lothian] Apparently 'Meldrum's (personal name) haugh (*halh*, OE)', but who Meldrum was is not known.

Drybridge [Grampian] Village founded in the mid-19th century near a bridge over a road: not being a bridge over a river (as was far more common in Scotland), it was thus a 'dry bridge'.

Dryburgh [Borders] Apparently 'Dry (*dryge*, OE) borough (*burh*, OE)', no more, no less.

Dryhope [Borders] 'Dry (*dryge*, OE) valley (*hop*, OE)'.

Drymen [Central] 'At the ridge (*drumein*, dative/locative of *druim*)'.

Duart [Mull] 'Black (*dubh*) height (*ard*)'.

dubh 'black', 'dark'; Welsh cognates are *du, ddu*.

Dubh Eilean [Colonsay] 'Black (*dubh*) island (*eilean*)'; these elements are more commonly reversed.

Dubh-fhéith [Firth of Lorn] 'Black (*dubh*) slow-moving channel (*fhéith*)': a hazard to shipping between Luing and Mull.

Dubh Sgeir [Firth of Lorn] 'Black (*dubh*) skerry (*sgeir*)': a hazard to shipping between Minard Point on the mainland (Strathclyde) and Mull.

Duddingston [Lothian] Presumably 'Dudda's people's (*Dudda-ingas*, OE) town (*tun*, OE)'. The forename Dudda is well established in English place names.

Dufftown [Grampian] Town founded by James Duff, Earl of Fife, in 1813.

duie elided form of *duibh(e)*, genitive of *dubh*: 'black'.

duine 'man'.

Duirinish [Highland] 'Deer (*djur*, ON) ness (*nes*, ON)'.

Duisky [Highland] Probably 'Black (*dubh*) water (*uisge*)'.

Dull [Tayside] Probably 'Field (*dail*)'.

dum- elided form of *dùn*: 'castle', 'fortified premises'; 'mound'.

Dumbarton [Strathclyde] 'Fortified stronghold (*dùn*) of the Britons (*breatainn*)': this was the capital town of the Britons in the kingdom of Strathclyde.

Dumcrieff [Dumfries & Galloway] Possibly 'Mound (*dùn*) of the tree (*craoibhe*)'.

Dumfries [Dumfries & Galloway] 'Mound (*dùn*) of the copse (*phris*, genitive of *preas*)'.

dùn 'castle', 'fortified premises', 'pile', 'heap', 'mound', depending perhaps on the state of preservation/decay of the said fortifications. Welsh cognates include *dinas*, 'castle'; Irish ones include *daingeann*, 'stronghold', from which the English word *dungeon* derives. A purely English cognate is *down*, as in the South Downs.

Dunan [Skye] Possibly 'Little mound (diminutive of *dùn*)'.

Dunbar [Lothian] 'Castle (*dùn*) [on] the top (*barr*)': the now ruined castle stands on a rock above the harbour.

Dunbeath [Highland] 'Fort (*dùn*) [of] the birch tree (*beithe*)': the village takes its name from the nearby broch.

Dunbeg [Strathclyde] 'Castle (*dùn*), small (*beag*)': the name may refer to Dunstaffnage Castle, ½ mile north, although that 13th-century edifice is not all that small, or it may refer by way of comparison to the smaller outlying community.

106

Dunblane [Central] 'Fortified premises (*dùn*) of [St] Blane (personal name)'. Blane, or Blaan, was a late 6th-century bishop who founded a monastery in his native Bute.

Dunbog [Fife] 'Fortified premises (*dùn*) [on] a rise (*builg*)'.

Duncansby [Highland] 'Dungad's (personal name) community (*byr*, ON)': the name is Gaelic *donn chadh*, 'brown(-haired) warrior' (in Ireland later to become Duncan, Doonican, Donnegan, Donaghan and so forth), and may refer to a local 10th-century chieftain.

Duncrievie [Tayside] Presumably 'Mound (*dùn*) of the tree (*craoibhe*)'.

Dùn da Ghaoithe [Mull] 'Mound (*dùn*) of two (*dà*) marshes (*ghaoithe*)': the 'mound' is 2,512 feet (989 m) high!

Dundee [Tayside] Commentators to a person plump for 'Fortified town (*dùn*) [of] Daig (personal name)'. But who Daig was is not known (his name would mean 'fire'), and there would seem really to be no need to look further than the local river name (Tay) for a more convincing derivation for the element.

Dundonald [Strathclyde] 'Castle (*dùn*) of Donald (personal name)': Donald (*Domhnall*, meaning 'world-ruler') was the name of six kings of Scotland and one Scottish saint; Robert II died in this now-ruined castle in 1309.

Dundreggan [Highland] Presumably 'Mound (*dùn*) of the blackthorn (*dreagheainn*)'.

Dùn Dubh [Strathclyde] 'Mound (*dùn*), dark (*dubh*)'.

Dunkeld [Tayside] 'Fort (*dùn*) [of] the Caledonians (*Chailleainn*)'.

Dunlop [Strathclyde] Possibly 'Mound (*dùn*) on a bend (*lùib*) [of the river]'.

Dunmore [Strathclyde; Central] 'Mound (*dùn*), big (*mór*)'.

Dunoon [Strathclyde] 'Castle (*dùn*) [on] the river (*obhainn*, variant of *abhainn*)': traces of an ancient castle lie on a rock above the pier.

Duns [Borders] 'Fortified premises (*dùn*)': the '-s' is a later addition possibly meant as a plural; the name may refer to an ancient tower now incorporated in the modern castle.

Dunsinane [Tayside] 'Fort (*dùn*) [on] the breast (*sineachan*)'.

Dunvegan [Skye] Possibly 'Castle (*din*, Brythonic Gaelic), small (*bychan*,

Brythonic Gaelic)': the present castle, however, is comparatively modern and rather large.

Durness [Highland] 'Deer (*djur*, ON) ness (*nes*, ON)'.

Dury [Shetland] 'Deer (*djur*, ON) island (*ey*, ON)'.

Dykehead [Tayside; Grampian] 'Ditch (*dic*, OE) head (*heafod*, OE)'.

Dysart [Fife] 'Retreat (*diseart*)'.

E

each 'horse'; this would appear to be cognate with Latin *equus*.

eadan (also *eadidh*) 'slope', 'brow'; the element seems to be a variant of *aodann*, q.v.

eadar 'between'.

eadidh (also *eadan*) 'slope', 'brow'.

eag 'notch', 'serration'; the word is cognate with a very ancient root going back farther than Sanskrit *akh* 'a sharp point'.

eagach 'notched', 'serrated'.

Eagan Bearneas [Highland] Presumably 'Notched (*eagan*, plural form) gaps (*bearneas*)': the gaps are in the mountain chain between Achnashellach Forest and West Monar Forest.

eaglais (Irish also *eaglis, aglish*; Welsh *eglwys*; Cornish *eglos*; French *église*; etc.) 'church', derived from Latin/Greek *ecclesia,* 'called together' as an assembly.

-eagles assimilated form of *eaglais*: 'church'.

Eag na Maoile [Coll] 'Notch (*eag*) on the (*na*) bare summit (genitive of *maol*)'.

ealadh 'tomb', 'grave'; because of the associations with grave-goods and the spoils of burial-mounds, the derivative *ulaidh* came to mean 'treasure'.

ear 'east'; cf Latin *oriens*.

earls- especially lowlands, 'earl's' and even, if early enough, 'jarl's'.

Earlston [Borders] 'Ercil's (personal name) fort (*dùn*)': the ruins of the tower known by Thomas the Rhymer, the 13th-century poet, still stand here.

Earn [Tayside/Central] Probably 'Water' from an ancient pre-Celtic source found in other river names (e.g. Findh-orn and Dev-eron); some commentators instead see 'Erin', a name for Ireland, as a possible derivation.

earran 'share', 'portion', thus 'plot of land'.

eas 'waterfall', 'chasm over which water may flow'.

Easaval [Uist] Probably 'Waterfall's (*easa*) fell (*mheall*)'.

Easdale [Strathclyde] Probably 'Æsi's (personal name, ON) dale (*dalr*, ON)': the personal name is well attested in Yorkshire.

easg (also *easga, easgaidh, easgainn*) 'marsh', 'bog', 'swamp'; the element is evidently cognate with *uisge*: 'water'.

easgaidh alternative form of *easg*, q.v.

easgainn alternative form of *easg*, q.v.

East – – – – See – – – – –.

easter 'farther to the east', 'eastern'; the word is derived in the north and west from ON, and elsewhere from English.

Easter Fearn [Highland] 'East of the (Eng) alder tree (*fearn*)': the alder tree must have been a landmark, for the streams each side of it are named the Wester and Easter Fearn Burns accordingly.

Easter Lednathie [Tayside] Possibly 'East of the (Eng) broad (*leathann*) ford (*ath[a]*)': there is now no Lednathie for this tiny village to be east of.

Easthouses [Lothian] The only strange thing about this OE name meaning exactly what it says is that it has only very recently become plural in form.

Ecclefechan [Dumfries & Galloway] 'Church (*eaglais*) of [St] Fechin (personal name)': the saintly 7th-century Irish abbot – also called Vigean – never actually came to Scotland, although his disciples did. (Some commentators nominate an otherwise unattested St Fiachan. In former years this name was in any case said to derive from Brythonic *eglwys-bychan*, 'little church'.)

Eccles [Border] 'Church (*eaglais*)'. The minuscule remains of a Cistercian convent destroyed in 1545 are still visible.

Ecclesmachan [Lothian] 'Church (*eaglais*) of [St] Machan (personal name)': St Machan was a 6th-century Irish-trained Roman-consecrated bishop resident in Campsie.

Eday [Orkney] 'Isthmus (*eith*, ON) island (*ey*, ON)': the island is almost split into two by a narrow causeway.

Edderton [Highland] 'Between (*eadar*) the mounds (*dùn*)': the village lies between Quarryhill (1,054 feet/321 m) and Struie (1,218 feet/371 m).

Eddleston [Borders] 'Eadwulf's (personal name, OE) farmstead (*tun*, OE)': the said Eadwulf (or Edulf) was landowner in the 12th century.

Eddrachillis [Highland] 'Between (*eadar*) two (*dà*) kyles (*chaolais*)': the village overlooks Badcall bay and numerous islands.

110

Eden Water [Borders] The river name Eden is found also in Cumbria and mid-Wales. In all cases the name is British and appears to mean something like 'strongly spouting', 'gushing forth'.

eder elided form of *eadar*: 'between'.

edin elided form of *aodann*: 'slope', mountain-face', 'hillside'.

Edinbane [Skye] Probably 'Slope (*aodann*), white (*bàn*)'. On some maps the name is spelled *Edinbain*.

Edinburgh [Lothian] 'Mountain-face (*aodann*) stronghold (*burh*, OE)': the OE element was a replacement for the original Gaelic *dùn*, which preceded what is now the first element (an arrangement that was centuries later transferred to Dunedin, New Zealand). As everybody knows, the castle is situated on top of a sheer rock-face above most of the present city.

Edmondstone [Orkney] Probably 'Eadmund's (personal name, OE) farmstead (*tun*, OE)'.

Ednam [Borders] 'Eden [Water] community (*ham*, OE)': the village stands on the Eden Water. The river name, which is British, may mean 'gushing'.

Edradynate [Tayside] Probably 'Between (*eadar*) two (*dà*) rocky braes (*aoneaidh*)'.

Edzell [Tayside] The town is on the River North Esk at the end of Glen Esk, where the river leaves the mountains and flows on to the coastal plain. Dare I suggest then that Edzell derives from a corruption of 'Esk-dale' in OE or ON? (There are one or two OE names in the vicinity.)

Egilsay [Shetland] 'Egill's (personal name, ON) island (*ey*, ON)'.

egles (also *eglis[h]*) elided forms of *eaglais*: 'church'.

Eididh nan Clach Geala [Highland] 'Brow (*eadidh*) of the (*na-n*) stone (*clach*), white (*geala*)': the 'brow' is some 3,039 feet (926 m) high.

eige 'file'.

Eigg [Inner Hebrides] 'Notched (*eag*)'. A rift or 'notch' runs right across the island.

eigheach 'wailing', 'making a noise', 'outcry'.

Eilanreach [Highland] Possibly 'Island (*eilean*), brindled (*riabhach*)'.

111

eileach   either 1)   'fish-trap', 'weir', thus also 'a narrow channel joining
two lochs or stretches of sea';
2)   mill-pool', 'dam';
or 3)   proto-Gaelic 'rocky', 'stony'.

Eileach an Naoimh [Inner Hebrides] 'Narrow channel (*eileach*) of the saints (*naoimh*)': on the island that forms one side of the channel is an anciently celebrated chapel.

eileag (also *eileirg*) 'deer-trap', 'enclosure into which deer might be herded for culling'.

eilean 'island': the word is said to be a corruption from ON *eyland* but the OE *iland/iegland* is equally close (and in both ON and OE the final element 'land' is totally unnecessary, for the first element by itself means 'island'). The original Gaelic for 'island' is *inis*.

Eilean a' Chalmain [Inner Hebrides] Probably 'Island (*eilean*) of the dove (*a' chalmain*)', although the final element may alternatively be one of the many references to St Columba.

Eilean a' Chladaich [Colonsay] 'Island (*eilean*) of the beaches (*chladaich*)'.

Eilean a' Chuirn [Islay] 'Island (*eilean*) of the cairn (*a' chuirn*)', although the final element could alternatively mean 'rocky rounded hill'.

Eilean a' Ghaill [Highland] 'Island (*eilean*) of the Gaels (*Ghaoidhail*)'.

Eilean an Ròin Mór [Highland] 'Island (*eilean*) of the seal (*ròin*), big (*mór*)': the final adjective applies to the 'island', not the 'seal'.

Eilean Aoidhe [Strathclyde] 'Island (*eilean*) of the isthmuses (*aoidhe*, genitive plural of *uidh*, itself an adaptation of ON *eith*)'.

Eilean Balnagowan [Strathclyde] 'Island (*eilean*) [of the] village (*baile*) of the (*na*) blacksmith (*gobhainn*)'.

Eilean Beag [Inner Hebrides] 'Island (*eilean*), small (*beag*)'.

Eilean Chaluim Chille [Lewis] 'Island (*eilean*) [of St] Columba's (*Choluim*) monastic cell (*chille*)'.

Eilean Craobhach [Islay] 'Island (*eilean*) of trees (*craobhach*)'.

Eilean Creagach [Inner Hebrides] 'Island (*eilean*) of crags (*creageach*)'.

Eilean Dallaig [Barra] Possibly 'Island (*eilean*) of the fields (*dalaich*)'.

Eilean Darach [Highland] 'Island (*eilean*), oak tree (*darach*)'.

Eilean Donan [Highland] Possibly 'Island (*eilean*), the little castle (diminutive of *dùn*)', although there was apparently a celebrated 7th - century monk called Donan (see **Kildonan**).

Eilean Dubh [Highland; Strathclyde (3)] 'Island (*eilean*), dark (*dubh*)'.

Eilean Dubh Mór [Inner Hebrides] 'Island (*eilean*), dark (*dubh*), big (*mór*)': the final adjective applies to the 'island, dark' – not just the 'island' – because there are other, lesser 'island, darks'.

Eilean Dùin [Strathclyde] 'Island (*eilean*) of the fort (*dùin*)'.

Eilean Garbh [Gigha] 'Island (*eilean*) [of] rough [water] (*garbh*)'.

Eilean Glas [Harris] 'Island (*eilean*), blue-green (*glas*)'.

Eilean Grianain [Inner Hebrides] 'Island (*eilean*) of the sunny mound (genitive of *grianan*)'.

Eilean Iosal [Inner Hebrides] 'Island (*eilean*), low (*íosal*)'.

Eilean Meadhonach [Inner Hebrides] 'Island (*eilean*) in the middle (*meadhonach*)': so named because it is between Eilean Beag and Eilean Mór.

Eilean Mór [Inner Hebrides (2); Highland (2); Strathclyde (2)] 'Island (*eilean*), big (*mór*)'.

Eilean Mór a' Bhàigh [Outer Hebrides] 'Island (*eilean*), big (*mór*) in the bay (*bhàigh*)'.

Eilean Mullagrach [Highland] Possibly 'Island (*eilean*) of the summits (*mullachraich*)'.

Eilean na Bà [Inner Hebrides] 'Island (*eilean*) of the (*na*) cow (*bà*)'.

Eilean na h-Airde [Inner Hebrides] 'Island (*eilean*) of the (*na*) height (*h-airde*)'.

Eilean na h-Aon Chaorach [Inner Hebrides] Presumably 'Island (*eilean*) of the (*na*) one single (*aon*) sheep (*chaorach*)'.

Eilean nam Muc [Inner Hebrides] 'Island (*eilean*) of the (*na-m*) pig (*muc*)'.

Eilean nan Bannaomh [Tayside] 'Island (*eilean*) of the (*na-n*) women (*ban*) saints (*naoimh*)': formerly there was a celebrated nunnery on the island.

113

Eilean nan Caorach [Strathclyde] 'Island (*eilean*) of the (*na-n*) sheep (*caorach*)'.

Eilean nan Gobhar [Highland] 'Island (*eilean*) of the (*na-n*) goat (*gobhar*)'.

Eilean nan Ròn [Highland; Oronsay] 'Island (*eilean*) of the (*na-n*) seal (*ròn*)'.

Eilean Righ [Strathclyde] 'Island (*eilean*), royal (*rìgh*)'.

Eilean Ruaridh Mór [Highland] Probably 'Island (*eilean*) of Rory Mór (personal name)', although the two final elements individually mean 'red' and 'big' respectively.

Eilean Sùbhainn [Highland] Probably 'Island (*eilean*) of raspberries (*subheain*)'.

Eilean Thuilm [Eigg] 'Island (*eilean*) of the small island (*t-huilm*, ON)'. It would seem that the first element was added later when the second had become no more than a name, also changing ON *holm[r]* to a Gaelic genitive form.

eileirg (also *eileag*) 'deer-trap', 'enclosure into which deer might be herded for culling'.

eilid 'hind', 'female deer'.

eirbhe alternative form of *airbhe*: 'dividing wall', 'partition', 'boundary'.

elan elided form of *eilean*: 'island'.

elch- elided form of proto-Gaelic *eileach*: 'rocky'.

Elcho [Tayside] 'Rocky (proto-Gaelic *eileach*)'.

Elgin [Grampian] 'Little Ireland (diminutive of *elg*)'.

Elie [Fife] 'Tomb (*ealadh*)'. The place is the site of a formerly well-known cemetery.

Elishader [Skye] Possibly 'Eilfr's (personal name, ON) house (*setr*, ON)'.

ellan elided form of *eilean*: 'island'.

Ellon [Grampian] Possibly 'Island (*eilean*)': the town is centred on the River Ythan.

Elrick [Grampian] 'Deer-trap (*eileirg*)'.

Elvanfoot [Strathclyde] 'Elvan [Water's] foot (Eng)': in the village, the Elvan Water joins with the Clyde. The river name may be Old Scandinavian for 'the river'.

Elvingston [Lothian] Possibly 'Ifwynn's (personal name, OE) farm (*tun*, OE)'. Ifwynn was a woman's name, but is attested in a Yorkshire place name.

Embo [Highland] 'Eyvind['s] (personal name, ODan) house (*bó*, ODan)'.

Enochdhu [Tayside] Possibly 'Moor (*aonach*), dark (*dubh*)': the village lies in the deep-cut valley between Strathardle and Glen Brerachan.

eòin genitive plural of *eun*, thus 'of the birds'.

eòrna 'barley'.

Eriboll [Highland] Presumably 'Erikr['s] (personal name, ON) settlement (*bol*, ON)': this would accord well with Arnaboll ('Arne's settlement') some 3 miles farther north.

Eriskay [Inner Hebrides] Probably 'Erikr's (personal name, ON) island (*ey*, ON)'.

-erno elided form of *airneach*: 'sloe'.

-errie elided form of *eirbhe*: 'boundary', 'partition', 'dividing wall'.

Esk [Grampian; Lothian; Dumfries & Galloway] A river name common in Scotland, as it is also in England (sometimes disguised as the Exe or Axe, etc.) and in Wales (Usk). The meaning is simply 'water': cf *uisge*.

Eskadale [Highland] Probably 'Marsh (*easga*) dale (*dail*, loan-word from ON or OE)'. The village lies in the valley formed by the junction of two rivers.

Eskbank [Lothian] '[River] Esk['s] bank (Eng)': the river name means 'water'. Cf *uisge*.

Eskdalemuir [Dumfries & Galloway] '[River] Esk dale (OE) moor (OE)': the river name means 'water'. Cf *uisge*.

Esknish [Islay] Probably 'Marshy (*easgaidh*) water-meadow (*inis*)': the village lies on the River Sorn.

Essich [Highland] Possibly 'Waterfall (*eas*) place (*achadh*)'.

-essie adapted form of *eas*: 'waterfall', 'ravine over which water flows'.

Ettrick [Borders] One commentator suggests 'Playful (*atre*, Brythonic Gaelic)', and as a description of the Ettrick Water – which is where the village name probably does derive from – that is not unreasonable. Moreover, a Brythonic form would accord perfectly with the nearby *Ettrick Pen*, 'the head (Brythonic *pen* for Goidelic *ceann*) of the Ettrick [Water]'.

115

Yet *atre* is otherwise unattested, and there are other possible elements (such as *uthrog*, 'wondrous'). And an OE derivation cannot be ultimately discounted: Ettrick might, for instance, be OE *ete-ric* 'grazing stream' or *Eat-ric* 'Eata's stream', one or other of which first elements certainly accounts for Etal (second element OE *halh*, 'haugh') in Northumbria only 45 miles away.

Ettrickbridge [Borders] 'Ettrick [Water] bridge (Eng)': for the possible meaning of the river name see **Ettrick**.

eun 'bird': possibly cognate with Latin *avian-*.

Evanton [Highland] The village was established around 1810 by a landowner named Evan Fraser of Balconie. (There is no excuse whatever to propose – as one commentator does – that the name derives from one Brythonic Gaelic element together with one OE element other than incidentally in this way.)

Ewe [Highland] The name has transferred to the sea-loch from what is now Loch Maree (the village at the head of which is still called Kinlochewe): a difficult name perhaps corresponding to a Brythonic Gaelic form meaning 'sheep' [cognate with Latin *ovis*, English *ewe*]; to an ON or OE form meaning 'yew'; or referring in some way to the nearby dominant Beinn Eighe.

Exnaboe [Shetland] Possibly 'Oxen (*uxni*, ON) house (*bó*, ODan)', although the first element may be a personal name.

Eye Water [Borders] The river name derives from OE *ea* 'river' – 'Water' was evidently added when the original meaning had been forgotten.

Eyemouth [Borders] 'Eye [Water's] mouth (Eng)': the river name means 'river'.

Eynort [Uist] Probably 'Ehen['s] (personal name, Old Scandinavian) fjord (*-ord*, corruption of ON *fjordr*)', although the personal name may instead be an ON version of the Welsh *Owain*.

F

fada 'long'.

fadhail 'salt-water ford': the word is an adaptation of ON *vathill*, 'wading-place'.

Failford [Strathclyde] '[Water of] Fail ford (Eng)': the meaning of the river name is unknown, but may be identical with that of the Fal in Cornwall.

faire 'spying', 'watching'.

Fair Isle [Shetland] 'Sheep (*faer*, ON) isle (in this case, probably an adaptation of ON *ey*, 'island')'

faithir (also *foithir*) 'shelving declivity', 'terraced slope'.

fàl 'hedge', 'palisade', 'enclosure'; the word is cognate with Latin *palum,* English *paling*, etc.

falamh 'empty' (modern Gaelic).

Falkirk [Central] 'Speckled (*fawe*, ME) church (*kirk*, ME)': it is not difficult to understand how *fawe-kirk* might (in the 15th century) evolve into Falkirk through a misplaced desire to 'pronounce it properly'.

Falkland [Fife] Possibly 'People's (*folc*, OE) land (Eng)', i.e. Crown property, which would be apt in this case, a Royal Burgh with a palace and a great history of occupation by the Scottish kings. (The name of Faulkland in Somerset derives from these sources.) But possibly instead 'Falcons' land', again from OE.

famhar 'giant'.

fàn 'gentle slope', 'flat area'.

fang 'sheep-pen'; in Scots the word has become *fank*. Evidently cognate with English *pen*.

Fanmore [Mull] Presumably '[The] Flat area (*fàn*), big (*mór*)'.

fannich elided form of *mhanach*: 'monk'.

faoghail adapted form of *fadhail*: 'salt-water ford'.

faoileag 'seagull'.

faoilinn 'beach'.

fas(adh) 'place', 'site', 'station', 'flat spot'.

Fascadale [Highland] Presumably 'Shelter (*fasgadh*) dale (*dail*)'.

fasgadh 'shelter'.

Fasnacloich [Strathclyde] 'Site (*fas*) of the (*na*) stone (*cloich*)'.

Fasnakyle [Highland] 'Place (*fas*) of the (*na*) narrows (*caol*)'.

Fasque [Grampian] Presumably 'Shelter (*fasgadh*)'

Fassfern [Highland] Presumably 'Place (*fas*) of the alder tree (*fearn*)'.

fassie adapted form of *fasadh*: 'place', 'site', 'station', 'flat spot'.

Fauldhouse [Lothian] 'Fallow land (*falh*, OE) house (Eng)'.

feadag 'plover'.

feadan 'streamlet', 'narrow glen in which a streamlet flows'.

feannag   either 1) 'potato-bed';
             or 2) 'crow'.

fear 'man': the word is cognate with the Latin *vir*.

fearn(a) 'alder tree'.

fearnan 'land'.

Fearnan [Tayside] Presumably 'Land (*fearnan*)': the village lies on hard ground between areas of more fertile growth.

Fearnbeg [Highland] 'Alder tree (*fearn*), small (*beag*)': the final adjective refers to the size of the village, in comparison with Fearnmore 1 mile north-west.

Fearnmore [Highland] 'Alder tree (*fearn*), big (*mór*)': the final adjective refers to the size of the village, in comparison with Fearnbeg 1 mile south-east.

fèith 'vein', therefore 'slow-moving stream', 'channel in a marsh', 'bog'.

Fèith a' Chaoruinn [Highland] 'Channel in the marsh (*fèith*) of the rowan trees (*chaoruinn*)'.

Fèith Gaineimh Mhór [Highland] 'Channel in the marsh (*fèith*) of the sand (*gainimh*), big (*mhór*)': this is the name of the major stream in a particularly swampy area.

fell (ON *fjall*) 'fell': the word was taken into Gaelic as *mheall*, and back-formed into a nominative *meall*, although the Gaelic then came to mean a relatively smaller and rounder hill. Cf Welsh *foel/moel*.

118

F

fenaig 'ridged'.

Fenwick [Strathclyde] 'Fen (*fen*, OE) farmstead (*wic*, OE)': the village has given its name to the river that runs through it – the Fenwick Water.

feòir genitive of *feur*, thus 'of grass'.

Feolin [Jura] Probably 'Beach (*faoilinn*)': the village is the Jura station for the ferry across the Sound of Islay.

ferin elided form of *fearnan*: 'land'.

Feriniquarrie [Skye] Possibly 'People of the Faeroe Islands (*faereyingr*, ON)'. Alternatively perhaps 'Land (*fearnan*) of the (*a'*) corrie (*coire*)'.

fern sometimes an elided form of *fearn*: 'alder tree'.

Fernilea [Skye] Probably 'Ferny (*fearna*, OE) meadow (*leah*, OE)'.

Fetterangus [Grampian] Presumably 'Terraced slope (*faithir*) [of] Angus (personal name)': the personal name means 'unique choice'; the original Angus was one of the sons of Erc, the original invaders from Ireland.

Fettercairn [Grampian] 'Terraced slope (*faithir*) [with a] thicket (*cardden*, Brythonic Gaelic)': presumably the first element was added after the second had become merely a name.

Feugh [Tayside] This river name may derive from the Brythonic *fothach*: 'lake'.

feur 'grass': this is evidently cognate with the Indo-European root **ver-* 'to grow'.

feusag 'beard'.

fh- Note that at the beginning of an element this combination is not pronounced, and that consequently anglicised forms of names beginning in this fashion may seem to be entirely different names.

fhada mutated form of *fada*: 'long': on some old maps this element has been anglicised to 'Attow'.

fheadan mutated form of *feadan* 'streamlet', 'narrow glen in which a streamlet flows'.

fhear mutated form of *fear*: 'man'.

fhèidh mutated form of the genitive of *fiadh*, thus 'of deer'.

fheòir mutated form of the genitive of *feur*, thus 'of grass'.

fhionn mutated form of *fionn*: 'white'.

fhir mutated form of the genitive of *fear*, thus 'of a man'.

Fhodla mutated form of *Fodla*, an old kenning for 'Ireland'.

fhraoich mutated form of the genitive of *fraoch*, thus 'of heather'.

fhuaran mutated form of *fuaran*: 'watery spot', thus 'spring', 'well'.

fhuathais mutated form of *fuathais*: 'ghost'.

fiacail 'tooth': this is a corruption of ON *(f)jökull*, 'spike', 'peak'.

fiacleach 'toothed', 'serrated', 'jagged'.

fiadh 'deer'.

Fife [Fife] Possibly 'Path *(fiamh)*'.

Fill Geo [Shetland] Possibly 'Foul[-smelling] *(full*, ON) ravine *(gjá* , ON)': with the proposed vowel-change in the first element, cf English 'fil-th'.

fin elided form of *fionn*: 'white', 'fair', thus 'fair-haired'.

Finalty Hill [Tayside] Possibly 'White *(fionn)* stream *(allt)* hill (Eng)', although there may be a third Gaelic element *tigh* 'house', and 'hill' may be an adaptation of *mheall* 'fell' – the 'hill' is 2,594 feet (791 m) high!

Fincharn [Strathclyde] Presumably 'White *(fionn)* cairn *(charn)*'.

Findhorn [Grampian] 'White *(fionn)* water *(eren*, ancient pre-Celtic river name)': the village derives its name from the river on whose mouth it stands. The attribution of whiteness to the second element may be in deliberate contrast to the attribution of blackness in *Deveron* (q.v.), the river that has an estuary some 36 miles eastwards.

Fingal's Cave [Staffa] '[The] Fair[-haired] *(fionn)* stranger's *(gael)* cave (Eng)': such white-haired strangers were the blond Vikings, the real Norsemen, as opposed to the darker-haired Danes, who were the *dubh-gael*, or Dougal.

Finglas [Central] 'White *(fionn)* stream *(glas*, Brythonic Gaelic)': the river name contrasts with the 'black stream', or Douglas.

Finnieston [Strathclyde] The Revd John Finnie was guardian of the landowner of the district here in 1768.

Finsbay [Harris] Possibly 'Finn's (personal name, OE) bay (Eng)'. Both elements may in fact be assimilated from ON (meaning the same).

120

Finstown [Orkney] The village is said to be named after one David Phin, an Irish ex-soldier who built an inn here in the early 1800s.

Fintry [Central; Grampian] Apparently '[The] White (*fionn*) house (*tref*, Brythonic Gaelic)', although the Brythonic element is surprising.

Finzean [Tayside] Possibly 'White (*fionn*) head (*ceann*)': the tiny village stands on a bit of a ridge.

fiodhag 'bird-cherry [a low-growing wild fruit tree]'.

fionn 'white', 'fair', thus 'fair-haired': there is another cognate form in Gaelic, *bàn*; the Welsh equivalent is *gwyn*; but cf also the OE *hwit*, from which Eng *white*, possibly akin to both *wheat* and *wood*.

Fionn Bheinn [Highland] '[The] White (*fionn*) mountain (*bheinn*)'.

Fionn Loch Mór [Highland] 'White (*fionn*) loch, big (*mór*)': this to contrast with *Gorm Loch Mór* ('blue loch, big') ½ mile north-west.

Fionnphort [Mull] '[The] White (*fionn*) harbour (*port*)'.

fireach 'hilly country', 'undulating terrain'.

firth 'estuary': adaptation in Gaelic or ME from ON *fjordr*.

Firth [Shetland] 'Fjord (adaptation of ON *fjordr*)': ironically, because the name was applied to the settlement to one side of the 'fjord', the bay has since been named Firth's Voe (where *voe* is an adapted form of ON *vágr*, 'bay').

Firth of Forth [Fife/Lothian/Central] The estuary of what is now the River Forth was probably first described as 'Fjord (ON)'; once the river name had been back-formed, however, the estuary was then described in Middle English as a *frith* or *firth*, ironically exactly the same word.

fisher exactly that: 'one who fishes', through OE or ME.

Fiskavaig [Skye] 'Fish (*fiskar*, ON) bay (*vágr*, ON)'.

fitheach 'raven'.

Fiunary [Highland] 'White (*fionn*) shieling (*àiridh*)'.

Fladda [Inner Hebrides] Probably 'Flat (*flatr*, ON) island (*ey*, ON)'.

Fladdabister [Shetland] Probably 'Flat (*flatr*, ON) settlement-steading (*bol-stathr*, ON)', although the first element might be a corruption of an ON nickname.

Flashader [Skye] Possibly 'Flat's (personal nickname, ON) house (*setr*, ON)'.

121

fliuch 'wet'.

Flodabay [Harris] Probably 'Torrent (*floth*, ON) bay (*vágr*, ON)': the village lies where a strong mountain stream enters the Little Minch, in a bay now ironically known as Loch Flodabay.

Flodday [Barra (2)] Possibly 'Torrent (*floth*, ON) island (*ey*, ON)', referring presumably to the strong currents around each island: the first element is unlikely to be 'fleet' although it could instead be 'float'.

Flodigarry [Skye] 'Float (*floti*, ON) enclosure (*garthr*, ON)': this suggests some form of fish farming using nets held in position by floats – but the first element can also mean 'fleet', 'raft of ships', and most commentators go for 'fleet enclosure' without bothering to mention which fleet, when or how.

Flotta [Shetland; Orkney] Probably 'Fleet (*flota*, ON) island (*ey*, ON)': both of the islands are roughly semicircular and might shelter a fleet.

flugga (ON) 'cliffs', 'precipices'.

fo 'subject to', 'secondary', 'under', 'lesser'.

Fochabers [Grampian] Apparently a hybrid name: 'Lake (*fothach*, Brythonic Gaelic), marsh (*abor*)': presumably the first element was originally the whole name and the second was added when the meaning had been forgotten (and the terrain had changed).

Fodderty [Highland] Presumably 'Terraced slope (*fothair*) house (*tigh*)', although the final element may alternatively represent a dative/locative case-ending only.

Fodla 'Ireland': an old kenning for the name of the whole island.

Fogla Skerry [Shetland] 'Birds' (*fugla*, ON) skerry (*sker*, ON)'.

Foinaven [Highland] Possibly 'Peat (*mhòine*) mountain (*bheinn*)'.

for- sometimes an elided form of *fothair*: 'terraced slope', 'shelving declivity'.

Ford [Strathclyde] Presumably 'Ford (ME)': the village lies where the road along Loch Awe (the name of which may mean 'Ford' in Gaelic) crosses the river at the loch's southern end.

Fore Holm [Shetland] Probably 'Front (*fora*, ON) island (*holmr*, ON)': the island lies in front of a long peninsula.

Forfar [Tayside] 'Terraced slope (*fothair*) [for] spying (*faire*)'.

Forres [Grampian] 'Lesser (*fo*) shrubland (*ras*)'.

122

Forse [Highland] 'Waterfall (*fors*, ON)'.

Forsinain [Highland] Possibly 'Waterfall (*fors*, ON) on the (*an*) river (*abhainn*)': if so, the river is now ironically called the Forsinain Burn. But the area may in fact have come to be called 'Fors' and this and the place name below then simply qualify different geographical features around it: 'Fors's river' and 'Fors's height'.

Forsinard [Highland] 'Waterfall (*fors*, ON) on the (*an*) height (*ard*)': the latter elements were evidently added when the first element had become just a name.

Fort Augustus [Highland] Town renamed after the 1715 Rebellion in commemoration of William Augustus, Duke of Cumberland – 'Butcher Cumberland' as his nickname in Scotland proclaimed him, but the 'Conqu'ring hero' that Mr Handel would have had the citizens of London hail. The town stands on the fortified road built by General George Wade between Fort William and Inverness: its original name was Kilcummin.

Fort George [Highland] Garrison community set up in quarters designed by Robert Adam in the time of George II, after whom it was named.

Forth [Fife/Lothian/Central] The river name probably derives from the description of its estuary: 'Fjord (adapted form of ON *fjordr*)'. See also **Firth of Forth**.

Forth [Strathclyde] Probably 'Ford (OE)': the area has several OE names.

Fortingall [Tayside] Hybrid name: 'Encampment (*gwerth*, Brythonic Gaelic) of the (*an*) churchyard (*ceall*)'.

Fortrose [Highland] Apparently 'Beneath (*foter*) the headland (*ros*)': the headland itself is Rosemarkie (q.v.) and the village above it has the same name; but the lesser community beneath the headland has now become far greater in size and importance.

Fort William [Highland] The original fort was established in 1655 by General Monk but required to be rebuilt a generation later for William of Orange, after whom it was then named.

Foss [Tayside] 'Flat spot (*fas*)'.

Foula [Shetland] 'Bird (*fugl*, ON) island (*ey*, ON)'.

-four elided form of 1) *phùir*, genitive of *phòr*, thus 'of pasture';
2) *feòir*, genitive of *feur*, thus 'of grass'.

123

Foveran [Grampian] Probably 'Spring (*fobharan*, proto-Gaelic)': the village is on a stream now called the Foveran Burn. The modern Gaelic for this element is *fuaran*.

Fowlis [Tayside] 'Lesser (*fo*) stream (*glais*)'.

Foyers [Highland] 'Terraced slope (*fothair*)'.

fraoch 'heather', 'heathland'.

Fraserburgh [Grampian] Town renamed in 1592 to honour the new landowner and developer, Sir Alexander Fraser: its original name was Faithlie.

Freester [Shetland] Possibly 'Fræthi's (personal name, ODan) steading (*stathr*, ON)'. The personal name is well attested in place names in Yorkshire.

Fresgoe [Highland] Possibly 'Fræthi's (personal name, ODan) chine (*gjá* ON)'.

Freuchie [Fife] 'Heathery (*fraochach*)'.

-fries adapted form of *phris*, genitive of *phreas*, thus 'of the copse'.

Friockheim [Tayside] The name was, before 1830, just Friock, said to derive from the surname of a baillie in Forfar (whose name, Freke, may in turn therefore have derived from *fraoch*, 'heather' – if there ever was such a baillie). In 1830 one John Andson, on returning from years spent in Germany, decided as the major tenant of the area to add the German for 'home' on at the end, thus ending up with a place name that belongs more to the Nibelungenlied than to Scottish nomenclature.

frith 'deer-forest': this is simply a loan-word from OE.

fuar 'cold': this is probably cognate with the (Latin-based) English words that begin *fr-*, such as 'frigid' and 'freeze'.

fuaran 'watery spot', therefore 'spring', 'well'.

Fuar Larach [Strathclyde] '[The] Cold (*fuar*) site of ruins (*làrach*)'.

fuathais 'ghost'.

Fugla Ness [Shetland (2)] 'Birds' (*fugla*, ON) ness (*nes*, ON)'.

Fugla Stack [Shetland] 'Birds' (*fugla*, ON) stack [sharp rock] (*stakkr*, ON)'.

124

Furnace [Strathclyde] The village was the site of a well-known iron-smelting plant from the 17th century until around 1813.

fyne probably 'marshy', from the ON equivalent of OE *fynig*: 'marshy', 'mouldy'.

Fyvie [Grampian] 'Path (*fiamh*)'.

G

-gaard elided form of ON *garthr*: 'enclosure'.

gabhar (also *gobhar*; Welsh *gafr*) 'goat': the word is evidently cognate with Latin *capri-* and English *heifer*.

gaibhre (also *goibhre*) genitive of *gabhar* (*gobhar*), thus 'of a goat'.

gaimhne genitive of *gamhainn*, thus 'of a young cow', 'of a stirk'.

gaineamh 'sand'.

gaineamha(i)ch 'sandy'.

gainimh genitive of *gaineamh*, thus 'of sand'.

gair-   either 1)   elided form of *gearr*: 'short';
       or 2)   adapted form of Brythonic Gaelic *caer*: 'fort', 'castle', 'stronghold'.

gairbhe (also *ghairbh*) mutated form of the genitive of *garbh*, thus 'of rough (water)'.

Gairloch [Highland] 'Short (*gearr*) loch': the village is named after the sea-loch on which it stands.

Gairlochy [Highland] The village lies at the end of Loch Lochy, a loch with an unusually ancient name: 'Black (*loch,* proto-Gaelic) goddess (*dheva,* proto-Gaelic). So for the first element in the village name, the Brythonic element *caer*, 'fort' seems likely.

Galashiels [Borders] 'Gala [Water]'s huts (*skali-s,* ON)'. It has been suggested that the huts were the homes of fishermen on the Gala Water.

gall 'Gael', 'stranger', 'foreigner': it was because they called other folk this that the Gaels themselves became known as such – indeed, the whole country of Wales (Pays de Galles) became known as such.

Galloway [Dumfries & Galloway] 'Stranger (*gall*) Gaels (*Ghaidhil*)' – that is, the Gaels of this area seemed 'foreign' to Irish Gaels.

Galmisdale [Eigg] Either 'Galmi's (personal name, ON) dale (*dalr,* ON) or, possibly, 'Gavelman's (OE) dale (OE)'. A *gavelman* was a co-inheritor of property for which rent was payable.

gamhainn 'young cow', 'stirk'.

126

gamhna variant genitive form of *gamhainn*, thus 'of the young cow', 'of the stirk'.

gaoith(e) genitive form of *gaoth*, thus 'of the wind', 'of the marsh'.

gaoth 'wind'; also 'bog', 'marsh'.

gar- elided form of 1) *garradh*: 'enclosure', 'garden', 'wall';
              2) ON *garthr*: 'enclosure', 'place of containment';
              3) Brythonic Gaelic *garth*: 'garden', 'enclosure';
    or 4) OE *geard*: 'yard', 'hedge', 'fence';

garaidh 'den', 'shelter', 'lair', 'hide-out'.

Garbat [Highland] Possibly 'Rough [water] (*garbh*) stream (*allt*)': the tiny village is on the Black Water.

garbh 'rough' in the context of water.

Garbhallt [Strathclyde] 'Rough [water] (*garbh*) stream (*allt*)'.

Garbh Bheinn [Highland] '[The] Rough [water] (*garbh*) mountain (*bheinn*)'.

Garbh-bheinn [Skye] '[The] Rough [water] (*garbh*) mountain (*bheinn*)'.

Garbh Eileach [Inner Hebrides] 'Rough [water] (*garbh*) fishing-gap (*eileach*)'.

Garbh Eilean [Inner Hebrides] 'Rough [water] (*garbh*) island (*eilean*)'.

Garbh Shlios [Highland] 'Rough [water] (*garbh*) bank (*slios*)'.

Gardenstown [Grampian] Village set up in 1720 by one Alexander Garden of Troup.

Garelochhead [Strathclyde] 'Gare Loch['s] head (Eng)': the name of the loch means 'Short loch'.

Gargunnock [Central] Probably 'Enclosure (*garradh*) of the rounded hill (*cnuic*)', although one commentator suggests alternatively 'Enclosure (*garradh*) of the little mound (*dùin-ock*)'.

Garliestown [Dumfries & Galloway] Village set up in around 1760 by the then Lord Garlies, later to become Earl of Galloway.

Garlogie [Grampian] Probably 'Enclosure (*garradh*) hollow (*lagaidh*)'.

Garrabost [Lewis] Possibly 'Enclosure (*garthr*, ON) settlement-steading (*bol-stathr*)'.

garradh 'enclosure', 'garden', 'wall': the word has many cognates, not least in Brythonic Gaelic, ON and OE, some of which are also found in place names in Scotland. The ultimately basic meaning is probably 'somewhere to allow things to grow'.

Garrisdale Point [Inner Hebrides] Possibly 'Giartharr's (personal name, ON) dale (ON) point (Eng)'. The personal name is the Scandinavian equivalent of OE Gurth.

Garrow [Tayside] Probably 'Rough [water] (*garbh*)': the tiny village is on the River Quaich.

garry elided form of 1) *garradh*: 'enclosure', 'garden', 'wall'
                     2) ON *garthr*: 'enclosure', 'place of containment';
        or 3) Brythonic Gaelic *garw*: 'rough (water)' [the word is cognate with Gaelic *garbh*].

Garrygualach [Highland] Probably '[Loch] Garry fork (*gobhlach*)': at this point the loch changes direction and a river flows into it – the whole scene looking like a fork in the loch. The loch name means 'rough (water)'.

Garrynamoine [Uist] Probably 'Enclosure (*garradh*) of (*na*) peat (*mòine*)'.

Garscadden [Strathclyde] 'Enclosure (*garradh*) for herring (*sgadain*)'.

Garscube [Strathclyde] Apparently 'Garden (*garradh*) of the sheaf (from a Gaelic source)'.

gart- (also *gort*) elided form of *garradh*: 'enclosure', 'garden', 'wall'.

Gartcosh [Strathclyde] Apparently 'Garden (*garradh*) of the foot (*cois*)': possibly an area for walking round.

Gartcraig [Strathclyde] 'Enclosure (*garradh*) of the crag (*creige*)'.

Garth Head [Orkney] 'Enclosure (*garthr*, ON) head[land] (Eng)'.

Gartloch [Strathclyde] 'Enclosure (*garradh*) loch'.

Gartmore [Strathclyde] 'Enclosure (*garradh*), big (*mór*)'.

Gartnavel [Strathclyde] 'Garden (*garradh*) of (*na*) apples (*avail*)'.

Gartocharn [Strathclyde] 'Enclosure (*garradh*) of the cairn (*chairn*)'.

Gartsherrie [Strathclyde] 'Enclosure (*garradh*) of the young horses (*searraich*)'.

Gartymore [Highland] Possibly 'Enclosure (*garradh*) of the house (*tighe*), big (*móire*)".

garv adapted form of *garbh*: 'rough (water)'.

Garvald [Lothian] 'Rough [water] (*garbh*) stream (*allt*)'.

Garvard [Colonsay] Presumably 'Rough [water] (*garbh*) height (*ard*)'.

Garve [Highland] 'Rough [water] (*garbh*)': the village is on the scenic Black Water.

gasg 'tongue of land'.

-gask anglicised version of *gasg*: 'tongue of land'.

Gasstown [Dumfries & Galloway] Village set up in around 1810 by a local landowner, Joseph Gass.

Gatehouse of Fleet [Dumfries & Galloway] 'Roadhouse (*geata-hus*, OE) on the [Water of] Fleet': the river name means 'stream'. Before 1790, when the village was founded, there was just one lonely house at the side of the road.

-gath elided form of *gaoth*: 'bog', 'marsh'.

Gavinton [Borders] Village begun as an area of resettlement by the landowner, David Gavin, in around 1760, when he wished to develop an adjacent site already occupied.

gead 'narrow strip of land'.

gèadh 'goose'; cognate with English *goose* and *gander*.

geal 'white', but particularly 'shining white'.

Geal Charn [Highland (2)] '[The] White (*geal*) cairn (*charn*)': some cairn – it is 3,443 feet (1,049 m) high.

gearr either 1) 'short';
         or 2) 'a hare'.

gearraidh 'strip of land between two forms of terrain'; particularly in Lewis: 'outer pastures'; the word is an adaptation of ON *gerthi*.

gearrsaich 'hare'.

geata 'gate', but also 'road': a loan-word from Scandinavian through English; in the lowlands the word became *yett*.

Gelder [Grampian] 'White (*geal*) water (*dobhar*)'.

geò (also *geodha*) 'chine', 'ravine', 'chasm', 'rift'. The word is an adaptation of ON *gjà*.

Geodha Daraich [Skye] 'Ravine (*geodha*) of the oak trees (*daraich*)'.

129

Geodha Mór [Highland] 'Ravine (*geodha*), big (*mór*)'.

Geodha nan Each [Skye] 'Ravine (*geodha*) of the (*na-n*) horse (*each*)'.

Geodha Ruadh [Highland] 'Ravine (*geodha*), red-brown (*ruadh*)'.

Geo Dubh [Harris] 'Ravine (*geò*), dark (*dubh*)'.

geòidh genitive form of *gèadh*, thus 'of the goose'.

ghabhair (also *ghobhair*) mutated form of the genitive of *gabhar* (*gobhar*), thus 'of a goat'.

ghaill (also *ghoill*) mutated form of the genitive of *gall*, thus 'of a stranger', 'of a foreigner'.

ghaimhne mutated form of the genitive of *gamhainn*, thus 'of a young cow', 'of a stirk'.

ghairbh masculine genitive of *garbh*, thus 'of rough (water)'.

ghamhna mutated form of the genitive of *gamhainn*, thus 'of a young cow', 'of a stirk'.

gharbh feminine form of *garbh*: 'rough (water)'.

gharraidh mutated form of the genitive of *garradh*: 'enclosure', 'garden', 'wall'.

gheal feminine form of *geal*: 'white', but particularly 'shining white'.

gheòidh mutated form of the genitive of *gèadh*, thus 'of the goose'.

ghil   either 1)   (also *ghile*) mutated form of the genitive of *geal*, thus 'of the white . . . ';
          or 2)   mutated form of *gil*: 'watercourse', 'burn', 'dry stream-bed'.

ghille mutated form of *gille* (q.v.): originally 'boy', 'lad', and then 'servant', 'devotee'.

ghiubhas (also *ghiuthas*) mutated form of *giubhas (giuthas)*: 'fir tree'.

ghiubhsaich (also *ghiuthsaich*) mutated form of the genitive plural of *giubhas* (*giuthas*), thus 'of fir trees'.

ghiuthas See *ghiubhas* above.

ghiuthsaich See *ghiubhsaich* above.

130

ghlais either 1) (also *glaise*) mutated form of the genitive of glas, thus 'of the blue-green . . . ';
  or 2) mutated form of *glais*: 'stream'.

ghlas either 1) feminine form of *glas*: 'blue-green';
  or 2) mutated form of the Brythonic Gaelic *glas*: 'stream'.

Ghlas-bheinn [Highland] 'Blue-green (*ghlas*) mountain (*bheinn*)'.

ghlo mutated form of *glo*: 'mist'.

ghobhair (also *ghabhair*) mutated form of the genitive of gabhar (*gobhar*), thus 'of a goat'.

ghobhlaich mutated form of the genitive of *gobhlach*, thus 'of the forked...'.

ghoill (also *ghaill*) mutated form of the genitive of *gall*, thus 'of a stranger', 'of a foreigner'.

ghorm feminine form of *gorm*: 'blue', 'grey-blue'.

ghru 'gloomy'.

ghuib mutated form of the genitive of *gob*, thus 'of the beak', and thus also 'of the point...'.

Giffnock [Strathclyde] 'Little ridge (*cefn-ock*, Brythonic Gaelic: the second element is a diminutive suffix)'.

Gifford [Lothian] Village founded in the late 1700s and named after the local land owners, the Gifford family.

gil either 1) (also *gill*) 'watercourse', 'burn', 'dry stream-bed'. The word is ON.
  or 2) elided form of *gille*: 'servant', 'devotee'.

Gilchriston [Lothian] 'Gilchrist['s] (personal name) farmstead (*tun*, OE)': the name Gilchrist means 'servant of Christ'.

gile (also *ghil*) genitive of *geal*, thus 'of the white . . . '.

gill (also *gil*) 'watercourse', 'burn', 'dry stream-bed'. The word is ON.

Gillabol [Highland] 'Stream (*gil*, ON) settlement (*bol*, ON)'.

Gillaval [Harris] 'Stream (*gil*, ON) fell (*fjall*, ON)'.

Gill Burn [Highland] Apparently a hybrid name: the two elements both mean 'stream', the first in ON, the second from OE.

131

gille originally 'boy', 'lad', and thus (like 'knave', and indeed like 'boy' in the US at times) 'servant', 'devotee'; this word was later anglicised with a special meaning to become *gillie* or *ghillie*.

gillean 'boys', 'young men' (see *gille*).

Gills [Highland] Probably 'Stream-beds (*gill-s*, ON)': the village lies on Gills Bay, into which many streamlets flow.

Gilmanscleuch [Borders] Probably 'Gillemon's (personal name, OE) ravine (*cloh*, OE)'. The name Gillemon is unusual but is attested in English place names; even then, the name is thought to derive from an ON adaptation of the Gaelic *gille*, 'servant', plus the word 'man'.

Gilmerton [Lothian; Tayside] 'Devotee (*gille*) of [the Virgin] Mary['s] (*Moire*) farmstead (*tun*, OE)'.

gilp (Irish *gilb*) 'chisel'.

Girvan [Strathclyde] According to one commentator, a terrible corruption of 'Rough [water] (*garbh*) stream (*allt*)'. Another commentator plumps instead for proto-Gaelic 'Thicket (*garan*), white (*vind*)'.

giubhas (also *giuthas*) 'fir tree'.

gùiran 'cow parsley', but also 'barnacle goose'.

giuthas (also *giubhas*) 'fir tree'.

glac 'hollow': the word may well be cognate with *lag*, q.v.

glais 'stream', although this probably represents a loan-word adaptation of Brythonic gaelic *glas* (see below).

Glais Bheinn [Highland] '[The] Stream (*glais*) mountain (*bheinn*)': at least eight major mountain streams flow down from this 1,570 feet (479 m) height.

Glamis [Tayside] 'Cleft (*glamhus*)': yet although the village stands to one side of the vast Strathmore, there is no ravine-like chasm anywhere near. The name is presumably cognate with OE *cleofan*, 'cleave', Greek *glyphein*, 'to carve'.

glas   either 1)   'blue-green';
          or 2)   Brythonic Gaelic for 'stream', cognate with Gaelic *glais*, q.v.

Glas Bheinn [Highland (2)] '[The] Blue-green (*glas*) mountain (*'bheinne*)': on some maps this name is spelled *Glasven*. Another mountain, *Ghlas-bheinn*, lies some 22 miles north of the more northerly of these two but is less than half that one's height.

Glas Bheinn Mhór [Skye] '[The] Blue-green (*glas*) mountain (*bheinn*), big (*mhór*)'.

Glas-charn [Highland] '[The] Blue-green (*glas*) cairn (*charn*)': the 'cairn' is a mountain 2,076 feet (633 m) high.

Glasdrum [Strathclyde] Presumably 'Blue-green (*glas*) ridge (*druim*)'.

Glas Eilean [Highland (3)] 'Blue-green (*glas*) island (*eilean*)'.

Glas-eileanan [Western Isles] 'Blue-green (*glas*) islands (plural of *eilean*)'.

Glasgow [Strathclyde] 'Blue-green (*glas*) hollows (*cau*)'. Not many blue-green hollows in the area now, eh? Some commentators profess to find a 'familiarative-diminutive' sense in the final element (i.e. 'dear little hollows').

Glas-loch Mór [Highland] 'Blue-green (*glas*) loch, big (*mór*)'.

Glas Maol [Tayside/Grampian] '[The] Blue-green (*glas*) bare top (*maol*)': bare top or not, Glas Maol reaches 3,504 feet (1,068 m).

Glas Meall Mór [Tayside] '[The] Blue-green (*glas*) fell (*meall*), big (*mór*)'.

Glasnakille [Skye] Probably 'Stream (*glais*) of the (*na*) [monk's] cells (*cille*)': it is possible that this name derives actually from the Brythonic equivalents – there is an ancient fortification near by.

Glass [Highland] 'Stream (from the ancient Brythonic *glas*)'; the river is inevitably now called the River Glass.

Glas Tulaichean [Tayside] '[The] Blue-green (*glas*) humps (*tulaichean*)': the humps together form a mountain of 3,449 feet 91,051 m) in height.

Glasven [Highland] '[The] Blue-green (*glas*) mountain (*bheinn*)'. On some maps the name appears as either Glas Bheinn or Ghlas-bheinn (and in any case there are two mountains with the name).

gleann 'glen'; the modern Welsh is *glyn*.

Gleann a' Choilich [Highland] 'Glen (*gleann*) of [the Abhainn] a' Choilich': the river name probably means 'of the cock'.

Gleann Airigh [Strathclyde] 'Glen (*gleann*) [of the] shieling (*àirigh*)'.

Gleann an Dubh Lochain [Highland] 'Glen (*gleann*) of the dark (*dubh*) little loch (diminutive of loch)'.

Gleann Beag [Highland] 'Glen (*gleann*), small (*beag*)'.

133

Gleann Bhruthadail [Lewis] Possibly 'Glen (*gleann*) of brae (*bhruthach*) dale (*dail*)', but this might be itself an assimilation of ON *breithr-dalr* 'broad-dale'.

Gleann Camgharaidh [Highland] 'Glen (*gleann*) of the crooked (*cam*) hide-out (*gharaidh*)': the river name associated with the glen is likely to be back-formed.

Gleann Còsaidh [Highland] Probably 'Glen (*gleann*) with recesses (*chòsaidh*)': the river name associated with the glen is like to be back-formed.

Gleann Dà-Eig [Tayside] Possibly 'Glen (*gleann*) [with] two (*dà*) notches (*eig*)'.

Gleann Dà-Ghob [Tayside] 'Glen (*gleann*) [with] two (*dà*) mouths (*ghob*)'.

Gleann Dubh [Highland (2)] 'Glen (*gleann*), dark (*dubh*)': the more northerly glen of the two skirts Glendhu Forest and ends at Loch Glendhu . . . ; the more southerly contrasts with the associated **Gleann Geal**.

Gleann Fearnach [Tayside] 'Glen (*gleann*) of the alder tree (*fearn*) field (*ach*)'.

Gleann Fhiodhaig [Highland] 'Glen (*gleann*) of bird-cherries (*fhiodhaig*)'. The bird-cherry is a wild fruit shrub.

Gleann Geal [Highland] 'Glen (*gleann*), white (*geal*)': this contrasts with **Gleann Dubh**, which forks off northwards.

Gleann Màma [Highland] 'Glen (*gleann*) of the mountain gap (*màma*)': the glen runs through what is almost a gorge.

Gleann Meadhonach [Skye] 'Glen (*gleann*) in the middle (*meadhonach*)'.

Gleann Mór [Highland; Tayside] 'Glen (*gleann*), big (*mór*)'.

Gleann Mór Barvas [Lewis] 'Glen (*gleann*), big (*mór*), [that leads to the village of] Barvas': the village name probably means 'burial mounds (*barpa-s*)'.

Gleann nam Fiadh [Highland] 'Glen (*gleann*) of the (*na-m*) deer (*fiadh*)'.

Gleann Sithidh [Highland] 'Glen (*gleann*) of [the Abhainn] Sithidh': the river name probably means 'of the fairy-hill'.

Glen Affric [Highland] 'Glen (*gleann*) of [the River] Affric': the river-name most probably means 'the ford of the boar'.

134

Glenalmond [Tayside] 'Glen (*gleann*) of the river (*amhainn*)', only of course the name of the river is now by back-formation the Almond.

Glenancross [Highland] Presumably 'Glen (*gleann*) of the (*an*) cross (*crois*)'.

Glen Aray [Strathclyde] 'Glen (*gleann*) of [the River] Aray': the river name is ancient and found all over Europe in cognate forms (e.g. Ara, Ahre, etc.)

Glen Arnisdale [Highland] 'Glen (*gleann*) [that leads to the village of] Arnisdale': the village name is ON.

Glen Artney [Tayside] 'Glen (*gleann*) of Arthur (personal name, diminutive)': the personal name accounts for why the name of the river running through the glen is unrelated; it is the Water of Ruchill.

Glen Avon [Grampian] 'Glen (*gleann*) of [the River] Avon'; the name of the river of course means 'river' and has thus been back-formed.

Glenbarr [Strathclyde] 'Glen (*gleann*) of Barr [Water]'; indeed the valley following Barr Water to the village is perversely called Barr Glen. The river name means 'summit'.

Glenbeg [Highland] 'Glen (*gleann*), small (*beag*)'.

Glen Bernisdale [Skye] Presumably 'Glen (*gleann*), Björn's (personal name, ON) dale (*dalr*, ON)': the initial element was evidently added afterwards.

Glenbervie [Grampian] 'Glen (*gleann*) of [the] Bervie [Water]': the river name may, if it is Brythonic, mean 'boiling', 'seething'.

Glenborrodale [Highland] 'Glen (*gleann*), fort (*borg*, ON) dale (*dalr*, ON)': the initial element was evidently added afterwards; the local pronunciation is, amazingly, 'Glenba-roddle'.

Glenbranter [Strathclyde] 'Glen (*gleann*) of the poor (*brann*) land (*tìr*)'.

Glenbreck [Borders] Presumably 'Glen (*gleann*), speckled (*breac*)': although the village is on the River Tweed, it is unlikely that the second element refers to trout (as it can also mean) because it is so far inland.

Glen Cannich [Highland] 'Glen (*gleann*) of [the River] Cannich': the river name may be Brythonic and mean 'white water'.

Glencaple [Dumfries & Galloway] Presumably 'Glen (*gleann*) of the horses (*capuill*)'.

Glen Carron [Highland] 'Glen (*gleann*) of [the River] Carron': the river name may mean 'of the cairn'.

135

Glencarse [Tayside] Presumably 'Glen (*gleann*) of the Carse [of Gowrie]'; the Carse (from a word that means 'fertile lowland area') is a large area of coastal flatland between Dundee and Perth, bordered inland by the Braes of the Carse.

Glencassley [Highland] Presumably '[The] Glen (*gleann*) with a stone fort (*caiseal*, adapted from Latin)', in which case both the glen and the largish river running through it were named after the fort (which is not the modern Glencassley Castle).

Glen Clachaig [Mull] 'Glen (*gleann*), stony (*clachaig*)', although it is possible that the glen was actually named after the stream that runs through it.

Glencoe [Highland] Probably 'Glen (*gleann*), narrow (*comhann*)', or so most commentators opine.

Glen Coul [Highland] Possibly 'Glen (*gleann*), back (*cùl*)'.

Glencraig [Fife] 'Glen (*gleann*) of the crag (*creige*)'.

Glen Croe [Strathclyde] Possibly 'Glen (*gleann*) of the sheep-pen (*cròtha*)'.

Glen Damff [Tayside] 'Glen (*gleann*) of the stag (*daimh*)'.

Glendaruel [Strathclyde] Probably 'Glen (*gleann*) of the (*na*) [River] Ruel': the river name is thought to mean 'of blood', in reference to a local battle between Norsemen and Celts in the year 1160.

Glendavan [Grampian] Possibly 'Glen (*gleann*) of the little stag (diminutive of *damh*)'.

Glendevon [Tayside] 'Glen (*gleann*) of [the River] Devon': the village lies at one end of the glen. The river name is from an ancient double root meaning 'black river' (and is identical with the name of the river in Leicestershire and Northamptonshire).

Glendhu [Highland] 'Glen (*gleann*), dark (*dubh*)': the actual glen through Glendhu Forest and leading to Loch Glendhu is spelled *Gleann Dubh*.

Glen Diebidale [Highland] Possibly 'Glen (*gleann*) [of] deep (*djupr*, ON) dale (*dalr*,ON)': the river and the local Forest are named after the dale.

Glen Dochart [Central] Possibly 'Glen (*gleann*) of the forbidding top', the second (double) element coming from the ancient Gaelic roots that went also to make the surname Docherty.

136

Glen Docherty [Highland] Possibly 'Glen (*gleann*) of the forbidding top', the second (double) element coming from the ancient Gaelic roots that went also to make the surname Docherty.

Glendoe [Highland] 'Glen (*gleann*) of [Allt] Doe': Allt Doe is the name of a short but steep stream leading into Loch Ness; the stream name probably means 'dark'.

Glen Douglas [Strathclyde] 'Glen (*gleann*) of [the] Douglas': the river name is ancient Gaelic and means 'dark stream'.

Gleneagles [Tayside] 'Glen (*gleann*) of the church (*eaglais*)'.

Glen Elchaig [Highland] 'Glen (*gleann*) of [the River] Elchaig': the river name may mean 'rocky'.

Glenelg [Highland] 'Glen (*gleann*) of [Greater] Ireland (*elg*)'; the village was a centre for early migrations from Ireland.

Glen Esk [Grampian/Tayside] 'Glen (*gleann*) of [the River] Esk': the river name is an ancient one, related to river-names in England such as the Exe and Axe, and in Wales the Usk: it means simply 'water'. Cf *uisge*.

Glen Fenzie [Grampian] Possibly 'Glen (*gleann*) of the sheep-folds (*fainge*)'.

Glenfiddich [Grampian] 'Glen (*gleann*) of Fidich (personal name)'; the river name associated with the glen is back-formed.

Glen Finglas [Central] 'Glen (*gleann*) of [the River] Finglas': the river name is ancient Gaelic and means 'white stream'.

Glen Finlet [Tayside] Possibly 'Glen (*gleann*) of the white (*fionn*) slope (*leathad*)'.

Glenfinnan [Highland] Apparently 'Glen (*gleann*) of Fingon (personal name)': Fingon is said to have been a 14th-century abbot of Iona; but cf **Kilfinnan**. His name probably means 'white-headed'.

Glen Fyne [Strathclyde, Argyll] Probably 'Glen (*gleann*) [that leads to Loch] Fyne': the loch name seems to derive from the ON for 'marshy'; the river in the glen also takes its name from the loch.

Glen Fyne [Strathclyde, Clydeside] Probably 'Glen (*gleann*) [that leads to Ard](fh)yne [Point]': the element *fyne* appears to be ON for 'marshy'; the Ardyne Burn runs through the glen.

Glen Garry [Highland; Tayside] 'Glen (*gleann*) of [the River] Garry'; the river name derives from the ancient root of modern *garbh*: 'rough [water]'.

137

Glen Goibhre [Highland] 'Glen (*gleann*) of [the Allt] Goibhre': the stream name means 'of the goat'.

Glen Golly [Highland] Possibly 'Glen (*gleann*), forked (*gobhlach*)': the description would not be inappropriate.

Glen Gour [Highland] 'Glen (*gleann*) of [the River] Gour': the river name may, if it is Brythonic, mean 'sinuous' or 'sloping', or if it is Scottish Gaelic then the element may be a personal name or mean 'goat'.

Glen Kin [Strathclyde] Presumably 'Glen (*gleann*) at the head (*cinn*)'.

Glen Kinglas [Strathclyde] 'Glen (*gleann*) at the head (*cinn*) of the stream (*glais*)'.

Glenlatterach [Grampian] Possibly 'Glen (*gleann*) on the slope (*leitreach*)': the reservoir of this name is on the side of Pikey Hill.

Glen Lean [Strathclyde] Probably 'Glen (*gleann*), broad (*leathann*)'.

Glenlivet [Highland] Apparently 'Glen (*gleann*) of the slippery smooth place (*liobhaite*)'; the name of the River Livet may thus have been back-formed.

Glen Loch [Tayside] 'Glen (*gleann*) of [Loch] Loch': the loch name is actually proto-Gaelic and means 'black'.

Glen Lochay [Central] Probably 'Glen (*gleann*) of [the River] Lochay', in which the river name may be proto-Gaelic and mean 'black goddess'.

Glen Lochy [Strathclyde] 'Glen (*gleann*) of [the River] Lochy': the river name is proto-Gaelic and means 'black goddess'.

Glen Logie [Tayside] 'Glen (*gleann*) of the hollow (*lagaidh*)'; the river name associated with the glen is likely to be back-formed.

Glen Lonan [Strathclyde] Presumably 'Glen (*gleann*) of the little marsh (diminutive of *lón*)'.

Glenlood Hill [Borders] Possibly 'Glen (*gleann*) of the hillside (*leothaid*)', with the final element added later when the original meaning had been forgotten.

Glen Loy [Highland] 'Glen (*gleann*) of the calf (*laoigh*)': the river name associated with the glen is likely to be back-formed.

Glen Lui [Grampian] Possibly 'Glen (*gleann*) of the calf (*laoigh*)': if this is the case, the river name associated with the glen is likely to be back-formed.

Glen Luss [Strathclyde] 'Glen (*gleann*) [that leads to the village of] Luss': the village name means 'herbs'.

Glen Lussa [Strathclyde] 'Glen (*gleann*) of herbs (*luss*)': the river name associated with this glen is back-formed.

Glen Lyon [Tayside] 'Glen (*gleann*) of [the River] Lyon': the river name may mean 'liable to flooding', from a Brythonic Gaelic source.

Glen Mark [Tayside] Presumably 'Glen (*gleann*) of the horse (*marc*)': the river name associated with the glen is likely to be back-formed.

Glen Markie [Highland] Presumably 'Glen (*gleann*) of the horse (*marc*)': the river name associated with the glen is likely to be back-formed.

Glenmore [Strathclyde; Skye] 'Glen (*gleann*), big (*mór*)'.

Glen More [Highland (3); Strathclyde] 'Glen (*gleann*), big (*mór*)': this is the Gaelic for the 'Great Glen', also known (at least in part) as the Caledonian Canal.

Glenmoy [Tayside] Presumably 'Glen (*gleann*) on the plain (*moigh*, dative/locative of *magh*)', but the terrain is not particularly appropriate.

Glenmuck [Borders] 'Glen (*gleann*) of the pigs (*muice*)'; the stream name associated with the glen is likely to be back-formed.

Glen Muick [Grampian] 'Glen (*gleann*) of the pigs (*muice*)'; the river name associated with the glen is likely to be back-formed.

Glenmuirshaw [Strathclyde] 'Glenmuir [Water]'s haugh [that is, strip of land within a bend of a river]': the area is indeed within a bend of the Glenmuir Water, the name of which means 'glen on the moor'.

Glenmoy [Tayside] Possibly 'Glen (*gleann*) on the plain (*moigh*, dative of *magh*)', but there is little flat terrain in the area.

Glen Nant [Strathclyde] 'Glen (*gleann*) of [the] Nant': the stream name is Brythonic and means simply 'stream'.

Glen Nevis [Highland] 'Glen (*gleann*) [beneath Ben] Nevis'. Most commentators reckon the mountain name to be back-formed from the Water of Nevis. This seems both illogical – the Water of Nevis is not particularly spectacular in comparison with the majesty of the highest mountain in Great Britain – and etymologically unreasonable. See **Nevis**.

Glen Ogle [Central] 'Glen (*gleann*), high (uchel, Brythonic Gaelic)'. The name is sometimes spelled Ogil.

Glen Oykel [Highland] 'Glen (*gleann*) of [the River] Oykel': the river

139

name is Brythonic and means 'high'. There is also a Strath Oykel farther down the same river, and it is possible that the description 'high' refers either to the glen or the strath rather than to the river.

Glen Quaich [Tayside] 'Glen (*gleann*) of the cup-shaped hollow (*cuaich*)'; the river name associated with this glen is likely to be back-formed.

Glen Quoich [Highland] 'Glen (*gleann*) of the cup-shaped hollow (*cuaich*)'; the River Quoich flows through Glen Quoich to meet Loch Quoich in just such a depression. The hollow, and thus the glen, probably gave the name to both the river and the loch.

Glenrothes [Fife] A made-up name: 'Glen of the *raths*' – although there are *raths* (circular stone forts) in the area, there is no glen to speak of. In fact, even the *raths* are a red herring, for the reference is actually to the Earls of Rothes, who were local landowners, and thus also to the short-lived Rothes Colliery in the vicinity.

Glen Roy [Highland] 'Glen (*gleann*) of [the River] Roy': the river name means 'red'.

Glenshee [Tayside (2)] 'Glen (*gleann*) of the fairy-hill (*sidhe*)'.

Glen Shiel [Highland] 'Glen (*gleann*) of [the River] Shiel': the river name means 'shelter'.

Glen Sletdale [Highland] 'Glen (*gleann*) [of] flat (*slétta*, ON) dale (*dalr*, ON)'.

Glen Sligachan [Skye] 'Glen (*gleann*) [that leads to the village of] Sligachan': the name of the village means 'place of shells'.

Glen Sluain [Strathclyde] Possibly 'Glen (*gleann*), slippery (*sleamhainn*)'.

Glen Strae [Strathclyde] Possibly 'Glen (*gleann*) [leading to the] Strath [of Orchy]', in which case the river-name associated with this glen is back-formed.

Glen Tarbert [Highland] 'Glen (*gleann*) of the portage (*tairbeart*)': the glen represents a short cut between Loch Linne and Loch Sunart; the river-name associated with the glen is back-formed.

Glen Tarsan [Strathclyde] Presumably 'Glen (*gleann*), cross-wise (*tarsuinn*)': the glen forms the cross-bar of a T-shaped depression.

Glen Torridon [Highland] The glen and its river are named after the village of Torridon at the end.

Glenuig [Highland] 'Glen (*gleann*) of the bay (*uig*, adaptation of ON *vík*)';

ironically, the bay to which the glen leads and on which the village is sited is now called Glenuig Bay.

Glen Ure [Strathclyde] 'Glen (*gleann*) of [the River] Ure': the river name is presumably identical with the Ure in Yorkshire, a tribal appellation.

Glen Urquhart [Highland] 'Glen (*gleann*) [that leads to] Urquart [Bay]': the name of the bay (and the castle on its shore) means 'near the thicket'; the river that runs down the glen is the River Enrick.

glinne genitive form of *gleann*, thus 'of the glen'.

glo 'mist'.

Gluss [Shetland] Possibly 'Shiny (*glys*, ON)': the name applies not only to the village some way inland, but also to the fjord where its river meets the sea and the island to one side; the name probably therefore describes one or other aspect of water – either the river or the fjord.

gob 'mouth', 'beak', and therefore 'point', 'sharp headland'. (The word appears to be cognate with the English *gab*.)

Gob a' Chuaille [Highland] Possibly 'Point (*gob*) of the recesses (*chùaile*)'.

Gob Aird an Tolmachain [Harris] Presumably 'Point (*gob*), height (*aird*) of the island (*an t-holm*, use of the ON element) fields (*achain*)'. The point projects into West Loch Tarbert and overlooks a number of islands.

gobhal 'fork', 'divide', 'twist'.

gobhann 'blacksmith'.

gobhar (also *gabhar*; Welsh *gafr*) 'goat': the word is evidently cognate with Latin *capri-* and English *heifer*.

gobhlach 'forked', 'twisting', 'sinuous'.

Gob na Creige [Lewis] 'Point (*gob*) of the (*na*) crag (*creige*)'.

Gob na h-Airde Móire [Harris] 'Point (*gob*) of the (*na*) height (*airde*), big (*móire*)'.

Gob na h-Oa [Skye] Presumably 'Point (*gob*) of the (*na*) bay (*òbha*)'.

Gob Rubha Bhatasgeir [Lewis] 'Point (*gob*) [of the] headland (*rubha*) [of the] boat (*bhàta*, adapted form of ON *bàtr*) skerry (*sgeir*, adapted form of ON *sker*)'.

-goe (also *geò*) elided form of ON *gjá*: 'chine', 'chasm', 'short fjord'.

141

Golspie [Highland] 'Gulli's (personal name, ON) farmstead (*byr*, ON)'.

Gordonstoun [Grampian] Estate renamed in 1638 by Sir Robert Gordon; perhaps he thought it sounded better than the Bog of Plewlands.

Gordonstown [Grampian] Village set up in 1770 by a landowner called Gordon from Badenscoth.

Gorebridge [Lothian] 'Goat's (*gobhair*) bridge (Eng)': this is what at least one commentator says – but much more likely the bridge is over a stream once/still called the Gore (which may thus have been 'the goat's stream').

gorm 'blue', 'grey-blue', or even 'blue-green'.

Gorm Loch [Highland] 'Blue (*gorm*) loch'.

Gorm-loch Beag [Highland] 'Blue (*gorm*) loch, small (*beag*)': this to distinguish it from Gorm-loch Mór some 2 miles south.

Gorm Loch Mór [Highland] 'Blue (*gorm*) loch, big (*mór*)': this to contrast with Fionn Loch Mór ('White loch, big')1/2 mile south-east.

Gorm-loch Mór [Highland] 'Blue (*gorm*) loch, big (*mór*)': this to distinguish it from Gorm-loch Beag some 2 miles north.

gort (also *gart-*) elided form of *garradh*: 'enclosure', 'garden', 'wall'.

goul elided form of *gobhal*: 'fork', 'divide'.

gour elided form of *gobhar*: 'goat', or of its genitive *gobhair*, thus 'of a goat'.

Gourock [Strathclyde] Apparently 'The pimple (*guireoc*)': the unflattering description may refer to Kempock Point.

Govan [Strathclyde] Presumably 'The blacksmith (*gobhann*)'.

gow elided form of 1) *cau:* 'hollows';
                 2) Brythonic Gaelic *cae:* 'enclosure', 'field', 'house';
         or 3) *gobha(nn):* 'blacksmith'.

gowan elided form of *gobhann:* 'blacksmith'.

gower elided form of *gobhar:* 'goat'.

gowrie elided form of the genitive of the personal name Gabran, son of Fe(a)rgus, one of the pioneering Celtic invaders from Ireland.

142

Grahamston [Central] District reputed to be named after one Sir John de Graham killed in the vicinity in 1298.

Grampian Mountains [Grampian] The name of this range of mountains is in fact a misreading by the early 16th-century historian Hector Boece of *Mons Graupius*, cited by Tacitus as the battlefield at which Agricola thrashed the Picts in around AD 84. The actual site of the battle is not known. The range was previously known as The Mounth – a name that is still used as part of the names of individual passes and mountain-chains in the Grampians.

gran(n)da 'ugly'.

Grangemouth [Central] '[The] Grange [Burn's] mouth (Eng)': the stream name is also English (*grange* derives from Latin, 'a place to store grain'). The town stands where the stream, named after nearby Abbot Grange (part of Newbattle Abbey), meets the much larger River Carron.

Grantown-on-Spey [Highland] The town was built as a model village on land owned by the Grant Family in 1766. The meaning of the river name is unknown.

Grantshouse [Borders] When the railway came through here in the 19th century, a name had to be found for its station: it took one from the nearby Tammy Grant's Inn. Tammy Grant is thought merely to have been a local celebrity of the 18th century.

Grassy Cletts [Orkney] 'Grassy (OE/ON) rocks (*klettr-s*, ON)'.

Greenburn [Lothian] '[The] Green (Eng) stream (*burna*, OE)': this possibly to distinguish from Whitburn ('White stream') and Stoneyburn near by – the area has many English names.

Greenlaw [Borders] 'Green (Eng) mound (*hlaw*, OE)'.

Greenock [Strathclyde] Probably just 'Sunny (*grianaig*)', although most commentators make it a 'Sunny place' or a 'Sunny knoll' or some such, attributing the final syllable to one or other element.

Greeta River [Lewis] 'Gravel (*gríot*, ON [English *grit*]) river (á, ON)' with the unnecessary 'River' thereafter added much later when the original meaning had been forgotten. The river is alternatively called by an elided form of the same name, the Creed.

Gretna [Dumfries & Galloway] 'Gravelly (*greoten*, OE) haugh [that is, a fertile strip in the bend of a river] (*halth*, OE)'. The River Sark runs to one side of the town.

143

Gretna [Dumfries & Galloway] 'Gravelly (*greoten*, OE) haugh [that is, a fertile strip in the bend of a river] (*halth*, OE)'. The River Sark runs to one side of the town.

grian 'sun'. An extremely unlikely word for 'sun', which in Indo-European languages is fairly constantly derived from the root that gives English words like 'solar', 'helium' and of course 'sun'. Perhaps the Gaelic means rather 'the light' and is related instead to words in English that begin *gl-*, such as 'gleam', 'glitter', 'glow'; cf Welsh *goleun-* 'light'.

grianan 'sunny knoll', evidently a derivative of *grian*.

Grianan [Lewis] 'Sunny knoll (*grianan*)'.

Grimersta [Lewis] 'Grímr's (personal name, ON) steading (*stathr*, ON)': the personal name was one also applied to the chief god Othinn (Odin), the 'masked one'.

Grimister [Shetland] Presumably 'Grímr's (personal name, ON) steading (*stathr*, ON)'. But the personal name was one also applied to the chief god Othinn (Odin), the 'masked one'.

Grimsay [Uist] Possibly 'Grímr's (personal name, ON) island (*ey*, ON)'.

Grimshader [Lewis] Possibly 'Grímr's (personal name, ON) house (*setr*, ON)'.

Griskerry [Shetland] Possibly 'Pig (*gríss*, ON) skerry (*sker*, ON)': the first element was sometimes used in ON as a nickname.

Grobister [Orkney] Possibly 'Gully (*gróf*, ON) settlement-steading (*bol-stathr*)'.

gronn 'marsh', 'muddy ground'.

gruagach 'fairy-woman', 'sorceress', 'witch'.

Gruinard [Highland] 'Green (*groenn*, ON) fjord (*-ard*, adaptation of ON *fjordr*)'. Nothing like a fjord, the bay has ironically now had the word 'Bay' additionally tacked on to its name. No fewer than two Gruinard Rivers also flow into the bay.

Grunasound [Shetland] Presumably 'Green (*groenn*, ON) inlet (*sund*, ON)'.

Gruna Stack [Shetland] Presumably 'Green (*groenn*, ON) stack [that is, sharp, conical hill] (*stakkr*, ON)': in fact, the stack is more a skerry, being a sharp rock out to sea off North Roe, Mainland.

Gualann [Strathclyde] 'Shoulder of a hill (*gualainn*)'.

Guallann Mhór [Strathclyde] 'Shoulder of a hill (*gualainn*), big (*mhór*)'.

Guardbridge [Fife] 'Enclosure (ME, the same word as 'yard') bridge (Eng)': the first bridge over the River Eden dates from around 1420.

Guildtown [Tayside] Village set up in 1818 on the land of the local corporation, known in Scotland as 'the guildry'.

Gullane [Lothian] Apparently 'Little loch (*gollan*)', one of which there is said to have been there.

Gunnista [Shetland] 'Gunni's (personal name, ODan) steading (*stathr*, ON)'. Gunni is a name well attested in place names in Lincolnshire and Norfolk.

-gussie elided form of *ghiubhsaich* or *ghiuthsaich*, genitive plurals respectively of *giubhas* or *giuthas*, thus 'of fir trees'.

-gyll elided form of *g(h)aidheal*: 'the Gaels'.

H

h- separating consonant between two vowels. Thus, for example in Altnaharra, the -h- separates the elements *na* and *airbhe*.

Habost [Lewis] 'Higher (*hár*, ON) settlement-steading (*bol-stathr*, ON)'.

Haddington [Lothian] 'Hada's people's (*Hada-inga*, OE) farmstead (*tun*, OE)'.

Haddo [Grampian] 'Half (OE) a *dabhach* (an agricultural area of land)'.

-halladale 'holy (*halig*, ON) dale (*dalr*, ON)'. This remains the derivation even when these elements are preceded by the Gaelic Strat(h)- (*srath*, 'valley').

Ham [Shetland] 'Harbour (*hamn*, ON)'.

Hamilton [Strathclyde] Either 'Plateau-like (*hamel*, OE) hill (*dun*, OE)' or 'Hamela['s] (personal name, OE) farmstead (*tun*, OE)'. In any case, the name is transferred from Hamilton, Leicestershire, England in 1548, at which date the contemporary village changed its name from Cadzow.

Hamnavoe [Shetland] 'Harbour (*hamn*, ON) bay (*vágr*, ON)'. Present-day Norwegian has mutated to *havn*, as Eng *haven*, but Swedish retains *hamn*. Both the two villages of this name in Shetland (one on Mainland, the other on Yell) are indeed thereby well described.

Handwick [Fife] 'Cock (*hana*, OE) settlement (*wic*, OE)'. The OE word for 'cock' later became modern Eng *hen*.

Haroldswick [Shetland] 'Harald's (personal name, ON) bay (*vík*, ON)'. The bay that this village is at the head of is now called Harold's Wick.

-harra (also ***-harrie***) elided form of *h-airbhe*: 'dividing wall', 'partition', 'boundary'.

-harrie See *-harra*.

Harris [Western Isles] 'Higher [island] (*h-earaidh*)'. Harris has considerably more and higher mountains than Lewis. The Gaelic may in turn be an adaptation of ON *hár-ey* 'higher island'. This would then strongly suggest the meaning 'low island' for Lewis. But all commentators derive 'Lewis' from Gaelic meaning something entirely different.

146

Hatton [Grampian] 'Hall (OE) farmstead (*tun*, OE)'. This was a common name in the 16th and 17th centuries for the large farmhouse in which the laird lived.

haugh (also *heugh*) elided form of OE *halh*, 'corner', 'angle', 'nook', or of OE *haga*, 'enclosure'. The first of these alternatives is by far the more common, and in northern England and Scotland frequently refers to alluvial land within the curve of a meandering river.

Hawick [Borders] 'Enclosure (*haga*, OE) settlement (*wic*, OE)'.

Ha Wick [Orkney] 'High (*ha*, ON) bay (*vík*, ON)'.

Heanish [Tiree] Presumably 'High (*há*, ON) headland (*nes*, ON)'. The headland south of the village is now called Rubha Tràigh an Dùin, 'Promontory (Goidelic Gaelic) of the beach of the hill (Brythonic Gaelic)'.

Hedderwick [Fife] 'Heather (*hathir*, ME)) settlement (*wic*, OE)'.

Helensburgh [Strathclyde] A village renamed by Sir James Colquhoun of Luss in 1776, while laying out a New Town on the site, after his wife Lady Helen (Sutherland). It was formerly called Mul(r)ig.

Hellabrick's Wick [Shetland] 'Helpric's (personal name, OE) farm (*wic*, OE)'; the personal name is attested in a place name in Lincolnshire. The final element could alternatively derive from ON *vík*, 'bay'.

Helliness [Shetland] Possibly 'Holy (*helig*, ON) cape (*nes*, ON)', although the first element might instead be a personal name.

Helmsdale [Highland] 'Hjalmund's (personal name, ON) dale (*dalr*, ON)'.

Heriot [Lothian] Possibly 'Army (*here*, OE) pass (*geat*, OE)'.

Hestaval [Lewis] Probably 'Horse (*hestr*, ON) fell (*fjall*, ON)'.

heugh (also *haugh*) elided form of OE *halh*, 'corner', 'angle', 'nook', or of OE *haga*, 'enclosure'. The second OE word is the origin of modern Eng *hedge*.

Hillbrae [Grampian] The second element appears to be a translation of the first: the areas around the two villages of this name in the Region are comparatively full of both English and Gaelic names. And both villages are indeed at some height.

Hilton [Grampian] 'Hill (*hyll*, OE) farmstead (*tun*, OE)'. A popular name in the 16th and 17th centuries for the secondary farm on the slopes above the Hatton, or 'hall farmstead', where the laird lived.

147

Hjoag [Shetland] 'Hill (*haugr*, ON)'.

Hobbister [Orkney] Presumably 'Bay (*hóp*, ON) settlement-steading (*bolstathr*, ON)'. The bay below the tiny village is called Waulkmill Bay.

Hobkirk [Borders] 'Shelter (*hóp*, ON) church (*kirkja*, ON)'.

holm elided form of ON *holmr*: 'little island'.

Holmsgarth [Shetland] 'Islands (*holms*, ON) enclosure (*garthr*, ON)'.

holy- modern form of OE *halig*: 'holy' and, similarly derived, 'hallow(ed)'.

Holyrood [Lothian] 'Holy (*halig*, OE) cross (*rod*, OE)'. Many churches still contain a rood screen on which there is a crucifix.

hop (also *hope, ob*) elided form of ON *hóp*: 'bay', thus 'shelter' and 'valley'.

Hope [Highland] 'Valley (*hóp*, ON)'. Loch Hope is in an extremely fine valley (Strath More) sweeping seawards from Ben Hope.

Hopeman [Grampian] Apparently a corruption of French *haut mont*, 'high hill', the name given to a village founded by one William Young of Inverugie in 1805.

-horn in Lowland areas, elided form of OE *erne*: 'house'.

-horn in Highland river-names, elided form of *eren*: 'water'.

Hornish Point [Western Isles] Presumably 'Horn (ON) headland (*nes*, ON) point (Eng)', the last element being added much later when the sense of the original elements had been forgotten.

hourn said to mean 'hell', 'Hades'.

-house either 1) OE or ME 'house';,
　　　　　　 or　 2) occasionally an elided form of *fhuathais*: 'ghost'.

Houston [Strathclyde] 'Hugo's (personal name, OE) farmstead (*tun*, OE)'. Once the property of Hugo de Paduinan.

hov- in Orkney and Shetland, elided form of ON *hof*: '(pagan) temple'.

howe in Lowland areas, elided form of OE *halh* 'corner', 'angle', 'nook', or of OE *haga*, 'enclosure'. See **haugh**.

howe in coastal and north Highlands, elided form of ON *haugr*: 'hill', 'mound', 'barrow'.

Hoxa [Orkney] 'Barrow (*haugr*, ON) isthmus (*eith*, ON)'.

Hoy [Orkney] 'High (*ha*, ON) island (*ey*, ON)'.

148

Humbie [Lothian] 'Hundi's (personal name, ON) farm (*byr*, ON)'. The personal name Hundi means 'Dog' (and corresponds to the Eng *hound*).

Huntingtower [Tayside] Site from the 15th century of the hunting tower of the Ruthven family of Ruthven Castle.

Huntly [Grampian] 'Huntsman's (*hunta*, OE) wood (*leah*, OE)'. Another name transferred north, this time from a site in Berwickshire by the Gordon family.

hurich 'yew trees'.

Hutchesontown [Strathclyde] Part of Glasgow deriving its name from the Hutcheson Hospital there, founded by George and Thomas Hutcheson in about 1647.

Hyndland [Strathclyde] Part of Glasgow that represents *land* that lies be*hind* (or back from) the River Clyde; Middle English.

I

i- elided form of *ath(a)*: 'ford'. E.g. I-brox.

i- elided form of ON *ey*: 'island'. E.g. I-colmkill (see **Iona**).

iar 'west'.

iarann 'iron'; the word has many Germanic cognates.

iaruinn genitive form of *iarann*, thus 'of iron'.

ibert elided form of *iobairt*: 'offering', '(land) donated to the church'.

Ibrox [Strathclyde] 'Ford (*ath[a]*) of the badger (*bruic*)'. Brock is still the common name of the badger in England, but few realise that that is because badgers are variegated in coloration. Cognate is another Gaelic word: *breac* 'speckled'. Cf the name for the bear, Bruin, which means (and is the same word as) 'brown'.

idri elided form of *eadar*: 'between'.

imrich 'removing', 'flitting'.

inbhir 'place where one water meets a greater', 'confluence', 'mouth of the river'. The Brythonic equivalent is *aber*, and is surely the same word, so it is surprising that some commentators derive the Goidelic term from an earlier Celtic **eni-beron*, 'in-bearing' – but they may be right. In place names this element is virtually always anglicised to *inver*.

inch elided form of *innis*: 'island', 'water-meadow'.

Inch [Lothian; Grampian] 'Island (*innis*)'.

Inch, North and **South** [Tayside] 'Water-meadow (*innis*)'.

Inchcape Rock [North Sea, south-east of Arbroath] 'Island (*innis*) [like a] beehive (*skeppa*, ON), rock (Eng)'. The sandstone reef, now more commonly called Bell Rock, is exposed only at low tide: did the Old Norsemen have long, low beehives?

Inchcailloch [Central] 'Island (*innis*) of the nuns (*cailleach*)'. The second element can also mean 'old women' or 'hags', being a mutation of the Latin *palliata* 'cloaked', referring either to nuns' habits or old crones' weeds.

Inchcolm [Fife] 'Island (*innis*) of [St] Columba'. The island bears the ruins of the abbey of St Columba, founded in 1123.

Inchfad [Central] Presumably 'Island (*innis*), long (*fada*)'.

Inchgarvie [Lothian] 'Island (*innis*), rough [water] (*garbh*)'.

Inchkeith [Firth of Forth] Presumably 'Island (*innis*) of Keith', although the name Keith is a version of a Brythonic Gaelic word for 'wood' (cf modern Welsh *coed*).

Inchkenneth [Mull] 'Island (*innis*) [of St] Caioneach (personal name)'. The saint was Irish, was a friend of St Columba of Iona, and is associated with several churches in the west of Scotland. The name is the origin of the present-day forename 'Kenneth', although in Roman Catholic literature he is referred to as 'Canice': it means 'fair'.

Inchlaggan [Highland] Presumably 'Water-meadow (*innis*) of the hollow (*lagain*, genitive of *lagan*)'.

Inchlonaig [Strathclyde] Presumably 'Island (*innis*), marshy (*lonneach*)'.

Inchmarnock [Strathclyde] Presumably 'Island (*innis*) of my (*mo*) [St] Ernoc', on an analogy with Kilmarnock (some 24 miles away).

Inchmichael [Tayside] 'Water-meadow (*innis*) of Michael'. The name Michael means 'Who is like El?' in Hebrew, and is not a particularly Scottish pronunciation – Mitchell is more common in names.

Inchmore [Highland] Presumably 'Water-meadow (*innis*), big (*mór*)'.

Inchmurrin [Strathclyde] 'Island (*innis*) [of St] Mirin (personal name)'. Mirin was an Irish abbot who in the 7th century founded a monastery at Paisley. His ruined chapel is on the island.

Inchnadamph [Highland] 'Water-meadow (*innis*) of the (*na*) stag (*damh*)'. The third element can also mean 'ox', but the area is one where stags used to roam and oxen must have been far less common.

inghean (also *inghinn, nighean*) 'young girl', 'daughter'.

inghinn See *inghean*.

Ingliston [Lothian] 'Ingialdr's (personal name, ON) farm (*tun*, OE)'.

inis elided form of *innis* 'island', 'water-meadow'.

Inishail [Strathclyde] Presumably 'Island (*innis*), rock[y] (*h-ail*)'.

Innerleithen [Borders] 'Confluence (*inbhir*) of the [River] Leithen [and the Tweed]'. The river name is presumably a version of *leathann*, 'broad'.

Innerwick [Tayside] Probably 'Confluence (*inbhir*) of [the] Mhuic [Water and the River Lyon]'. The stream name is from *muice*, genitive of *muc*: 'pig',

151

but the stream flows down from Meall a' Mhuic ('Fell of the pig') through the Lairig a' Mhuic ('Pass of the pig'), and the mountain name is probably the primary eponym.

innis (also *inis*; Irish *ennis*; Welsh *ynys*; cf Latin *insula*) 'island', 'water-meadow'.

innse (also *inse*) genitive form of *innis*: 'island', 'water-meadow'.

Insch [Grampian] 'Water-meadow (*innis*)'.

inse (also *innse*) genitive form of *innis*: 'island', 'water-meadow'.

Insh [Highland] 'Water-meadow (*innis*)'.

inver anglicised form of *inbhir*: 'place where one water meets a greater', 'confluence', 'mouth of the river'. The Brythonic equivalent is *aber*, and is surely the same word, so it is surprising that some commentators derive the Goidelic term from an earlier Celtic **eni-beron* 'in-bearing' – but they may be right.

Inver [Grampian] 'Confluence (*inbhir*)'. The village is situated where the Feardar Burn meets the River Dee.

Inver [Highland] 'Confluence (*inbhir*)'. The village is at the mouth of a large estuary, itself at the mouth of the Dornoch Firth.

Inverailort [Highland] Hybrid and possibly corrupt name. The village is not far from where the River Eilt flows into the sea-loch now called Loch Ailort, and may therefore once have been called Invereilt – 'Mouth (*inbhir*) of the Eilt'. However, the influence of the Vikings meant that the sea-loch came to be called a fjord – *-ort*, Gaelic version of ON – and the village name may have been adapted accordingly.

Inveralligin [Highland] 'Mouth (*inbhir*) of the Alligin [Water]'. The village is situated where the Alligin Water flows into Upper Loch Torridon. The stream name derives from the mountain whence it flows, Beinn Alligin, the name of which is probably an ancient word related to *ail* 'rock(y)'.

Inveraray [Strathclyde] 'Mouth (*inbhir*) of the [River] Aray'. The town is situated where the river runs into Loch Fyne. With the river name, cf Ayr (cognate with European river names Aar, Ara, Ahre, etc.).

Inverbeg [Strathclyde] '[River-]Mouth (*inbhir*), small (*beag*)'.

Inverbervie [Grampian] 'Mouth (*inbhir*) of the Bervie [Water]'. The town is situated on Bervie Bay. The name was originally Aberbervie, however, so it seems right to look for a Brythonic meaning to the river name. So cf modern Welsh *berw* 'boiling', 'seething'.

152

Inverdruie [Highland] 'Confluence (*inbhir*) of the [River] Druie [and the River Spey]'. The village is situated at the confluence, just over the Spey from Aviemore. The river name may come from *druidhe*: 'thrushes'.

Inveresk [Lothian] 'Mouth (*inbhir*) of [the River] Esk'. The town is close to where the river flows into the Firth of Forth. The river name is from the root of *uisg*: 'water', and is identical to Usk in Wales, and Esk, Exe and Axe in England.

Invergarry [Highland] 'Mouth (*inbhir*) of the [River] Garry'. The town is situated where the river flows into Loch Oich in the Great Glen. The river name is from *garbh*: 'rough [water]'.

Invergordon [Highland] An 18th-century settlement founded and named by Sir Alexander Gordon. It is quite close to – but not at – the sea end of the Cromarty Firth.

Inverkirkaig [Highland] 'Mouth (*inbhir*) of the [River] Kirkaig'. The village is situated where the river flows into the sea-loch Loch Kirkaig. The river name is strangely Old Norse and presumably refers more to the sea-loch: 'Church (*kirkja*, ON) bay (*vágr*, ON)'.

Inverness [Highland] 'Mouth (*inbhir*) of the [River] Ness'. The town is situated where the river flows into the Moray Firth and at the end of the Beauly Firth. The river name is from an ancient *nesta* thought to mean 'roaring [one]', 'rushing [one]'. That the normally placid river can indeed turn ferocious was proved in 1988 when the mainline railway bridge over the Ness at Inverness was swept away in a storm. Floods recurred in 1990.

Inveroran [Strathclyde] 'Mouth (*inbhir*) of the little water (*dhobhran*)'. The Inveroran Hotel is upon a streamlet that near by flows into Loch Tulla. The river name is a diminutive of *dobhar*: 'water' (Brythonic Gaelic).

Inverroy [Highland] 'Confluence (*inbhir*) of the [River] Roy [and the River Spean]'. The River Roy runs between the 'parallel roads' of Glen Roy, but actually meets the Spean at Roybridge, a mile east of Inverroy. The river name is from *ruaidhe*: 'red'.

Inveruglas [Strathclyde] 'Mouth (*inbhir*) of the [Inver]uglas [Water]'. The village is situated where the Inveruglas Water flows into Loch Lomond. The river name evidently derives from that of the village, although in origin it was apparently *dhubh glas*: 'black stream' (Brythonic Gaelic).

Inverurie [Grampian] 'Confluence (*inbhir*) of the [River] Urie [and the River Don]'. Two rather large rivers meet in the town: the Don goes on some 16 miles to Aberdeen. The river name is probably from *uidhre*, genitive of *odhar*: 'grey', 'dun-coloured'.

iobairt 'offering', 'sacrifice', '[land] donated to the church'. The word derives from Latin *offertus*.

iochdar 'lower (part)', 'bottom'. Opposite of *uachdar*, q.v.

iodhlann 'granary', 'cornyard'.

iola 'fishing grounds', 'fishing-bank'.

iolair 'eagle'.

iolan elided form of *iodhlann*: 'granary', 'cornyard'.

iomaire 'ridge'.

Iona [Strathclyde] Possibly 'Jonah', the Biblical name meaning 'dove' in Hebrew. There would be reason behind this, for until around 1800 the island was known as Icolmkill – 'Island (*ey*, ON) of [St] Columba's churchyard (*cille*)' – and the name Columba is Latin for 'dove'. But that may be fanciful coincidence, for some commentators believe that Iona is a spelling mistake for 'Ioua', although they don't know what that might mean. The churchyard contains the burial sites of many Scottish kings.

ionga 'nail'.

iosal 'low'. (Cf Welsh *isel*.)

Irongath [Central] 'Area (*earann*) of bog (*gaoth*)'.

Irvine [Strathclyde] Elided form of a river name that may contain the element *uaine*: 'green'. Alternatively, the name may mean no more than 'The river' or be Brythonic Gaelic and correspond to modern Welsh *yr wyn*, 'The white [one]'. The town stands at the mouth of the River Irvine, in Irvine Bay.

Islay [Strathclyde] 'Ile's (personal name, ON) island (*ey*, ON)'.

isle genitive of *iosal*: 'low'.

iubhar 'yew tree'. Cognate with Welsh *yw* and Eng *yew*.

J

Jedburgh [Borders] '[River] Jed borough (*burh*, OE)', although earlier it was Jed *worth* 'outlying settlement'. It has been suggested that the river name derives from *gead* 'pike', 'spear' (itself an adaptation of ON *gaddr*), although there is just as good a truly Gaelic place-name element *gead* 'strip of land'. But apart from the Teviot – into which the Jed eventually flows – all the other river names around here are back-formed from English roots (e.g. Oxnam Water, Kale Water, etc.) and in any case the pronunciation J- is distinctively English. But if English, the meaning of the name is obscure.

Jemimaville [Highland] Named in the 1820s by Sir George Munro after his wife Jemima.

John o' Groats [Highland] Place named after John de Groot, one of three brothers of apparently Dutch extraction but relatively Scottish Christian-names (Malcolm, Gavin and John) who came to live in Caithness in the 1490s under patronage of James IV. The family prospered and became well-known factors and landowners.

Johnstone [Strathclyde] 'John's town (OE)'. The name for the community has been in use since the late 13th century, although the town itself was established only in the 1780s as a commercial venture.

Joppa [Lothian] Name transferred from the Biblical Joppa (now Jaffa, part of Tel-Aviv, Israel) in the early 1780s. The name is thought to mean 'beautiful' (in Hebrew, *yapho*').

Juniper Green [Lothian] First recorded in 1812, the village evidently grew up on a green where there had been juniper bushes. Now it is the name of an entire district.

Jura [Inner Hebrides] Said to be 'Doirad['s] (personal name) island (*ey*, ON)': if Doirad is a Gaelic personal name, it could well mean 'broken-hearted (*deoirid*)'. But the first element may instead merely be an ON word *djur* 'deer', and 'deer island' (with both elements ON) does seem quite likely, really. 'Jura' is the stem from which the geological term 'Jurassic' derives.

K

katrine elided form of *ceathairne*: originally 'band of peasants' and later 'reivers', 'robbers', 'highway-bandits': the English word *cateran* (which is a singular) derives from the medieval Gaelic, through medieval Latin.

keal elided form of *ceall*: 'of the church graveyards', 'of the [monks'] cells', 'of the churches', genitive plural of *cill*.

keil(l)- adapted form of 1) *cill(e)*: '[monk's] cell', 'church graveyard' 'church';

or 2) *caol*: 'narrows', 'kyle'.

Keillmore [Strathclyde] 'Cell [or church] (*cill*), big (*mór*)'. The village stands on the shore of Loch na Cille.

keith elided form of Brythonic Gaelic *coed*: 'wood' [i.e. stand of trees]. But in that the Brythonic Gaelic for 'wood' [i.e. timber] is *gwydd*, and evidently from the identical root, all are presumably cognate with English *wood*.

Keith [Grampian] 'Wood (*coed*, Brythonic Gaelic)'.

Keithock [Grampian] Probably 'Wooded (*coediog*, Brythonic Gaelic)'. The tiny village is very close to the city with a classic Brythonic name, Brechin.

-keld elided form of a word meaning 'of the Caledonians'. (Commentators have suggested a form *Chailleann* for the original, but without a -d it seems extremely unsatisfactory.) The name Caledonia may in turn derive from a root that means 'wooded shelter' – *celydd* in modern Welsh.

Kelso [Borders] Apparently 'Chalk (*calc*, OE) hill (*-how*, OE)'; indeed, a section of the town is still known as 'the Chalkheugh'.

Kelty [Fife] 'Hard (*caled*, Brythonic Gaelic)'. The name is sometimes said to refer to water, although there are no major expanses of water anywhere near. See also **Kirkcaldy**.

ken- (also *kin-*) adapted form of *ceann*: 'head', in all the senses of the word: as the head of the body or the family; the head of a river or a loch; and the 'head' that is a head[land] or point. The word is cognate with the English *chin*, and corresponds to the Welsh/Cornish (Brythonic Gaelic) *pen-*.

Kenmore [Tayside] 'Head (*ceann*), big (*mór*)'. The town is the larger of the two communities one each end of Loch Tay (the other is Killin, q.v.).

156

Kenmore [Highland; Dumfries & Galloway] 'Head (*ceann*), big (*mór*)': both these communities are situated on the shore beneath a large headland.

Kennacraig [Strathclyde] 'Head (*ceann*) of the (*na*) crag (*creag*)'.

Kennet [Fife] Possibly 'Fair', from an ancient Brythonic Gaelic word found now as Welsh *Gwynedd* and *Gwent* (cognate with Latin *candidus* 'shining white'), the first element in the city name Winchester, and perhaps corresponding to the river name Kennett. The word is also the derivation of the forename Kenneth.

Kennoway [Fife] 'Head [i.e. perhaps 'chief'] (*ceann*) field (*achadh*)'. The town is situated where the foothills begin to rise behind the coastal plain, and so one might have expected the second element in the place name to have been *mhagh* 'plain' – an element that in some other names has resulted in the corrupted form '-oway'. But an earlier form of 'Kennoway' was 'Kennachy'.

Kentallen [Highland] Probably 'Head (*ceann*) of the little sea (*an t-sàilan*)': the village stands at the end of a creek off the sea-loch Loch Linnhe, 4 miles west of the Ballachulish bridge.

Kentra [Highland] Presumably 'Head (*ceann*) [of the] sands (*tràigh*)'. The village overlooks a wide, sandy bay with a thin sea-entrance, on the northern shore of the Ardnamurchan Peninsula.

keol- adapted form of *caol*: 'narrows', perhaps better known as 'kyle'.

Keoldale [Highland] 'Narrows (*caol*) dale (*dalr*, ON)'. The village is situated on the eastern shore of the Kyle of Durness – the Keol of the name – 2 miles south-west of Durness (another very ON name).

keppoch adapted form of *ceapach*: 'tillage plot', 'plantation', 'garden'.

Keppoch [Highland] 'Tillage plot (*ceapach*)'.

Kerrysdale [Highland] '[River] Kerry's dale (ON)'. If the river name is older than the village name, as is likely, it might derive from the same source as Irish Kerry: probably *Gabran*, the son of King Fe(a)rgus of Ulster, whose name in Scotland is more commonly corrupted to -gour or -gowrie. But if ON, the name might refer instead to *ciarr*: 'brushwood', 'muddy place where brushwood grows', the origin of the surname Kerr.

Kershope Burn [Borders] 'Cress (*caerse*, OE) valley (*hop*, OE) stream (*burna*, OE)'. The burn forms the border between England and Scotland for some eight or nine miles.

157

Kettla Ness [Shetland] 'Ketil['s] (personal name, ON) ness (*nes*, ON)'. The personal name means 'cauldron' and presumably was first used as a nickname.

Kettletoft [Orkney] 'Ketil['s] (personal name, ON) site for a house (*topt*, ON)'. The personal name means 'cauldron' and presumably was first used as a nickname.

kil-   elided form of 1) *cill*: 'church grounds', 'church graveyard, '[monk's] cell', 'church'; this element often introduces a saint's name; the form may be said to be dative (locative) and thus the element to mean 'at the cell', but there is little sense here in making that distinction;

                  2) *coille*: 'wood', 'forest';
                  3) *cùil*: 'recess', 'nook';
                  4) *cùl*: 'back', 'ridge';
    or, rarely, 5) *caol*: 'narrows', better known as 'kyle'.

Kilbarchan [Strathclyde] Possibly 'Cell [or church] (*cill*) of [St] Brychan (personal name)'. There is no known Scottish saint of this name – but then there is only a legendary holy king of this name in Wales – and yet in all British lands there are variants of the name Brychan (such as Brechin, Brecon, Wrekin and Virocon-) in religious connotations.

Kilbirnie [Strathclyde] Most commentators plump for 'Cell [or church] (*cill*) of [St] Brendan (personal name)'. There were two Irish saints of this name, contemporary with each other in the mid-6th century, both with genuine Scottish connections. The name means, apparently, 'dweller by a beacon'. A St Brendan's Fair used to be held annually. On the other hand, much closer to the actual pronunciation and to earlier forms of the place name, there was also a Saint Birinus (or Berin or Birin, a name that would probably mean either 'brown' or 'bear' [cf Bruin, Björn, etc.]), first Bishop of Dorchester (Oxfordshire), who had strong connections with the crusading missionary King Oswald of Northumbria in the mid-7th century (who in turn also features in Scottish place names: see **Kirkoswald**).

Kilbride [Highland; Strathclyde; Western Isles] 'Cell [or church] (*cill*) of [St] Bridget/Bridie (personal name)'. Saint Bridget is another saint who may never have actually lived. Much of her story is bound up with that of the ancient Celtic goddess of fire, Brigit, daughter of the sun god, goddess also of the hearth and of poetry, whose worship the church was trying to take over. Saint Bridget then (not surprisingly) became patron saint of poets, blacksmiths and healers. It may well have been after her that the British (originally Brigantes) first got their name.

Kilchainie [South Uist] 'Cell [or church] (*cill*) of [St] Caioneach (personal name)'. This saint was Irish, was a friend of St Columba of Iona, and is associated with several churches in the west of Scotland. The name is the origin of the present-day forename 'Kenneth', although in Roman Catholic literature he is referred to as 'Canice': it means 'fair'.

Kilchattan [Bute; Colonsay] 'Cell [or church] (*cill*) of [St] Chattan (personal name)'. Chattan was the founder of a monastery at Kingarth, on the shore of what is now Kilchattan Bay, on the Isle of Bute (some 40 miles south-east of the village on Colonsay) in the 6th century.

Kilchennich [Tiree] 'Cell [or church] (*cill*) of [St] Caioneach (personal name)'. This saint was Irish, was a friend of St Columba of Iona, and is associated with several churches in the west of Scotland. The name is the origin of the present-day forename 'Kenneth', although in Roman Catholic literature he is referred to as 'Canice': it means 'fair'.

Kilchenzie [Strathclyde] Probably 'Cell [or church] (*cill*) of [St] Caioneach (personal name)'. A 'Cainnech' was the friend of St Columba of Iona; it was he who was titular patron of Kilchennich in Tiree, Kilchainie in Uist and Inchkenneth in Mull. The name is the origin of the present-day forename 'Kenneth', although in Roman Catholic literature he is referred to as 'Canice': it means 'fair'.

Kilchiaran [Islay] 'Cell [or church] (*cill*) of [St] Ciaran (personal name)'. There were two Irish saints of this name, both famous for their way with animals – but not for any connection with Scotland. The name is spelled also Kieran or Kiaran, and is said to mean 'dark'.

Kilchoan [Highland] 'Cell [or church] (*cill*) of [St] Congan (personal name)'. St Congan, or Comgan or Coan, founded a monastery in Lochalsh after being banished from Ireland in the 8th century. He was buried on Iona by his nephew, St Fillan.

Kilchoman [Islay] 'Cell [or church] (*cill*) of [St] Congan (personal name)'. St Congan, or Comgan or Coan, founded a monastery in Lochalsh after being banished from Ireland in the 8th century. He was buried on Iona by his nephew, St Fillan.

Kilchurn [Strathclyde] 'Narrows (*caol*) of the cairn (*chuirn*, genitive of *carn*)'. Picturesque spot on Upper Loch Awe.

Kilconquhar [Fife] Apparently 'Cell [or church] (*cill*) of Conchobar

159

(personal name)'. But as a potential saint's name, Conchobar is not recorded in Celtic or Roman Catholic literature, although it is a well-attested forename – particularly as the name of a famous (mythical) king of Ulster – and means 'high desire'.

Kilcoy [Highland] 'Back (*cùl*) [of] the wood (*coille*)'.

Kilcreggan [Strathclyde] 'Cell [or church] (*cill*) on the little rock (diminutive of *creag*)'.

Kildonan [Highland; Eigg; Arran] 'Cell [or church] (*cill*) of [St] Donan (personal name)'. Donan, or Donnan, was an Irish monk who founded a community on Eigg but was eventually martyred there in 618. The name may be a form of 'Donald' (meaning 'world-ruler').

Kildonnan [Uist] 'Cell [or church] (*cill*) of [St] Donan (personal name)'. Donan, or Donnan, was an Irish monk who founded a community on Eigg but was eventually martyred there in 618. The name may be a form of 'Donald' (meaning 'world-ruler').

Kildrummy [Grampian] 'Head (*ceann*) [of] the ridge (*druim*)'. Formerly known as Kindrummie, the village is on the very edge of the Correen Hills.

Kilfinan [Strathclyde] 'Cell [or church] (*cill*) of [St] Finan (personal name)'. The most famous saint of this name was abbot of Iona in the mid-7th century, an associate of King Oswald of Northumbria, although a century earlier there had been another saint of this name in Aberdeen. The name means 'white(-haired)'.

Kilfinnan [Highland] 'Cell [or church] (*cill*) of [St] Finan (personal name)'. The most famous saint of this name was abbot of Iona in the mid-7th century, an associate of King Oswald of Northumbria, although a century earlier there had been another saint of this name in Aberdeen. The name means 'white(-haired)'.

Kilkenneth [Tiree] 'Cell [or church] (*cill*) of [St] Caioneach (personal name)'. This saint was Irish, was a friend of St Columba of Iona, and is associated with several churches in the west of Scotland. The name is the origin of the present-day forename 'Kenneth', although in Roman Catholic literature he is referred to as 'Canice': it means 'fair'.

killie- adapted form of *coille*: 'wood', 'forest'.

Killiecrankie [Tayside] 'Wood (*coille*) [of] aspen trees (plural of *critheann*)'.

Killiemor [Mull] Presumably 'Wood (*coille*), big (*mór*)'.

160

Killilan [Highland] Probably 'Cell [or church] (*cill*) of [St] Fillan (personal name)'. It was to the intercession of St Fillan that Robert the Bruce attributed his victory at Bannockburn. See also **Kilchoan** and **Kilchoman**.

Killin [Central; Highland] Probably 'Cell [or church] (*cill*), white (*fionn*)', although it remains possible that the church was instead dedicated to an otherwise unattested St Finn.

Kilmalcolm [Strathclyde] 'Cell [or church] (*cill*) of my (*ma*) Columba (personal name)'. Columba was possibly the most famous and most influential Irish/Scottish saint. He founded many religious communities, particularly that on Iona, and greatly encouraged the copying of sacred texts. The name means 'dove' (from Latin; cf the Spanish *palomo* 'dove', through the Brythonic equivalent).

Kilmaluag [Skye] 'Cell [or church] (*cill*) of [St] Maluag (personal name)'. Maluag, or Moluag, was an Irish monk who came to Scotland and set up a community on Lismore, building what amounted to a cathedral there in the latter half of the 6th century.

Kilmarie [Skye] Possibly 'Cell [or church] (*cill*) of [St] Maelrubha (personal name)'. Maelrubha was an Irish monk who founded a monastery at Applecross (some 20 miles north-east of Kilmarie) and established a church on Loch Maree (which is named after him). He died in the early 8th century.

Kilmarnock [Strathclyde] 'Cell [or church] (*cill*) of my (*mo*) Ernon (personal name)'. There is no saint of this name, or anything like it, with Scottish connections.

Kilmartin [Strathclyde] Presumably 'Cell [or church] (*cill*) of Martin (personal name)', and named after St Martin of Tours, for there is no other saint of this name (which means 'of Mars') with Scottish connections.

Kilmelford [Strathclyde] Probably '[The] Church (*cill*) of [the village of] Melfort [½ mile north-west]': the village itself seems to have been named after the loch on which it stands – 'sandbank fjord' in ON.

Kilmichael [Strathclyde] Presumably 'Cell [or church] (*cill*) of Michael (personal name)' and named after the archangel, for there is no saint of this name (which means 'Who is like El?') with Scottish connections.

Kilmory [Strathclyde] Presumably 'Cell [or church] of Mary (personal name)' and named after Jesus's mother, for there is no saint of this name (which possibly means 'of bitterness') with Scottish connections.

Kilninian [Mull] 'Cell [or church] (*cill*) of [St] Ninian (personal name)'. Ninian was a 5th-century British bishop and missionary to the Picts in

161

Galloway. His major community was the 'Candida Casa' established at Whithorn. The name is a British corruption of Latin *Vivianus*, 'lively'.

Kilninver [Strathclyde] 'Cell [or church] (*cill*) [of] the (*an*) confluence (*inbhir*)'. The village overlooks the spot at which the River Euchar flows into the sea-loch Loch Feochan.

Kilpatrick [Arran] 'Cell [or church] (*cill*) of [St] Patrick (personal name)'. Except by dedication, there is no connection here with the famous St Patrick, bishop and missionary to Ireland. Patrick means 'aristocrat'.

Kilpheder [Uist] 'Cell [or church] (*cill*) of [St] Peter (personal name)' and presumably named after the prime disciple of Christ, for there is no saint of this name (which means 'rock') with Scottish connections.

Kilphedir [Highland] 'Cell [or church] (*cill*) of [St] Peter (personal name)' and presumably named after the prime disciple of Christ, for there is no saint of this name (which means 'rock') with Scottish connections.

Kilsyth [Strathclyde] 'Cell [or church] (*cill*) of Syth (apparently a personal name)'. There is no saint of this name, or anything like it, with Scottish connections although there are two saints (Osyth and Sitha/Zita) with Home Counties or East Anglian associations.

Kilwinning [Strathclyde] 'Cell [or church] (*cill*) of [St] Finnian (personal name)'. St Finnian, educated at Candida Casa (Whithorn) under St Ninian, was in turn the teacher of St Columba during the 6th century. He should not be confused with St Finan, the abbot of Iona in the mid-7th century, an associate of King Oswald of Northumbria. The name means 'white(-haired)'.

kin- (also *ken-*) adapted form of the dative (locative) of *ceann*: 'head', in all the senses of the word: as the head of the body or the family; the head of a river or a loch; and the 'head' that is a head[land] or point. The word is cognate with the English *chin*, and corresponds to the Welsh/Cornish (Brythonic Gaelic) *pen-*. In place names the real meaning, because of the grammatical case involved, is actually 'at the head', but there is little sense now in making that distinction.

Kincaple [Fife] Presumably 'Head (*ceann*) of the horse (*capuill*)'.

Kincardine [Highland; Fife] 'Head (*ceann*) of the thicket (*cardden*, Brythonic Gaelic)'.

Kincraig [Highland] 'Head (*ceann*) of the crag (*creige*)'.

Kingairloch [Highland] 'Head (ceann) of the short (*gearr*) loch (*locha*)'. The area is inland of and surrounding the short sea-loch Loch a' Choire.

K

Kingarth [Strathclyde] 'Head (*ceann*) of the thicket (*cardden*, Brythonic Gaelic)'.

King Edward [Grampian] 'Head (*ceann*) of the boundary (*eadaradh*)'. The true derivation of this name is reflected more closely in the name of the nearby Kinedart Castle.

Kinghorn [Fife] 'Head (*ceann*) of the muddy ground (*gronn*)'. The town overlooks the mudflats of the Firth of Forth.

Kinglassie [Fife] 'Head (*ceann*) of the stream (*glas*, Brythonic Gaelic)'.

Kings Muir [Borders] 'King's (ME) moor (ME)'.

Kingston [Grampian] Name transferred from Kingston-upon-Hull by the founders of the local shipyard in 1784 who meant the yard to emulate the success of those of the Humberside city.

Kingussie [Highland] 'Head (*ceann*) of the fir trees (*ghiuthsaich*)'.

Kinknockie [Grampian] 'Head (*ceann*) of the rounded hill (*cnuic*)'.

Kinloch [Highland (3); Tayside] 'Head (*ceann*) of the loch (*locha*)'.

Kinlochard [Central] 'Head (*ceann*) of Loch Ard'. The loch name means 'height' or, as an adjective, 'high', and may refer to the nearby Ben Venue (2,386 feet/727 m).

Kinlochewe [Highland] 'Head (*ceann*) of Loch Ewe' – only Loch Ewe has now for centuries (since St Maelrubha's time, around 700) been known instead as Loch Maree. Still, the River Ewe very properly continues to flow from the loch to the sea at Inverewe.

Kinloch Hourn [Highland] 'Head (*ceann*) of Loch Hourn'. The name of this exceptionally scenic sea-loch is said by some to mean 'of Hell'.

Kinloch Laggan [Highland] 'Head (*ceann*) of Loch Laggan'. The loch name means 'little hollow' and indeed there is a little hollow at the head of the loch.

Kinlochleven [Highland] 'Head (*ceann*) of Loch Leven'. The loch name probably means 'liable to flooding' and derives from Brythonic Gaelic.

Kinlochluichart [Highland] 'Head (*ceann*) of Loch Luichart'. Strangely for a loch well inland, the loch name means 'ship-harbour'.

Kinlochmore [Highland] 'Head (*ceann*) of the loch (*locha*), big (*mór*)'.

Kinloch Rannoch [Tayside] 'Head (*ceann*) of Loch Rannoch'. The loch name means 'ferny'.

163

Kinloss [Grampian] 'Head (*ceann*) of herbs (*lussa*)'. The village is at the top of a large, enclosed sea-bay now called Findhorn Bay, representing the estuary of the River Findhorn. Otherwise there is little excuse for it to be a 'head' of any kind. (The River Lossie flows by at a distance of some 13 miles.)

Kinnaird [Tayside] 'Head (*ceann*) of the crag (*aird*)'. The village is on the edge of the Braes of the Carse.

Kinnell [Tayside] 'Head (*ceann*) of the rock (*aila*)'.

Kinnoull [Tayside] 'Head (*ceann*) of the rock (*aila*)'.

Kinross [Tayside] 'Head (*ceann*) of the promontory (*rois*)'. The promontory in front of the town projects into Loch Leven.

Kintail [Highland] 'Head (*ceann*) of the briny (*an t-sàile*)'. The area is at the end of the sea-loch Loch Duich.

Kintore [Grampian] Possibly 'Head (*ceann*) of the hill (*torra*)'.

Kintyre [Strathclyde] 'Head (*ceann*) [of the] land (*tìr*)'. The Mull of Kintyre is very much an enormously elongated headland.

Kinuachdrachd [Jura] Presumably 'Head (*ceann*), upper (*uachdar*) field (*achadh*)'.

Kippen [Central] 'Little stump (diminutive of *ceap*)'.

Kirbister [Orkney] 'Church (*kirkja*, ON) settlement-steading (*bol-stathr*, ON)'.

Kirbuster [Orkney] 'Church (*kirkja*, ON) settlement-steading (*bol-stathr*, ON)'.

kirk 'church', a Scots word derived in various areas either from OE *cirice* or *cyrice* or from ON *kirkja*. (In English it was the influence of the Normans that changed the k- sounds to ch-.) The Gaelic for 'church' is *eaglais* (derived from Latin/Greek *ecclesia*).

Kirk [Highland] 'Church'.

Kirkaig [Highland] 'Church bay (*-aig*, adaptation of ON or OE)'.

Kirk Burn [Highland] 'Church stream (*burna*, OE)'.

Kirkbean [Dumfries & Galloway] Possibly 'Church of [St] Bean (personal name)'. There was a saint of this name who in the 11th century was bishop of what is now Aberdeen.

K

Kirkcaldy [Fife] Apparently 'Fort (*caer*, Brythonic Gaelic) [of the] hard (*caled*, Brythonic Gaelic) stronghold (*din*, Brythonic Gaelic)'.

Kirkcolm [Dumfries & Galloway] 'Church of [St] Columba (personal name)'. Columba was possibly the most famous and most influential Irish/Scottish saint. He founded many religious communities, particularly that on Iona, and greatly encouraged the copying of sacred texts. The name means 'dove' (from Latin; cf the Spanish *palomo* 'dove', through the Brythonic equivalent).

Kirkconnel [Dumfries & Galloway] Possibly 'Church of [St] Conan (personal name)'. There was a 7th-century bishop of this name who proselytised in the Hebrides and in the Isle of Man. But 'Connel(l)' is a well-established Gaelic name too.

Kirkcowan [Dumfries & Galloway] 'Church of [St] Congan (personal name)'. St Congan, or Comgan or Co(w)an, founded a monastery in Lochalsh after being banished from Ireland in the 8th century. He was buried on Iona by his nephew, St Fillan.

Kirkcudbright [Dumfries & Galloway] 'Church of [St] Cuthbert (personal name, OE)'. Missionary and Prior of Lindisfarne, Cuthbert was famous for preaching and teaching in the 7th century. He is buried in Durham Cathedral. His name means 'famous-bright'.

Kirkgunzeon [Dumfries & Galloway] 'Church of [St] Finnian (personal name)'. St Finnian, educated at Candida Casa (Whithorn) under St Ninian, was in turn the teacher of St Columba during the 6th century. He should not be confused with St Finan, the abbot of Iona in the mid-7th century, an associate of King Oswald of Northumbria. The name means 'white(-haired)'.

Kirkhill [Tayside] 'Church hill (OE)'. The village is in an area of several OE names (e.g. Hillside, Barnhead).

Kirkhope [Borders] 'Church valley (*hop*, OE)'.

Kirkibost [Highland; Lewis; Uist] 'Church (*kirkja*, ON) settlement-steading (*bol-stathr*, ON)'.

Kirkintilloch [Strathclyde] 'Fort (*caer*, Brythonic Gaelic) [at the] head (*ceann*) of the hillock (*tulaich*)'.

Kirkmichael [Tayside; Strathclyde] 'Church of Michael (personal name)', presumably named after the archangel, for there is no saint of this name (which means 'Who is like El?') with Scottish connections.

Kirk o' Shotts [Strathclyde] 'Church of [the] steep slopes (*sceots*, OE)'. But many English place names ending in -shot(t) derive in fact from OE *sceat*, 'clump of trees', 'waste ground with trees on it'.

165

Dictionary of Scottish Place Names

Kirkoswald [Strathclyde] 'Church of Oswald (personal name)'. The name is that of the 7th-century religious-minded missionary King Oswald of Northumbria, an associate of St Finan and of St Birinus (see **Kilfinan** and **Kilbirnie**).

Kirkton [Highland (3); Borders; Dumfries & Galloway; Grampian (3); Tayside; Fife; Strathclyde] 'Church farmstead (*toun*, ME)'.

Kirktown [Grampian] 'Church farmstead (*toun*, ME)'.

Kirkwall [Orkney] 'Church (*kirkja*, ON) bay (*vágr*, ON)'.

Kirriemuir [Tayside] 'Quarter (*ceathramh*), big (*mór*)'. A *ceathramh* was an area of land that was the fourth part of a *dabhach*: 192 Scots acres.

Kittybrewster [Grampian] Possibly 'Ketilbjörn's (personal name, ON) steading (*stathr*, ON)'.

knap adapted form of *cnap*: 'hillock', a form in turn loaned from ON *knappr*. The initial k- should be pronounced.

Knapdale [Strathclyde] 'Hillock (*knappr*, ON) dale (ON)'. Not a particularly suitable name for a large area containing several summits at more than 1,500 feet (457 m). But there are also considerable tracts of undulating lowland.

Kneep [Lewis] 'Steep overhanging rock (*gnípa*, ON)'.

knock version of *cnoc*: 'rounded hill'. Both k's should be pronounced – the word is, after all, the origin of the English place name Cannock.

Knock [Lewis; Strathclyde; Grampian] 'Rounded hill (*cnoc*)'.

Knockan [Highland] 'Little rounded hill (diminutive of *cnoc*)'.

Knockandhu [Grampian] 'Little rounded hill (diminutive of *cnoc*), black (*dhubh*)'.

Knockando [Grampian] Said, rather unconvincingly in the light of the derivation above, to be 'Rounded hill (*cnoc*) of the market (*cheannachd*)'.

Knockbain [Highland] Possibly 'Rounded hill (*cnoc*), fair (*bàn*)'.

Knockdee [Highland] Probably 'Rounded hill (*cnoc*), black (*dubh*)'.

Knockenkelly [Arran] Probably 'Rounded hill (*cnoc*) [in] the (*an*) forest (*coille*)'.

Knockentiber [Strathclyde] 'Rounded hill (*cnoc*) [of] the (*an*) well (*tiobar*)'.

Knockfin [Highland] Presumably 'Rounded hill (*cnoc*), white (*fionn*)'.

166

K

Knockingallstane [Highland] Probably 'Rounded hill (*cnoc*) [by] Comgall's (personal name) town (*tun*, OE)'. St Comgall with his pupil St Columba preached to the chieftain Brude in Inverness at the end of the 6th century. (He should not be confused with Comgan, also known as Co[w]an.)

Knocknaha [Strathclyde] Probably 'Rounded hill (*cnoc*) of the (*na*) ford (*h-ath[a]*)'. Two rivers meet at the village.

Knockrome [Jura] Probably 'Rounded hill (*cnoc*), crooked (*crom*)'.

knowe elided form either of *cnoc* or of the English *knoll*, both meaning roughly the same thing: a tump or rounded hill.

Knoweside [Strathclyde] 'Knowe's (*cnoc-s* or OE) side (ME)'. The village is on the side of a 923 feet (281 m) hill overlooking Culzean Bay.

Knoydart [Highland] 'Cnut['s] (personal name, ON) fjord (*-art*, Gaelic corruption of the ON *fjordr*)'.

kyle adapted form of *caol*: 'narrows', 'strait', sometimes alternatively found in place names as an apparent plural 'kyles' actually from an alternative singular form *caolas*. Cf Modern Welsh *cul*, 'narrow', 'lean'.

Kyleakin [Highland] '[The] Kyle (*caol*) [of] Haakon (personal name)'. Haakon IV Haakonsson, King of Norway, Greenland and Iceland, sailed with a large fleet to the Hebrides in 1263 with the intention of reasserting the traditional sway of the Norsemen in the area. But he was defeated at Largs, and retired to Orkney where he then almost immediately died.

Kylerhea [Highland] '[The] Kyle (*caol*) of Reathann (*Rheithainn*, personal name)'. A name from Celtic mythology and legend.

Kylesku [Highland] Apparently '[The] Kyle (*caolas*), thin (*cumhann*)'. Virtually the same place as Kylestrome, q.v. Perhaps the presence of Garbh Island in the middle of the loch thus seemed to divide the crossing into two kyles.

Kylesmorar [Highland] '[The] Kyle (*caolas*) [of North] Morar'. The village is on the Morar side of a narrows in Loch Nevis, a very remote spot indeed. Morar, an area named after its central loch, means 'big water'.

Kyles Scalpay [Western Isles] '[The] Kyle (*caolas*) [of] Scalpay'. The village is on the mainland shore overlooking the channel to the island of Scalpay. Scalpay is said to mean 'ship[-like] island'.

Kylestrome [Highland] Probably '[The] 'Kyle (*caol*) [of] the point (*sròn*)'. The narrows lies in the shadow of Ben Strome (1,374 feet/419 m) and the tiny village used to be known rather as Stromeferry. See also **Kylesku**.

167

L

labhar 'loud': possibly cognate with English *laugh*, itself cognate with *clash*.

Labost [Lewis] Probably 'Low (*lagr*, ON) settlement-steading (*bol-stathr*, ON)'.

lacha 'wild duck'.

Ladykirk [Borders] '[Our] Lady['s] (Eng) church (Scots)': the church was built in about 1500 under the patronage of King James IV.

lag (also *lagaidh*) 'hollow', probably cognate with English *low* and *lie*.

lagan diminutive of *lag*: 'hollow'.

Lagavulin [Islay] 'Hollow (*lag*) of the mill (*a' mhuilinn*)'.

Lagg [Jura; Arran] 'Hollow (*lag*)'.

Laggan [Highland (2)] 'Little hollow (*lagan*, diminutive of *lag*)'.

làir 'mare'.

lairg (also *lorg*) 'thigh', 'shank'.

Lairg [Highland] 'Thigh (*lairg*)'.

Lairgmore [Highland] Presumably 'Thigh (*lairg*), big (*mór*)': the tiny village is on a promontory projecting much of the way across Loch Ness.

làirig 'pass'.

Làirig Ghru [Highland/Tayside] Said to be '[The] Pass (*làirig*), gloomy (*ghru*)'.

Lamancha [Borders] Name transferred from the Spanish province made famous by Don Quixote; the nearby Lamancha House – presumably its local origin – was built in 1663 (although one commentator dates the transference from 1736).

Lamba Ness [Shetland] 'Lambs' (*lamba*, ON) cape (*nes*, ON)'.

Lamlash [Arran] Amazingly, 'Island (*eilean*) of my (*mo*) [St] Laserian (personal name)'. What an elided form: *eilean* > 'La-'; *mo* > '-m-'; *Laserian* > '-lash'! St Laserian, or Laisren, was a shadowy Irish monk and mystic who proselytised chiefly in Ireland during the 7th century.

168

Lammermuir [Borders] Probably 'Lambs' (ME) moorland (ME)'.

Lanark [Strathclyde] 'Glade (*llanerch*, Brythonic Gaelic)'.

lang 'long' – but in place names the element may derive either from ON, OE, or the later Scots adaptations of either of these forms, all meaning the same.

Langbank [Strathclyde] Presumably 'Long (Scots) bank (Eng)': it is on the Firth of Clyde.

Langholm [Dumfries & Galloway] 'Long (Scots) water-meadow (Scots adaptation of the ON *holmr*, which originally meant 'island')'; the town is a centre in Eskdale.

Langshaw [Borders] Presumably 'Long (Scots) copse (Scots adaptation of OE *scaga*)'.

lann 'enclosure', 'farmed land': as a Gaelic word this is suspiciously close to Scandinavian place-name elements.

Lanrick [Central] 'Glade (*llanerch*, Brythonic Gaelic)'.

Lanrig [Lothian] 'Long (Scots) ridge (Scots adaptation of OE *hrycg*)': the village is spelled 'Longridge' on many maps.

Lanton [Borders] 'Long (Scots) town (Scots adaptation of OE *tun*)'.

laogh 'calf'.

lapach 'boy'.

Laphroaig [Islay] Possibly – but very tentatively – 'Loud (*labhar*) bay (corrupt form of ON *vágr*)'

làrach   either   1) 'ruins', 'devastated site';
          or   2) 'of the mare' (genitive of *làir*).

Larachbeg [Highland] Apparently 'Ruins (*làrach*), small (*beag*)'.

Larbert [Central] Commentators have plumped, puzzlingly, for 'Half (*leth*) wood (*pert*, Brythonic Gaelic)' but such an initial adjective seems nonsensical if the older element is the second: better, surely, to look for a Brythonic adjective – and there are two potentially suitable. The first is the Brythonic equivalent of Goidelic *leth*, *lled*: 'half', 'partly'; and the second is *llydan*: 'wide'.

larg- adapted form of *learg*: 'hillside', 'plain'.

Largie [Grampian] 'Hillside (*learg*)': the village is on the side of the Hill of Foudland.

169

Largo [Fife] 'Hillside (*learg*)': so much is the village on a hillside that it is divided into Upper and Lower Largo, on the slopes of Largo Law.

Largoward [Fife] Probably '[The village of] Largo [as above] outlying enclosure (*ward*, Scots)': the village is about 6 miles north-east of Largo.

Largs [Strathclyde] 'Hillside (*learg*)': the addition of the final '-s' would seem to have happened quite late.

Largybeg [Arran] Presumably 'Hillside (*learg*), small (*beag*)', and thus to distinguish it from Largymore (q.v.) 1 mile north.

Largymore [Arran] Presumably 'Hillside (*learg*), big (*mór*)', and thus to distinguish it from Largybeg (q.v.) 1 mile south.

Lasswade [Lothian] Probably 'Meadow's (*leah-s*, OE) ford (*[ge]waed*, OE)', although the first element might perhaps be OE *laess*: 'the lesser'; the village is close to the North Esk River.

Latheron [Highland] Possibly 'Barn (*hlatha*, ON) storehouse (OE *aern*)', perhaps even by way of a translation.

Latheronwheel [Highland] Presumably '[The village of] Latheron [as above] (stone-)circle (*hweol*, OE)': Latheron is 1 mile north-west and there are many hut-circles in the area.

Lauder [Borders] This would seem to be an adaptation of the name of the river on which it stands: the Leader Water. Probably therefore 'Elm (*leamh*, probably the Brythonic form) water (*dobhar*, Brythonic Gaelic)': the tautologous 'Water' would have been added afterwards.

Laurencekirk [Grampian] '[St] Laurence['s] (personal name) church (Scots)': the town was founded in the 1770s.

Laurieston [Central] Originally Laurenceton, the village was named in 1774 after its owner Sir Lawrence Dundas.

Laurieston [Dumfries & Galloway] William K. Laurie bought the land on which the village stands during the 18th century.

law elided form of OE *hlaw*: 'small hill', 'mound'.

Law [Strathclyde] 'Small hill (*hlaw*, OE)': actually 662 feet (202 m).

Lawers [Tayside] The village is named after the stream that runs through it down from Ben Lawers (in turn named after the village): 'Loud (*labhar*)'.

lax ON for 'salmon'.

Laxay [Lewis] 'Salmon (*lax*, ON) island (*ey*, ON)'.

170

Laxdale [Lewis] 'Salmon (*lax*, ON) dale (*dalr*, ON)'.

Laxfirth [Shetland] 'Salmon (*lax*, ON) fjord (Scots adaptation of ON *fjordr*)'.

Laxford Bridge [Highland] 'Salmon (*lax*, ON) fjord (adaptation of ON *fjordr*) bridge (Eng)': the place, and the river that flows under the bridge, are named after the sea-loch immediately westward.

Laxo [Shetland] 'Salmon (*lax*, ON) river (å, ON)'.

Laxobigging [Shetland] 'Salmon (*lax*, ON) river (å, ON) buildings (*byggin*, ON)'.

leaba (also *leabaidh*) 'bed', 'lair'.

leac 'flat stone', 'stone slab', 'flagstone', 'stepping-stone': cognate with Welsh *llech*, and possibly akin to Greek *lith*-. Cf also *clach*.

leacach 'stony'; 'stony place', 'stony slope', 'scree'.

Leachkin [Highland] Possibly 'Stony (*leacach*) head (*ceann*)'.

Leadhills [Strathclyde] 'Lead hills (ME)': the village and area were once famous for lead mining (and for the mining of gold and silver).

Lealt [Skye; Jura] Possibly 'Grey (*liath*) stream (*allt*)': both these villages are named after the watercourses on which they stand (which have subsequently had the words 'River' or 'Burn' added to their names).

leamh (also *leamhan, leamhain*; Old Irish *lem*; Welsh *llwyf*) 'elm', especially as a river name. In fact the word represents one of the best-attested river names in Europe, corresponding in Britain to names such as Lympne, Lemon, Leam, Lymn, and Lyming. (But probably not Lyme or Leven.)

lèana 'wet plain'.

lèanag (also *lianag*) diminutive of *lèana*, thus 'wet field', 'lush meadow'.

learg 'hillside', 'plain': this may or may not be akin to *lairg*: 'thigh'.

Leargybreck [Jura] Presumably 'Hillside (*learg*), speckled (*breac*)'.

leas (also *lios*) 'court', 'enclosed area', and thus 'garden'.

Leask [Grampian] Possibly 'Grey (*liath*) marsh (*easg*)': the village lies in the fertile valley of the Ythan.

leathad 'slope', 'hillside', 'brae'.

171

leathann (also *leathan)* 'broad'.

Lecht [Grampian] 'Cairn *(leacht,* associated with *leac:* 'stone')'.

leck elided form of *leac:* 'flat stone', 'stone slab', 'flagstone', 'stepping-stone'.

Leckfurin [Highland] Possibly 'Flagstone *(leac)* [by] the spring *(fuarain)'.*

Leckmelm [Highland] Possibly 'Stone *(leac)* of Maeldubh (personal name)' – a bit of an outlandish guess, this, but one Maeldubh was a Scotsman who founded the monastery named after him that became the city of Malmes-bury. The second element is less likely to be ON *malm,* 'ore', or Gaelic *muilinn,* 'mill' .

led- elided form of *leathad:* 'slope', 'hillside', 'brae'.

Ledaig [Strathclyde] Probably 'Slope *(leathad)* bay *(-aig,* corrupt form of ON *vágr)'.* The bay fronted by Ledaig is now called Ardmucknish Bay.

Ledbeg [Highland] 'Slope *(leathad),* small *(beag)'.* The Ledbeg River runs past Ledmore, q.v.

Ledmore [Highland] 'Slope *(leathad),* big *(mór)'.* Ledmore Junction (the junction of the A837 and the A835) lies just below a height of 1,306 feet (398 m).

Lednagullin [Highland] Presumably 'Slope *(leathad)* of the *(na)* hill-shoulder *(gualainn)'.*

Leebotten [Shetland] Possibly 'Shelter *(hlee,* ON) bottom *(botn,* ON)'.

Leith [Lothian] Probably 'Grey *(liath)'.*

-lemno elided form of *leamhan:* 'elm'.

Lennoxtown [Strathclyde] Renamed thus in the 1780s after the family of the dukes and earls of Lennox (a surname that probably derives either from *leamhnach,* 'elm-covered', or from an ancient root meaning 'flooding').

leothaid genitive form of *leathad,* thus 'of the slope'.

Lerwick [Shetland] 'Mud *(leir,* ON) bay *(vík,* ON)'.

Leslie [Grampian; Fife] Apparently 'Court *(leas)* pool *(linn)'.*

Lesmahagow [Strathclyde] 'Church *(eaglais)* of [St] Mahagow (personal name)'. There is no saint actually of this name, although one Machutus is normally cited. But Machutus was a Welshman who went to Brittany and became St Malo. There was an Irish St Mochta. I might suggest that the early Gaelic form of the name Michael is not dissimilar (cf *Mihangel* in Welsh). Some commentators propose that the name is rather *mo Fhegu,* 'my

172

[St] Fechin', but St Fechin – or Vigean – was another Irish monk of little or no connection with Scotland. All this distracts from the dreadful corruption initially of *eaglais* to 'Les-'.

Lethenty [Grampian] Possibly 'Broad (*leathann*) house (*tigh*)'.

letter elided form of *leitir*: 'slope', 'hillside'.

Letterewe [Highland] 'Hillside (*leitir*) [over Loch] Ewe' – except that the loch is now called Loch Maree.

Letterfearn [Highland] 'Hillside (*leitir*) [of the] alder-tree (*fearn*)'.

Leuchars [Fife] Probably '[Of] Rushes (*luachair*)': the place is not far from the estuary of the River Eden.

leum 'leap'.

Leven [Fife] The town takes its name from the river name Leven, and the river name may well have originated as a loch name. One commentator has convincingly suggested that the name means '[liable to] flooding', from an ancient Gaelic root; the name is unlikely to derive from *leamhan*, 'elm', although that word is also well attested as a river name.

Leverburgh [Harris] Renamed thus when Harris and Lewis were bought in 1918 by William H. Lever, Viscount Leverhulme.

Lewis [Western Isles] Said to be from *leog*, 'marsh', by way of being called 'The Lews'. But if Harris (q.v.) is possibly an adaptation of ON *hár-ey*, 'higher island', then Lewis might equally possibly be an adaptation of *lag-ey*, 'low island'.

Lhanbryde [Grampian] Presumably 'Church (*llan*, Brythonic Gaelic) of [St] Bridget (personal name)'. The area seems to have been a Brythonic one – Urquhart is only 1½ miles away. For information on St Bridget, see **Kilbride**.

liath (Welsh *llwyd*) 'grey', 'grey-blue'.

Liathach [Highland] 'Grey (*liath*) open space (*achadh*)'.

Liddesdale [Dumfries & Galloway/Borders] '[The River] Lyd's dale (OE)'. The river name (OE *hlyde*, from *hlud* 'loud', 'roaring') is no longer applied to the river in question, that river now being called Liddel Water (where 'Liddel' is itself a corruption of 'Lyd-dale').

Limekilns [Fife] Evidently there were limekilns (furnaces for making lime) here.

173

lin- elided form of 1) *linn(e)*: 'pool';
2) Brythonic Gaelic *llyn*: 'pool';
or 3) OE *lin*: 'flax', loaned in Gaelic as *lìon*.

Lincluden [Dumfries & Galloway] 'Pool (*linn*) on [the River] Cluden'. The meaning of the river name is unknown, although the name is evidently cognate with 'Clyde'.

Lindifferon [Fife] Apparently 'Pool (*llyn*, Brythonic Gaelic) valley (*dyffryn*, Brythonic Gaelic)'.

Lindores [Fife] Apparently 'Pool (*llyn*, Brythonic Gaelic) water (*dwr*, Brythonic Gaelic) + English plural '-s'.

Linlithgow [Lothian] Apparently 'Pool (*llyn*, Brythonic Gaelic) [in the] damp (*llaith*, Brythonic Gaelic) field (*cae*, Brythonic Gaelic)'.

Linmill [Central] 'Flax (*lin*, OE) mill (Eng)'.

linn (also *linne*; Welsh *llyn*) 'pool', 'lake', 'channel'.

Linn of Dee [Grampian] 'Pool (*linn*) on the [River] Dee': the river name represents the name of the ancient Celtic water-goddess; see **Dee**.

Linton [Strathclyde; Borders] 'Flax (*lin*, OE) town (*tun*, OE)'.

Linwood [Strathclyde] Hybrid name: 'Pool (*llyn*, Brythonic Gaelic) wood (Eng)'.

liobh 'smooth', 'slippery'.

lis- elided form of *lios*: 'court', 'enclosed area', thus 'garden'.

Lismore [Inner Hebrides] 'Court (*lios*), big (*mór*)': the 'big court' may well have been the large monastic community (including a cathedral) set up by St Maluag, or Moluag, in the latter half of the 6th century.

lith elided form of the Brythonic Gaelic *llaith*: 'damp', 'sodden', thus 'marshy'.

Littleferry [Highland] Presumably the place where there really was a little ferry – across the sea-mouth of Loch Fleet.

Littlemill [Highland] Presumably the place where there really was a little (water-)mill.

-livet elided form of *liobhaite*: 'of the slippery place'.

Livingston [Lothian] 'Leving's (personal name, OE) town (*tun*, OE)': the man Leving was apparently a fairly well-established landowner in his time.

174

loan Scots dialectal form of Eng *lane* – but the word can refer to virtually any collection of items in a line, such as houses or even hills.

loch 'lake': the word has cognates in most European languages, and in English is also connected with such words as *liquid, liquor,* etc. See also separate list of loch names beginning with this element.

Lochaber [Highland] Probably 'Loch (*loch*) marshes (*abor*)': the area contains many lochs.

Lochailort [Highland] The settlement is named after the sea-loch on which it stands; the name may mean 'Loch (*loch*), rock (*ail*) fjord (*-ort*, adapted form of ON *fjordr*)'. But see **Inverailort.**

Lochaline [Highland] The village is named after the loch on which it stands: the name means 'Loch (*loch*), green place (*ailean*)'.

lochan (diminutive of *loch*): 'a small loch'.

Lochan a' Chairn [Highland] 'Little loch (diminutive of *loch*) of the cairn (genitive of *carn*)'.

Lochan Dubh nan Geodh [Highland] 'Little loch (diminutive of *loch*), black (*dubh*), of the (*na*) ravine (*geodha*)'.

Lochan Fada [Highland] 'Little loch (diminutive of *loch*), long (*fada*)'.

Lochan Gaineamhach [Highland] 'Little loch (diminutive of *loch*), sandy (*gaineamhach*)'.

Lochan Thulachan [Highland] 'Little loch (diminutive of *loch*) [of] the little hillock (diminutive of *tulach*)'.

Locharbriggs [Dumfries & Galloway] Possibly 'Lockhart['s] (personal name, OScand) bridge (Scots)': see **Lockerbie.**

Lochawe [Strathclyde] The village is named after the loch on which it stands; the name may well mean 'Loch (*loch*) [of the] ford *ath[a]*'.

Lochboisdale [Skye] The village is named after the loch on which it stands; the name may mean 'Boia's dale'.

Lochbuie [Mull] The village is named after the loch on which it stands: the name means 'Loch (*loch*), yellow (*buidhe*)'.

Lochcarnan [Uist] The village is named after the loch on which it stands: the name probably means 'Loch (*loch*) of the little cairn (diminutive of *carn*)'.

Lochcarron [Highland] The village is named after the loch on which it stands: the name presumably means 'Of the cairn (genitive of *carn*)'.

175

Dictionary of Scottish Place Names

Lochdon [Mull] The village is named after the loch on which it stands: the name probably means 'Loch (*loch*), brown (*donn*)'.

Lochearnhead [Central] 'Lochearn['s] head (Eng)': for information on the derivation of 'Loch Earn', see **Earn** in the separate list of loch names.

Lochgair [Strathclyde] The village is named after the loch on which it stands: the name presumably means 'Loch (*loch*), short (*gearr*)'.

Lochgarthside [Highland] Presumably 'Loch (*loch*) cultivated enclosure (*garth*, Brythonic Gaelic) side (Eng)': the name of the loch on which it stands is (now) Loch Mhór.

Lochgelly [Fife] The town is named after the loch near which it stands: the name may mean 'White (*geal*)'.

Lochgilphead [Strathclyde] 'Loch Gilp['s] head (Eng)': for information on the possible derivation of 'Loch Gilp', see **Gilp** in the separate list of loch names.

Lochgoilhead [Strathclyde] 'Loch Goil['s] head (Eng)': for information on the possible derivation of 'Loch Goil', see **Goil** in the separate list of loch names.

Lochhill [Grampian] Presumably 'Loch (*loch*) hill (Eng)'.

Lochinvar [Dumfries & Galloway] 'Loch (*loch*) on the (*an*) summit (*bharr*)'.

Lochinver [Highland] 'Loch (*loch*) [at the] river-mouth (*inbhir*)': the port is at the mouth of the Abhainn na Clach Airigh.

Lochluichart [Highland] The village is named after the loch on which it stands: the name means 'Ship (*long*, a Gaelic misunderstanding of ON for 'ship') port (elided form of ME)'.

Lochmaddy [Uist] The port is named after the loch on which it stands: the name means 'Of the fox (*madaidh*)'.

Lochnagar [Grampian] 'Loch (*loch*) of the (*na*) rocky outcrop (*gaire*, probably akin to *garbh*)'. A surprising name for a mountain (3,791 feet/1,155 m).

Lochore [Fife] The town is named after the loch near which it stands: the name may mean 'Gold (*òr*)'.

Lochranza [Arran] The port is named after the loch on which it stands: the name may mean 'Ferny (*raineach*)'.

-lochry elided form of *cloichreach*: 'rocky', 'stony'.

176

Lochskipport [Uist] The port is named after the loch on which it stands: the name probably means 'Ship (*skip*, ON) port (elided form of ME)'.

Lockerbie [Dumfries & Galloway] Said to be 'Lockhart['s] (personal name, OScand) settlement (*by*, ODan; *byr*, ON)'. But Lockhart is by no means a well-attested name, so in view of the proximity of Middlebie (5 miles south-east), perhaps this is rather the 'lower' settlement – although against this it has to be said that Locharbriggs (possibly 'Lockhart's bridge') is only 9 miles west.

Logan [Strathclyde] 'Little hollow (*lagan*)': this is the derivation of the Scots/Irish surname as well.

Loggie [Highland] Possibly 'Hollow (*lagaidh*)'.

Logie [Tayside; Fife] 'Hollow (*lagaidh*)'.

Logie Pert [Tayside] 'Hollow (*lagaidh*) [with a] thicket (*pert*, Brythonic Gaelic)'.

Logierait [Tayside] 'Hollow (*lag*) of the (*an*) circular fort (*ràth*)'. This is an area of stone circles and ancient ruins.

loisgte genitive form of *losg*, thus 'of the burned ground'.

loisk elided form of *loisgte*: 'of the burned ground'.

lòn 'standing water', 'pool'; the word is presumably cognate with *linn(e)*.

lonaig elided form of *lonneach*: 'marshy'.

Lonbain [Highland] Probably 'Standing water (*lòn*), white (*bàn*)'. The tiny village is about 21 miles south-west of Lòndubh, q.v.

Lòndubh [Highland] 'Standing water (*lòn*), black (*dubh*)'. The tiny village is about 21 miles north-east of Lonbain, q.v.

Lonemore [Highland] Possibly 'Pool (*lòn*), big (*mór*)'.

Lomond [Central; Fife] Probably 'Beacon', from an old Brythonic Gaelic source (*laomuinn*).

long   either 1)   loaned form from ON or OE meaning 'long';
           2)   Gaelic misunderstanding of ON word, thus meaning 'ship';
    or 3)   very corrupt form of Brythonic Gaelic *lann*: 'church'.

Longformacus [Borders] Apparently 'Church (*lann*, Brythonic Gaelic) [of the] meadow (*fothir*, Brythonic Gaelic) of Maccus (personal name, an Irish-Scandinavian form of Magnus)'.

177

Longhope [Orkney] The village is named after the sea-loch on which it stands: the name means 'Long (ON) bay (*hóp*, ON)'.

Longniddry [Lothian] 'Church (*lann*, Brythonic Gaelic), new (*nuadh*, Brythonic Gaelic) community (*tref*, Brythonic Gaelic)'.

Longside [Grampian] Village named by its founder in 1801 because it is situated along the side of a hill.

Lòn Liath [Highland] 'Pool (*lòn*), grey (*liath*)': the place is a bay on the Arisaig peninsula.

Lonmore [Skye] 'Pool (*lòn*), big (*mór*)'.

lonneach 'marshy', 'wet', 'with pools of water': a derivative of *lòn*, q.v.

Lorn(e) [Strathclyde] Area named after Loarn, son of Erc, brother of Fe(a)rgus, one of the traditional co-leaders of the invasion from Ireland.

losg (also *loisgte*) 'burnt [ground]'.

losgann 'frog'.

Lossiemouth [Grampian] '[River] Lossie['s] mouth (Eng)': the river name means 'of herbs'.

Lothian [Lothian] Area named after a man who may have been its historical founder: Leudonus.

Louisburgh [Highland] District named in the later 1700s after one local landowner, Lady Louisa Dunbar.

Lowthertown [Dumfries & Galloway] Village named in around 1840 after its local landowners, the Lowther family.

luachair 'rushes'.

luachrach 'with rushes'.

luaidhe 'lead'.

luath 'fast' (modern Gaelic).

lùb 'curve', 'bend'.

Luce [Dumfries & Galloway] 'Herbs (*luss*)'.

lugha 'smaller' (modern Gaelic).

lui elided form of *laoigh*, genitive of *laogh*, thus 'of the calf'.

luig genitive of *lag*, thus 'of a hollow'.

lum- elided form of Brythonic Gaelic *lann*: 'church'.

Lumphanan [Grampian] 'Church (*lann*, Brythonic Gaelic) of [St] Finan (personal name)'. The most famous saint of this name was abbot of Iona in the mid-7th century, an associate of King Oswald of Northumbria, although a century earlier there had been another saint of this name in Aberdeen. The name means 'white(-haired)'.

Lumphinnans [Central] Presumably 'Church (*lann*, Brythonic Gaelic) of [St] Finan (personal name)'. The most famous saint of this name was abbot of Iona in the mid-7th century, an associate of King Oswald of Northumbria, although a century earlier there had been another saint of this name in Aberdeen. The name means 'white(-haired)'.

Luncarty [Tayside] Apparently 'Ship (*long*, from a Gaelic misunderstanding of the ON for 'ship') port (elided form of ME)'. Strange name for an inland village.

Lund [Shetland] 'Grove (*lund*, OScand)'.

Luss [Strathclyde] 'Herbs (*luss*)'.

lussa elided form of *luss achadh*, 'place of herbs'.

Lybster [Highland] 'Leeward (*hlee*, ON) settlement-steading (*bol-stathr*, ON)'.

lyne adapted form of *linn*: 'pool'.

Lynturk [Grampian] 'Pool (*linn*) of the boar (*tuirc*)'.

Lyth [Highland] Probably 'Slope (*hlith*, ON)': the village is at the high point (all of 175 feet/53 m) in an extremely low-lying flat area.

Lythes [Orkney] Probably 'Slopes (*hlith-s*, ON)': the village is near the highest point on South Ronaldsay.

Loch

Loch

The following are loch names that on the map are preceded by this word:

a' Bhaid-luachraich [Highland] 'of the copse (*bhaid*) with rushes (*luachraich*)'.

a' Bhealaich [Highland (3)] 'of the pass (*bhealaich*)': in the northernmost case, the pass would seem to have been on the path between Badanloch Lodge and Crask Inn; in the next south, between Shieldaig and Torridon; and in the southernmost, between Glen Elchaig and Glen Affric.

a' Bhealaich Bheithe [Highland] 'of the pass (*bhealaich*), birch (*bheithe*)'.

a' Bhràige [Rona] 'of the upper part (*bhràige*)'.

a' Bhurra [Jura] Possibly 'of the fortified premises (*burh*, OE)'.

a' Chàirn Bhàin [Highland] 'of the cairn (*chàrn*), white (*bhàin*)'.

Achanalt [Highland] 'of [the village of] Achanalt', q.v.

a' Chaorainn [Highland] 'of the rowan trees (*chaorainn*)'.

Achilty [Highland] 'At the high (*uchel* + locative; Brythonic Gaelic) [place]'.

Achnamoine [Highland] 'Place (*achadh*) of the (*na*) peat (*mòine*)'.

a' Chnuic Bhric [Jura] 'of the rounded hill (*chnuic*), speckled (*bhric*)'.

a' Choire [Highland] 'of the corrie (*choire*)'.

a' Choire Mhóir [Highland] 'of the corrie (*choire*), big (*mhóir*)'.

a' Chroisg [Highland] 'of the crossing (*chroisg*)', presumably between Achnasheen and Kinlochewe.

Affric [Highland] Presumably named after the river that flows into the loch: the river name seems to mean 'ford of the boar', although the second element might instead represent the name of a water-nymph.

a' Garbh-bhaid Mór [Highland] 'of the rough [water] (*garbh*), clump of trees (*bhaid*, genitive of *bad*), big (*mór*)'.

a' Gheòidh [Jura] 'of the chine (*gheòdha*, an adapted form of ON *gjá*)'.

a' Ghlinne [Lewis] 'of the glen (*ghlinne*, genitive of *gleann*)'.

a' Ghorm-choire [Highland] 'of the blue (*ghorm*) corrie (*choire*)'.

180

Ailsh [Highland] Possibly 'Of the fairy (*aillse*)'.

Airigh na Beinne [Highland] 'Shieling (*àirigh*) of the (*na*) mountain (*beinn*)'.

Airigh na h-Airde [Lewis] 'Shieling (*àirigh*) of the (*na*) height (*aird*)'.

Akran [Highland] Possibly 'Little open space (diminutive of *achadh*)' – but this demands a certain amount of ON corruption . . . It is in an ON area.

Aline [Highland] 'Green place (*ailean*)'.

A' Mhuilinn [Highland] 'Of the mill (*mhuilinn*)'.

an Alltan Fheàrna [Highland] 'of the little stream (diminutive of *allt*) of the alder tree (*fearna*)'.

an Daimh [Highland; Tayside] 'of the stag (*daimh*)'.

an Dùin [Highland/Tayside] 'of the mound (*dùin*)'.

an Easain Uaine [Highland] 'of the waterfalls (plural of *eas*), green (*uaine*)'.

an Eòin [Highland] 'of the birds (*eòin*, genitive plural of *eun*)'.

an Laoigh [Highland] 'of the calf (*laoigh*)'.

an Leathaid Bhuain [Highland] 'of the slope (*leathaid*) of [Beinn a'] Bhùtha'.

an Leothaid [Highland] 'of the slope (*leathaid*)': the loch lies beneath Quinag (2,654 feet/809 m).

an t-Seilich [Highland] 'of the willow (*seilich*)'.

Ard [Central] 'Height (*ard*)'.

Arichlinie [Highland] Possibly 'Shieling (*àirigh*) pool (*linne*)'.

a' Sguirr [Raasay] 'of the skerry (*sguirr*, genitive of *sgeir*)'.

Assynt [Highland] Name transferred from its surrounding area, and thought to derive from *as-agus-int*, 'outs and ins', referring to the local topography.

a' Tuath [Lewis] 'of the north (*tuath*)'.

Avon [Grampian] 'River (*abhainn*)': ironically, the loch is named after the River Avon.

Awe [Strathclyde; Highland] Possibly a corrupt form of *ath[a]*, 'ford' – indeed, in the Sutherland example the village of Ford (which would seem to derive its name from English) is at its southern end.

181

Bà [Highland; Mull] 'Of the cow (*bà*, genitive of *bó*)'.

Bad a' Chreamh [Highland] 'Tuft (*bad*) of wild garlic (*chreamh*)'.

Bad a' Ghaill [Highland] 'Place (*bad*) of the stranger (*ghaill*)': the third element can also mean 'Gael'.

Badanloch [Highland] Presumably 'Tuft (*bad*) of the loch'.

Baddagyle [Highland] See **Bad a' Ghaill**.

Ballygrant [Islay] Named after the nearby village of Ballygrant.

Bay [Skye] 'Bay (ME)'.

Beinn a' Mheadhoin [Highland] 'Mountain (*beinn*) in the middle (*mheadhoin*)'.

Bhac [Tayside] '[On the] Peat-bank (*bhac*, adaptation of ON *bakki*)'.

Bodavat [Lewis] Possibly 'Hut (*both*, ON) water (*vatn*, ON)': the tautologous 'Loch' was evidently added afterwards.

Boisdale [Skye] Probably 'Boia's (personal name) dale (ON)', although there is a slight difficulty in that Boia is predominantly an OE name.

Breac [Highland] Either 'Speckled' (*breac*) or 'Trout' (*breaca*)'.

Breachacha [Coll] Presumably 'Trout (*breaca*) place (*achadh*)'.

Breivat [Lewis] 'Broad (*breithr*, ON) water (*vatn*, ON)': the tautologous 'Loch' was evidently added afterwards.

Broom [Highland; Tayside] Probably either from OE *brom*, 'broom shrub' or from a cognate ON word meaning 'thorny shrub'.

Brora [Highland] 'of [the town of] Brora', q.v.

Bruicheach [Highland] Possibly 'On the edge (*bruaich*) of the field (*achadh*)': the loch is not far from bordering a large fertile area (Boblainy Forest).

Buidhe [Highland] 'Yellow (*buidhe*)'.

Buidhe Mór [Highland] 'Yellow (*buidhe*), big (*mór*)'.

Buie [Mull] 'Yellow (*buidhe*)'.

Cairnbawn [Highland] See **a' Chàirn Bhàin**.

Calder [Highland] Apparently 'Hard (*caled*, Brythonic Gaelic) water (*dobhar*, Brythonic Gaelic)'.

Cam [Islay] 'Winding *(cam)*'.

Cama [Highland] 'Winding *(cam)*'.

Caolisport [Strathclyde] 'Narrows *(caolas)* port *(port)*': Port Cill Maluag is at the outer end of the loch.

Carloway [Lewis] Probably Karli['s] (personal name, ON) bay *(vágr, ON)*': the tautologous 'Loch' was evidently added afterwards.

Carnan [Uist] Probably 'Little cairn (diminutive of *carn)*'.

Carron [Highland] Possibly 'Of the cairn *(cairn,* genitive of *carn)*'.

Chaolartan [Lewis] Possibly 'Narrows *(caol)* [of] the little fjord (diminutive of *-art,* an adaptation of ON *fjordr)*'.

Choire [Highland] 'Corrie *(choire)*'.

Chon [Central] 'Of the dogs *(con,* genitive plural of *cù)*'.

Claidh [Harris] Possibly 'Of the burial-ground *(claidh,* genitive of *cladh)*'.

Clàir [Highland (2)] 'Of the plank ferry-crossing *(clàir)*'.

Clash [Highland] Possibly 'Narrow valley *(clais)*'.

Cluanie [Highland] Possibly 'Pastures (derivative of *cluain)*'.

Coire na Saithe Duibhe [Highland] 'Corrie *(coire)* of the *(na)* bitch *(saidhe),* black *(duibhe)*'.

Coirigerod [Lewis] Possibly 'Corrie *(coire)* [of] the *(a')* strip of land between moor and plain *(gearraidh,* adaptation of ON *gerthi)*'.

Con [Tayside] 'Of the dogs *(con,* genitive plural of *cù)*'.

Coruisk [Skye] Either 'Crane *(corr)* water *(uisge)*' or 'Corrie *(coire)* water *(uisge)*'.

Coulin [Highland] Possibly 'Back *(cùl)* pool *(linn)*'.

Coulter [Central] Possibly 'Back *(cùl)* land *(tìr)*'.

Craggie [Highland (3)] 'Of the crag *(creige,* genitive of *creag)*': the northernmost loch is just below Cnoc Craggie.

Craiginish [Strathclyde] 'Crag *(creag)* [of the] water-meadow *(inis)*': the final element can also mean 'island'.

Cròcach [Highland (3)] 'Branched *(cròcach)*'.

Cuaich [Highland] 'Of the cup-shaped hollow *(cuaich)*'.

183

Dictionary of Scottish Place Names

Culag [Highland] Possibly 'Back (derivative of *cùl*)'.

Damh [Highland] 'Stag (*damh*)'.

Davan [Grampian] Possibly 'Little stag (diminutive of *damh*)'.

Dee [Dumfries & Galloway] Ancient river name that probably means 'goddess'.

Derry [Dumfries & Galloway] 'Grove of trees (*doire*)'.

Diabaigas Airde [Highland] 'Of [the village of] Diabaig's height (*aird*)': the loch overlooks the scenic cove in which the village of Lower Diabaig nestles.

Dochard [Strathclyde] Possibly 'Forbidding top', from ancient Gaelic roots that went also to make the surname Docherty.

Dochart [Central] Possibly 'Forbidding top', from ancient Gaelic roots that went also to make the surname Docherty.

Don [Mull] Probably 'Brown (*donn*)'.

Doon [Strathclyde/Dumfries & Galloway] Probably 'Of the castle (*dùin*)': there is a castle on the shore of the loch.

Droma [Highland] 'Of the ridge (*druima*)'.

Druidibeg [Uist] Possibly 'Thrush (*druid*), small (*beag*)'.

Dubh [Highland] 'Dark (*dubh*)'.

Dubh a' Chuail [Highland] Possibly 'Dark (*dubh*), of the recesses (plural of *cùil*)'.

Dughaill [Highland (2)] Presumably 'Of the dark[-haired] (*dubh*) stranger (*ghaill*)': thus a Dane or an Irishman rather than a fair-haired Norseman.

Duich [Highland] Possibly a hybrid name: 'Black (*dubh*) bay (corrupt form of ON *vík*)'.

Dungeon [Dumfries & Galloway] Probably 'Stronghold (*daingeann*)'.

Dunvegan [Skye] Named after the castle: possibly 'Stronghold (*din*, Brythonic Gaelic), small (*bychan*, Brythonic Gaelic)'.

Earn [Tayside/Central] Probably 'Water' from an ancient pre-Celtic source found in other river names (e.g. Findh-orn and Dev-eron); some commentators instead see 'Erin', a name for Ireland, as a possible derivation.

Eilde [Highland] Probably 'Of the hinds (plural of *eilid*)'.

184

Loch

Eileanach [Highland (2)] 'With islands (*eileanach*)'.

Eriboll [Highland] Named after the village of Eriboll, q.v.

Erisort [Lewis] Probably 'Eirikr's (personal name, ON) fjord (*-ort*, adaptation of ON *fjordr*)'.

Esk [Tayside] Probably 'Marsh (*easg*)', but it could be the ancient river name found elsewhere as Exe, Usk, Axe etc.

Ewe [Highland] The name has transferred to the sea-loch from what is now Loch Maree (the village at the head of which is still called Kinlochewe): a difficult name perhaps corresponding to a Brythonic Gaelic form meaning 'sheep' [cognate with Latin *ovis*, English *ewe*]; to an ON or OE form meaning 'yew'; or referring in some way to the nearby dominant Beinn Eighe.

Eye [Highland] Probably 'Island (*ey*, ON)'.

Fad [Bute] Presumably 'Long (*fada*)': it is the longest on the island.

Fada [Highland; Skye; Uist] 'Long (*fada*)'.

Féith an Leothaid [Highland] 'Bog (*féith*) of the slope (*leathaid*)': the loch lies beneath Beinn Gharbh (1,769 feet/539 m).

Finlaggan [Islay] Presumably 'White (*fionn*) little hollow (diminutive of *lag*)'.

Finlas [Strathclyde] Possibly 'Of the white (*fhionn*) stream (*ghlais*, Brythonic Gaelic)'.

Finsbay [Harris] Presumably 'Finn's (personal name) bay (*vágr*, ON)': Finn is a Celtic name meaning 'white(-haired)'.

Fleet [Highland] Possibly 'Of the fleet (ON or ME)'.

Flodabay [Harris] Probably 'Fleet (*flota*, ON) bay (*vágr*, ON)', although the first element might alternatively be 'Torrent (*floth*, ON)'.

Freuchie [Tayside] 'Heather (*fraoch*) place (*achadh*)'.

Frisa [Mull] Probably 'Of the bushes (*phrisa*)'.

Fuaran [Mull] 'The cold (*fuar*)'.

Fyne [Strathclyde] Probably 'Marshy', from the ON equivalent of OE *fynig*, 'marshy', 'mouldy'.

Gaineamhach [Highland (2); Strathclyde] 'Sandy (*gaineamhach*)'.

Gair [Strathclyde] Presumably 'Short (*gearr*)': a small, rounded inlet off Loch Fyne.

Gairloch [Highland] Possibly 'Short (*gearr*) loch': as sea-lochs go, it is a short loch – but the element can also mean 'hare'; the name is really that of the village on the shore.

Garbhaig [Highland] 'Rough [water] (*garbh*) bay (-*aig*, adaptation of ON *vágr*)'.

Garry [Highland; Tayside] 'Rough [water] (*garw*, Brythonic Gaelic, cognate with *garbh*)'.

Garten [Highland] Probably 'Tilled ground (*garth-en*, Brythonic Gaelic)': the loch was named after the River Garten.

Garve [Highland] 'Rough [water] (*garbh*)'.

Gelly [Fife] Possibly 'White (*geal*)'.

Gilp [Strathclyde] Possibly 'Chisel (*gilp* or *gilb*)'.

Glascarnoch [Highland] 'Blue-green (*glas*) rocky hills [cairns] (plural of *carn*)'.

Glass [Highland] 'Blue-green (*glas*)'.

Glencoul [Highland] Possibly 'Glen (*gleann*), back (*cùl*)'.

Glendhu [Highland] 'Glen (*gleann*), dark (*dubh*)'.

Goil [Strathclyde] Possibly 'Of the Lowlander (*goill*)', although the name might alternatively derive from the area name *Cowal*, itself a version of the ancient Scottish personal name, Comgall, who was the son of Fe(a)rgus, a pioneer Scottish invader from Ireland.

Gorm [Islay] 'Blue (*gorm*)'.

Gowan [Highland] Probably 'Of the blacksmith (*gobhainn*)'.

Gruinart [Islay] Presumably 'Green (*gröna*, ON) fjord (*fjordr*, ON)' as corrupted in Gaelic: the tautologous 'Loch' was evidently added afterwards.

Grunavat [Lewis] Presumably 'Green (*gröna*, ON) water (*vatn*)': the tautologous 'Loch' was evidently added afterwards.

Hoil [Tayside] Possibly 'Forest (*choille*)'.

Hope [Highland] 'Shelter (*hóp*, ON)'.

Hourn [Highland] Said by some to mean 'Of Hell' – but it lies exactly opposite the very ON Loch na Dal on Skye, and could therefore represent no more than the ON for 'horn'.

Inchard [Highland] 'Water-meadow (*inis*) fjord (*-ard*, adaptation of ON *fjordr*)'.

Insh [Highland] 'Water-meadow (*innis*)'.

Inshore [Highland] Probably 'Water-meadow (*innis*), gold (*òr*)'.

Invar [Dumfries & Galloway] '[On] The summit (*an bharr*)'.

Inver [Highland] 'River-mouth (*inbhir*)': the port lies at the end of the Abhainn na Clach Airigh.

Iubhair [Central] 'Of the yew tree (*iubhair*)'.

Kanaird [Highland] Probably 'Head (*ceann*) [of the] height (*aird*)', but the sea-loch is named after the River Kanaird that flows down Strath Kanaird.

Katrine [Central] 'Robbers (*ceathairne*, originally meaning 'band of peasants')'.

Ken [Dumfries & Galloway] Presumably 'Head (*ceann*)', although the artificial loch is really named after Kenmure Castle at its top end.

Kennard [Tayside] Presumably 'Head (*ceann*) [of the] height (*ard*)'.

Kildonan [Uist] '[of the] Church (*cill*) of [St] Donan (personal name)': Donan founded a monastery on Eigg in the early 7th century.

Killin [Highland] Possibly 'Church (*cill*) pool (*linn*)', but there is no church; the second element could instead be *fionn*, 'white'.

Kirkaig [Highland] 'Church (ON or OE) bay (*-aig*, corrupt form of ON or OE)'.

Knockie [Highland] 'Rounded hill (*cnoc*)'.

Laggan [Highland] 'Little hollow (diminutive of *lag*)'.

Langavat [Lewis (2)] 'Long (*langa*, ON) water (*vatn*, ON)': the tautologous 'Loch' was evidently added afterwards.

Laxavat Ard [Lewis] 'Salmon (*laxa*, ON) water (*vatn*, ON), height (*ard*)': the tautologous 'Loch' and the final word were evidently added afterwards.

Laxford [Highland] 'Salmon (*laxa*, ON) fjord (*fjordr*, ON)'.

Leacann [Strathclyde] 'Stony (*leacainn*)'.

Leathan [Skye] 'Broad (*leathann*)'.

Leathann an Sgorra [Islay] 'Broad (*leathann*), of the sharp peak (*sgorr*)'.

Lee [Tayside] Possibly 'Grey (*liath*)'.

Dictionary of Scottish Place Names

Leven [Highland; Tayside] Possibly 'Flooding' from a Brythonic Gaelic source.

Linnhe [Highland/Strathclyde] Presumably 'Pool (*linne*)'.

Loch [Tayside] 'Black (*loch*, proto-Gaelic)'.

Lochy [Highland] 'Black (*loch*, proto-Gaelic) goddess (*dheva*, proto-Gaelic)'.

Lomond [Central/Strathclyde] Apparently 'Beacon' from a Brythonic Gaelic source, and thus referring actually to Ben Lomond rather than the loch.

Long [Highland; Strathclyde] 'Ship (*long*, a Gaelic misunderstanding of ON for 'ship')'.

Loyne [Highland] Probably 'Of [the River] Loyne': the river name means 'of the marsh (*lòin*, genitive of *lòn*)'.

Lubnaig [Central] 'Sinuous (adjectival form from *lùb*)'.

Luichart [Highland] 'Ship (*long*, a Gaelic misunderstanding of ON for 'ship') port (elided form)'.

Lungard [Highland] 'Ship (*long*, a Gaelic misunderstanding of ON for 'ship') fjord (-*ard*, corrupt form of ON *fjordr*)'.

Lyon [Tayside] Possibly 'Flooding' from a Brythonic Gaelic source.

Maddy [Uist] 'Of the fox (*madaidh*)'.

Maree [Highland] '[Of St] Maelrubha (personal name)'. St Maelrubha, founder of a monastery at Applecross, built a church on an island in Loch Maree in the late 7th century – and thus caused the loch's name to change from Loch Ewe, q.v.

ma Stac [Highland] Apparently 'my (*ma*) stack [i.e. sharp peak]': the loch lies beneath Meall a' Chràthaich (2,226 feet/678 m).

Melfort [Strathclyde] 'Sandbank (*melr*, ON) fjord (*fjordr*, ON)'.

Merkland [Highland] 'Merk-land [i.e. land held in common by the villagers] (*marg-lann*)': the loch is thus named after adjacent territory.

Mhór [Highland] 'Big (*mhór*)'.

Moidart [Highland] 'Mud (*moda*, ON) fjord (*fjordr*, ON)'.

Morar [Highland] Possibly 'Big (*mór*) water (*dobhar*, Brythonic Gaelic)'.

188

More [Highland] 'Big (*mór*)'.

Morlich [Highland] 'Big (*mór*) hillock (*tulach*)'.

Mór na Caorach [Highland] 'Big (*mór*), of the (*na*) sheep (*caorach*)'.

Mór Sandavat [Lewis] 'Big (*mór*) sandy (*sanda*, ON) water (*vatn*, ON)': the tautologous 'Loch' and the following adjective were evidently added afterwards.

Moy [Highland] 'On the plain (*moigh*, dative/locative of *magh*)'.

Muck [Strathclyde] 'Of the pig (*muice*)'.

Muick [Grampian] 'Of the pig (*muice*)'.

na Beinne Baine [Highland] Presumably 'of the (*na*) mountains (plural of *beinn*), white (*bàine*)'.

na Cille [Strathclyde] Presumably 'of the [monk's] cells [or churches] (plural of *cill*)'.

na Claise Carnaich [Highland] 'of the (*na*) narrow valley (*clais*) with cairns (*carneach*)'.

na Claise Móire [Highland] 'of the (*na*) narrow valley (*clais*), big (*mór*)'.

na Craige [Tayside] 'of the (*na*) crag (*creige*, genitive of *creag*)'.

na Creige Dubhe [Highland] 'of the (*na*) crag (*creige*, genitive of *creag*), dark (*dubhe*)'.

na Dal [Skye] 'of the (*na*) dale (*dalr*, ON)'.

na Gainimh [Highland] 'of the (*na*) sand (*gainimh*)'.

na h-Achlaise [Highland] Probably 'of the (*na*) armpit (*h-achlais*)'.

na h-Oidhche [Highland] 'of the (*na*) night (*h-oidhche*)'.

na Keal [Mull] 'of the (*na*) [monks'] cells [or churches] (*ceall*, genitive plural of *cill*)'.

nam Bonnach [Highland] 'of the (*na-m*) end (*bonn*) field (*achadh*)': the loch borders a fertile area above the Beauly estuary.

nam Breac [Highland] 'of the (*na-m*) trout (*breaca*, plural)'.

nam Breac Dearga [Highland] 'of the (*na-m*) trout (*breaca*), red (*dearga*)'.

nan Ceall [Highland] 'of the (*na-n*) [monks'] cells [or churches] (*ceall*)'.

189

nan Clach [Highland (2)] 'of the (*na-n*) stone (*clach*)'.

nan Clàr [Highland] 'of the (*na-n*) plank ferry-crossing (*clàr*)'.

nan Eilean [Lewis] 'of the (*na-n*) island (*eilean*)'.

nan Eun [Highland (3); Tayside] 'of the (*na-n*) bird (*eun*)'.

Nant [Strathclyde] Possibly 'Stream (*nant*, Brythonic Gaelic)'.

nan Uamh [Highland] 'of the cave (*uamh*)'.

na Saobhaidhe [Highland] 'of the (*na*) fox earth (*saobhaidh*)'.

na Scaravat [Lewis] 'of the (*na*) skerry (*sker*, ON) water (*vatn*, ON)': the tautologous 'Loch na' was evidently added afterwards.

na Sealga [Highland] 'of the (*na*) hunt (*seilge*)': the loch is named after Strath na Sealga, to its south-east.

na Seilg [Highland] 'of the (*na*) hunt (*seilge*)'.

na Seilge [Highland] 'of the (*na*) hunt (*seilge*)'.

Ness [Highland] 'Roaring (Brythonic Gaelic)': it is evident that the loch is named after the River Ness.

Nevis [Highland] Possibly 'Cloudy and snowy': see **Nevis**.

Ochiltree [Dumfries & Galloway] 'High (*uchel*, Brythonic Gaelic) community (*tref*, Brythonic Gaelic)'.

Odhairn [Lewis] Possibly 'Little brownish (*odhair*), the ('*n*, ON)'.

of Mey [Highland] 'of sea-mew (*ma*, ON) island (*ey*, ON)'.

of Skene [Grampian] Skene is the name of the local area.

of Strathbeg [Grampian] 'of [the] valley (*srath*), small (*beag*)', but the loch is named after the valley.

of Toftingall [Highland] Presumably 'of [the] building-site (*topt*, ON) of the Gael', and presumably unusual in a predominantly ON area.

Ore [Fife] Possibly 'Gold (*òr*)'.

Poll [Highland] 'Pool (*poll*)': the element can also mean 'mud'.

Quoich [Highland] 'Of the cup-shaped hollow (*cuaich*)'.

Rannoch [Tayside] 'Ferny (*raineach*)'.

Ranza [Arran] Possibly 'Ferny (*raineach*)'.

190

Loch

Resort [Lewis] Perhaps 'Roe[deer]'s (*raa-s*, ON) fjord (*-ort*, corruption of ON *fjordr*)'.

Ruard [Highland] Probably 'Red-brown (*ruadh*) height (*ard*)'.

Ruthven [Highland] Presumably 'Red-brown (*ruadh*) mountain (*bheinn*)'.

Ryan [Dumfries & Galloway] This may – or may not – be the same name as Earn: an ancient river name meaning simply 'water' found also in the names Findh-orn and Dev-eron.

Scavaig [Skye] 'Claw (*ská*, ON) bay (*vágr*, ON)'.

Seaforth [Harris] 'Sea (*sjö*, ON) fjord (*fjordr*, ON)': the tautologous 'Loch' was evidently added afterwards.

Sealg [Lewis] Probably 'Shell (*skel*, ON)' although the word as it stands in Gaelic means 'hunt'; note, though, that 'shell' in Gaelic is *slige*.

Sgibacleit [Lewis] Possibly 'Ship (*skip*, ON) rock (*klettr*, ON)'.

Shandabhat [Lewis] Possibly 'Sand (*sanda*, ON) water (*vatn*, ON)': the tautologous 'Loch' was evidently added afterwards.

Shiel [Highland] 'Shepherd's hut (adaptation of *skáli*, 'shelter', ON)'.

Shieldaig [Highland] 'Of [the village of] Shieldaig', q.v.

Shin [Highland] Possibly 'of the storm (*sine*)'.

Skiach [Tayside] Probably 'Hawthorn (*sgitheach*)'.

Skipport [Uist] Possibly 'Ship (*skip*, ON) port (Eng)'.

Sletill [Highland] Possibly 'On the flatland (*slétta*, ON)'.

Sligachan [Skye] 'Shell (*slige*) place (*achadh*)'.

Snigisclett [Uist] Probably 'Snigill's (personal name, ON) rock (*klettr*)': the name is actually the word 'snail' used as a nickname.

Snizort [Skye] 'Sni's (personal name, ON) fjord (*-ort*, corrupt form of ON *fjordr*)': the name is likely to be a nickname.

Spey [Highland] 'Of [the River] Spey': the river name may mean something like 'spouting'.

Stack [Highland] 'Peak (*stac*)': the loch lies beneath Ben Stack (2,364 feet / 721m).

Stornoway [Strathclyde] 'Steerage (*stjorn*, ON) bay (*vágr*, ON)' – but it is surprisingly far south for an ON name, and may have been transferred.

191

Strandavat [Lewis] 'Beach (*strand*, ON) water (*vatn*)': the tautologous 'Loch' was evidently added afterwards.

Strathy [Highland] The name is back-formed from the village of Strathy, on Strathy Bay, inland of Strathy Point – the latter of which may have been the original holder of the name.

Suainavat [Lewis] Possibly 'Sven['s] (personal name, ON) water (*vatn*, ON)': the tautologous 'Loch' was evidently added afterwards.

Sunart [Highland] 'Sven['s] (personal name, ON) fjord (-*art*, adaptation of ON *fjordr*)'.

Sween [Strathclyde] Probably from an ON equivalent to the OE *swin*, 'creek', 'channel'; unlikely to be the personal name 'Sven'.

Tamanavay [Lewis] Possibly 'The ('*t*, ON) harbour (*hamn*, ON) bay (*vágr*, ON)'.

Tarbert [Strathclyde; Harris; Jura] 'Portage-crossing (*tairbeart*)'.

Tay [Tayside] Possibly 'Dark' from an ancient root corresponding to that of *Thames*: the loch is named after the River Tay.

Thom [Strathclyde] Named after Robert Thom, its construction engineer, in 1827.

Tollaidh [Highland] Possibly 'Of the hollows (derivative of *tuill*)'.

Torridon [Highland] Named after the village of Torridon (q.v.) at its end.

Tuath [Mull] 'North (*tuath*)'.

Tuim Ghlais [Highland] 'Of the mound (genitive of *tom*), blue-green (*glais*)'.

Tulla [Strathclyde] 'Mound (*tulach*)'.

Tungavat [Lewis] 'Tongue [of land] (*tunga*, ON) water (*vatn*, ON)': the tautologous 'Loch' was evidently added afterwards.

Uisg [Mull] 'Water (*uisge*)'.

Uisge [Highland] 'Water (*uisge*)'.

Uiskevagh [Uist] 'Water (*uisge*) bay (adaptation of ON *vágr*)'.

Ussie [Highland] Possibly 'Of the fir trees (*ghiuthsaich*)'.

Venachar [Central] Possibly 'Of the mountain (*bheinn*) fields (*achadh*)'.

Vrotachan [Grampian] Possibly 'Of the braes (*bhruthaichean*)'.

Watten [Highland] 'Water (*vatn*, ON)'.

Whinyeon [Dumfries & Galloway] Possibly 'Ash tree (*uinnseann*)'.

M

ma an occasional elided form of either 1) *magh* 'plain', or of its genitive *maighe*, thus 'of the plain'; or 2) *math* 'good'.

mac- 'son (of)'; the element occurs in a number of place names, especially in its mutated genitive form, *mhic*.

Macduff [Grampian] Town renamed by James Duff, Earl of Fife, in 1783, in commemoration of his father; the surname means 'son of Duff [the black (-haired one)]'. The original name of the place was Down (*dùn*, 'mound': ironically, the local viewpoint is now called the Hill of Down).

machair 'plain'.

macharach genitive form of *machair*, thus 'of the plain'.

Macharioch [Strathclyde] Possibly 'Plain (*machair*), brindled (*riabhach*)'.

machrach elided genitive form of *machair*, thus 'of the plain'.

Machrihanish [Strathclyde] Possibly 'Plain (*machair*) [of the] high (*há*, ON) ness (*nes*, ON)': if this is correct, the first element was evidently added later after the ON had become simply a name. One commentator alternatively suggests the somewhat unlikely 'Plain (*machair*) of the whisper (*a' sanais*)'.

madadh 'fox', 'dog', and even 'wolf'.

madaidh genitive form of *madadh*, thus 'of the fox', 'of the dog', 'of the wolf'.

-maddy anglicised version of *madaidh*: 'of the fox'.

magh 'plain', 'field': the word is evidently connected in some way with *machar*, q.v.

Magus Muir [Fife] Apparently 'Plain (*magh*) [with the] tongue of land (*gasg*), moor (ME)': the final element would have been added after the first two had become simply a name.

maighe irregular genitive form of *magh*, thus 'of the plain', 'of the field'.

maigheach 'hare'.

maighiche genitive form of *maigheach*, thus 'of the hare'.

193

Dictionary of Scottish Place Names

màim genitive form of *màm*, thus 'of the breast', 'of the rounded hill'.

Mainland [Shetland; Orkney] In each case the name of the major island of the group, the 'main land' whereas the others count as merely islands. The present-day English term derives from words meaning 'strong land' in either ON or OE.

mains 'manor farmhouse', 'laird's farmstead'; the word is cognate with the ME *demesne* and corresponds with the equally ME *toun*, 'farmstead' as used in place names referring to the houses of lesser folk – like Milton, Kirkton, Overton, Netherton, and so forth (q.v.).

Mains of Drum [Tayside] 'Manor farmhouse (*mains*, Scots) of (Eng) [the laird who lived at nearby] Drum [Castle]'. The name of the castle means 'ridge'.

mairig '[of the] boundary'; the word is evidently cognate with English *march*.

mal (also *mol, mul*) 'shingle beach'; the word derives from ON *möl*.

Mallaig[Highland] Possibly 'Shingle (*möl*, ON) bay (*-aig*, Goidelic adaptation of ON *vágr*)': the corruption of *möl* to *mal-* is attested in two place names in Yorkshire. Other commentators suggest 'Headland (*múli*, ON) bay (*-aig*, Goidelic adaptation of ON *vágr*)', although one would expect 'Mullaig' from those elements, and 'Speech (derivation not cited) bay (*-aig*, Goidelic adaptation of ON *vágr*)', which may or may not make sense.

-mally possible elided form of *maoile*, genitive of *maol*, thus 'of the bare summit'.

mam 'breast', and therefore 'rounded hill'; the word is evidently cognate with Latin *mamma*, English *mamma(ry)*.

Mambeg [Highland] 'Rounded hill (*mam*), small (*beag*)'.

Mam na Gualainn [Highland] 'Rounded hill (*mam*) of the (*na*) hill-shoulder (*gualainn*)'.

Mamore [Highland] 'Rounded hill (*mam*), big (*mór*)'.

Mam Ratagan [Highland] Apparently 'Rounded hill (*mam*) [of] Ratagan (personal name)'. The personal name can also be spelled Rattachan, which makes it look more like a surname than a forename, possibly meaning 'fields of the circular fort'.

Mam Sodhail [Highland] 'Rounded hill (*mam*) of the barn (genitive of *sodhal*, variant of *sobhal*)'.

194

M

manach 'monk'; the word derives ultimately from the ancient Greek *monachos*, 'recluse', 'hermit', thence Latin *monachus*, 'monk'.

mang 'faun'.

Mangersta [Lewis] Probably 'Trader's (*mangera*, OE [or the ON equivalent]) steading (*stathr*, ON)'; if this is correct, the first element is cognate with the present-day English *-monger*.

Mannofield [Grampian] Suburb named in around 1790 after the owner of the estate, one Robert Balmano.

maoile genitive form of *maol*, thus 'of the bare summit', 'of the bald top'.

maol 'bare summit', 'bald top'; the word is cognate with Welsh *moel*, but is probably also connected with Goidelic *meall*, 'lump', 'hill' which is akin to ON *fjall*, Eng *fell*. Some commentators also relate the word to ON *múli*, 'headland', 'promontory'.

Maol Breac [Strathclyde] 'Bare summit (*maol*), speckled (*breac*)'.

Maol Buidhe [Islay] 'Bare summit (*maol*), yellow (*buidhe*)'.

Maol Chean-dearg [Highland] 'Bare summit (*maol*) at the head (*cinn*) of [the Abhainn] Dearg': the river name means 'red'.

Maol nan Damh [Jura] 'Bare summit (*maol*) of the (*na-n*) stag (*damh*)'.

mara genitive form of *muir*, thus 'of the sea'.

marc 'horse'.

marconaich 'place of horses'.

marg 'merk-land'; merk-land is land held in common by a village and used only by communal consent.

Marg na Craige [Highland] Presumably 'Merk-land [i.e. land held in common by villagers] (*marg*) of the (*na*) crag (*creige*)'.

Margnaheglish [Arran] 'Merk-land [i.e. land held in common by villagers] (*marg*) of the (*na*) church (*h-eaglais*)'.

-maree elided form of the name [of St] Maelrubha; see **Loch Maree**.

Markinch [Fife] 'Horse (*marc*) water-meadow (*innis*)'.

Marvig [Lewis] Probably 'Sea (*marr*, ON) bay (*vík*, ON)'.

Marwick [Orkney] Probably 'Sea (*marr*, ON) bay (*vík*, ON)' because the bay above which the village stands is now called Mar Wick; the present form of the name nevertheless is more representative of 'Boundary (*maer*, OE) farm (*wic*, OE)' but again there is no apparent geographical logic for that.

Marybank [Highland] Village probably named at or around the same time as Maryburgh (q.v.), 4 miles north-east, and thus in commemoration of Queen Mary, daughter of James II, wife of William of Orange. The 'bank' is of the River Conon.

Maryburgh [Highland] Village named after Queen Mary (the Mary of William and Mary) in 1692. Her father, James II, had fled to France four years earlier, and was to die there nine years later.

Maryhill [Strathclyde] Suburb named in 1760 after the landowner who was actually called Mary Hill.

Marykirk [Grampian] Presumably '[St] Mary['s] (personal name, ME) church (Scots)'; Laurencekirk (q.v.) is only 4 miles north-east.

Maryport [Dumfries & Galloway] '[The Virgin] Mary['s] (*Maire*, personal name) harbour (*port*)'. A local chapel is dedicated to St Mary.

Marywell [Grampian; Tayside] Villages that had holy wells which were originally probably named after natural deities (see **Brideswell**) but which were overtaken by Christian religiosity and so renamed after the Virgin Mary.

màs 'buttock'.

math 'good' (modern Gaelic).

Mauchline [Strathclyde] 'Field (*magh*) of the pool (*linne*)'.

Maud [Grampian] Probably '[Place of] Foxes (plural of *madadh*)'. An interesting but far less likely alternative would be 'Coarse grey cloth (*maud*, Scots, from an earlier *maldy*)' if the town is where such cloth was made, or if somehow the surrounding countryside is visually reminiscent of it.

Mawcarse [Central] 'Plain (*magh*) [of] the carse [i.e. fertile land by a stretch of water] (Scots)'.

Maxwelltown [Dumfries & Galloway] Town renamed in 1810 in honour of the landowner, Marmaduke Maxwell; its name had previously been Bridgend.

may   either 1)   most often an elided form of *magh*: 'plain', 'field'.
        or 2)   rarely, in OE-influenced areas, either OE *maeddre*, 'madder(-plant)', OE *maegthe*, 'mayweed', or OE *maegth*, 'maidens'.

May, Isle of [Firth of Forth] Thought to be 'Sea-mew (*má*, ON) island (*ey*, ON)'.

Maybole [Strathclyde] Probably 'Plain (*magh*) of danger (*baoghail*)'.

meadhon 'middle'; the word is cognate with Eng *mid-*, Latin *medius* and many Germanic forms.

meadhonach 'in the middle', an extension of *meadhon*.

Mealfourvounie [Highland] Apparently 'Round hill (*meall*) [of the] cold (*fuar*) mountain-land (*mhonaidh*)'.

meall 'lump', 'round hill'; the word is cognate with ON *fjall*, Eng *fell* (cf the genitive mutated form *mhill*) and is probably also akin to *maol*, Welsh *moel*, 'bare summit'; cf also Eng *hill*, Latin *coll-*. See separate list of hill and mountain names beginning with this element.

meallan most commonly the plural or diminutive form of *meall*, thus 'round hills', 'fells', or 'little round hill', 'little fell'; but also alternatively an adaptation of *maol-an*, plural or diminutive form of *maol*, thus 'bare summits', 'bald tops', or 'little bare summit', 'little bald top'.

Meallan Buidhe [Highland (2)] '[The] Little round hill (*meallan*), yellow (*buidhe*)'.

Meallan Liath Coire Mhic Dhugaill [Highland] '[The] Little round hill (*meallan*), grey (*liath*), of Corrie MacDougal': the meaning of the final surname is 'son of the dark[-haired] foreigner'.

Meallan Liath Beag [Highland] '[The] Little round hill (*meallan*), grey (*liath*), small (*beag*)': this to contrast with Meallan Liath Mór some 15 miles west.

Meallan Liath Mór [Highland] '[The] Little round hill (*meallan*), grey (*liath*), big (*mór*)': this to contrast with Meallan Liath Beag some 15 miles east.

Mealna Letter [Tayside] 'Round hill (*meall*) of the (*na*) cliff (*leitire*)'.

meanach elided form of *meadhonach*: 'in the middle'.

meanbh 'small', 'thin'.

meann 'kid [i.e. young goat]'.

Mearns, The [Grampian] Name that was formerly an alternative to the county name Kincardineshire: 'The Stewardship (*an mhaoirne*)', an area administered by an officially appointed Steward.

Dictionary of Scottish Place Names

Meavig [Harris] Apparently 'Narrow (*mjór*, ON) bay (*vík*, ON)'.

Meigle [Tayside] Apparently 'Marsh (*mign*, Brythonic Gaelic) meadow (*dol*, Brythonic Gaelic)': it is appropriate that such a purportedly Brythonic name is attached to the place where Queen Guinevere is said to be buried, and that the village lies 2 miles north-east of another called Arthurstone.

meikle usually a Scots form of either OE *micel/mycel* or ON *mikill*, all meaning 'large', 'great(er)'

mèinn 'ore'; the word may be cognate with Eng *vein*, late Latin *vena*.

Meith Bheinn [Highland] Possibly 'Rich-soiled (*méith*) mountain (*bheinn*)'.

mel elided form of either   1) ON *melr*: 'sandbank', 'sand-dune';
                or   2) *maol*: 'bare summit', 'bald top'.

Melbost [Lewis] 'Sand-dune (*melr*, ON) settlement-steading (*bol-stathr*, ON)'.

Melby [Shetland] 'Sand-dune (*melr*, ON) community (*byr*, ON)'.

Melfort [Strathclyde] Probably 'Sandbank (*melr*, ON) fjord (*fjordr*, ON)': the village was thus named after the sea-loch on which it stands, a loch that is ironically now called Loch Melfort.

Melgarve [Highland] 'Bare summit (*maol*) [of] rough [water] (*garbh*)'.

Melldalloch [Strathclyde] Presumably 'Bare summit (*maol*) of the haugh [i.e. land in the bend of a river] (*dalach*, genitive of *dail*)'.

mellon corrupted form of either   1) *meallan*: plural or diminutive of *meall*: 'lump', 'round hill';
                             2) *maol-an*: plural or diminutive of *maol*: 'bare summit', 'bald top';
                or   3) *muileann*: 'mill'.

Melrose [Borders] 'Bare summit (*maol*) promontory (*ros*)'.

Melvaig [Highland] Presumably 'Sand-dune (*melr*, ON) bay (ON)'.

Melvich [Highland] 'Sandbank (*melr*, ON) bay (*vík*, ON)'; ironically, the bay on which the village stands is now called Melvich Bay.

Menstrie [Central] 'Plain (*maes*, Brythonic Gaelic) house (*tref*, Brythonic Gaelic)'.

meòir genitive form of *meur*, thus 'of the finger', 'of the branch', 'of the tributary', 'of the streamlet'.

198

M

Merkadale [Skye] Possibly 'Dark (*myrkr*, ON) dale (*dalr*, ON)', although the first element might instead be a personal name.

Merkland [Highland] 'Merk-land [i.e. land held in common by villagers] (*marg-lann*)'.

Methil [Fife] Apparently 'Boundary (*maid*, Brythonic Gaelic) wood (*choille*)'. But cf OScand *methal*, 'middle', and note that the town is directly between the other, partly older, urban areas of Buckhaven and Leven, and note also that Buckhaven has an apparently OScand name.

Methlick [Grampian] Possibly 'Boundary (*maid*, Brythonic Gaelic) slab of stone (*llech*, Brythonic Gaelic)'.

Methven [Tayside] Commentators have had various stabs at this one, both as a surname and as a place name. Least likely – but not impossible – is 'Mead [the drink] (*medd*, Brythonic Gaelic) stone (*vaen*, Brythonic Gaelic)', which may or may not make sense. Others have plumped for 'Plain (*magh*) of the river (*abhainn*)', which is at least Goidelic, or for 'Middle (*meadhon*)'. As a place name, therefore, its meaning remains unclear – although I would personally go for 'Boundary (*maid*, Brythonic Gaelic) stone (*vaen*, Brythonic Gaelic), which makes perfect sense and, as far as I know, has not been suggested to date despite the element quoted first under **Methil** and **Methlick** (see above). As a surname, and particularly in the variant form Methuen, it may well be Brythonic: *meddwyn* is 'drunkard' in Welsh (and is indeed related to *medd*, 'mead'; cognate is ancient Greek *methuein* 'to be tipsy').

meur 'finger', thus 'branch', 'tributary', and thus also 'streamlet'.

Mey [Highland] '[The] Plain (*magh*)'. The village has given its name to the Castle of Mey, the Loch of Mey and, on the coast, the Men of Mey.

mhachaire mutated genitive form of *machair*, thus 'of the plain'.

mhadaidh mutated genitive form of *madadh*, thus 'of the fox', 'of the dog', 'of the wolf'.

mhagh mutated form of *magh*: 'plain', 'field'.

mhaigh mutated variant genitive form of *magh*, thus 'of the plain', 'of the field'.

mhàim mutated genitive form of *màm*, thus 'of the breast', 'of the rounded hill'.

mhanaich mutated genitive form of *manach*, thus 'of the monk'.

199

mhaoile mutated genitive form of *maol*, thus 'of the bare summit', 'of the bald top'.

mhaoirne mutated form of what is now spelled Mearns: 'stewardship'.

mhara mutated genitive form of *muir*, thus 'of the sea'.

mharconaich mutated form of *marconaich:* 'place of horses'.

mhath mutated form of *math:* 'good' (modern Gaelic).

mheadhoin mutated genitive form of *meadhon*, thus 'of the middle'.

mheadhonach mutated form of *meadhonach:* 'in the middle'.

mheòir mutated genitive form of *meur*, thus 'of the finger', 'of the branch', 'of the tributary', 'of the streamlet'.

mhic mutated genitive form of *mac*, thus 'of the son [of]'.

mhill mutated genitive form of *meall*, thus 'of the lump', 'of the rounded hill', 'of the fell'.

mhinn mutated genitive form of *meann*, thus 'of the kid [i.e. young goat]'.

mhòid mutated genitive form of *mòd*, thus 'of the council', 'of the court', 'of the trial', 'of the assembly'.

mhòine mutated form of *mòine*, thus 'mossy ground', 'peat-bed'.

mhòir mutated masculine genitive form of *mòr*, thus 'of the big . . . '.

mholach mutated derivative of *mol*, 'mass', thus 'massive'.

mhonadh mutated form of *monadh:* 'mountain-land', 'hill', 'moorland'.

mhór mutated feminine form of *mór:* 'big'.

mhuice mutated genitive form of *muc*, thus 'of the pig'.

mhuilinn mutated genitive form of *muileann*, thus 'of the mill'.

mhuilt mutated genitive form of *molt/mult*, thus 'of the wether'.

mhullaich mutated genitive form of *mullach*, thus 'of the top', 'of the summit'.

mhurain mutated genitive form of *muran*, thus 'of the marsh-grass', 'of the sea-bent'.

Midbea [Orkney] Probably 'Middle (*meth-*, OScand) community (*by*, OScand)'.

200

Middlebie [Dumfries & Galloway] 'Middle (*methal*, OScand) community (*by*, OScand)'; it is tempting to relate this name to that of Lockerbie, some 5 miles north-west, and to suggest that that may be the 'lower' settlement as this is the middle one. But see **Lockerbie**.

Middleton [Strathclyde; Lothian] 'Middle (ME) town (*toun*, ME)'.

Mid Yell [Shetland] '[Village at the] Mid[dle of the island of] Yell': the island name means 'barren' (ON).

mig 'bog'.

Milesmark [Fife] Presumably 'Miles (Eng) mark [in the form of a stone or post] (Eng)', and equally presumably the mark showed 2 miles to Dunfermline.

mill   either   1)   English 'mill';
　　　　　 or   2)   genitive form of *meall*, thus 'of the lump', 'of the round hill', 'of the fell'.

Mill Buie [Grampian] 'Round hill (*meall*), yellow (*buidhe*)'.

Millburn [Strathclyde] Presumably 'Mill (ME) stream (*burn*, ME)'

Millheugh [Strathclyde] Presumably 'Mill (ME) corner (*heuch*, ME)'.

Milliken Park [Strathclyde] Village established in the 1850s and named after a landowner of the previous century, Major Milliken.

Millport [Great Cumbrae] Town established in the very early 1800s, when the harbour was built, and so called after the grain mill that used to stand above the harbour.

Millton [Grampian (2)] Unusual spelling of 'Mill (ME) farm (*toun*, ME)'; see also **Milton**.

Milltown [Grampian (5); Tayside; Dumfries & Galloway] Less common spelling of 'Mill (ME) farm (*toun*, ME)'; see also **Milton**.

Milngavie [Strathclyde] 'Mill (*muileann*) of the wind (*gaoithe*)', whereas most mills were water-driven. The second element can, however, alternatively mean 'of the marsh'. The only excuse for the spelling -gavie, incidentally, is that it is actually pronounced like the forename Guy and not phonetically.

Milton [Highland (6); Grampian (7); Central (2); Fife; Strathclyde (2); Dumfries & Galloway (2)] This is one of the examples of ME names that entered Scotland towards the end of feudal times, when the laird lived in the Mains (the demesne) or the hall farm (Halton or Hatton) and lesser beings

201

lived on farmsteads above (Overton), below (Netherton), by the church (Kirkton), or indeed by the mill (Milton).

mìn 'smooth'. The Irish equivalent is *mín*, and means also 'fine', 'delicate'.

Minard [Strathclyde] Probably 'Smooth (*mìn*) promontory (*ard*)': Minard Castle stands on a headland overlooking Minard Bay. Minard Point, 24 miles north-west, has had the extraneous element 'Point' added later.

Mintlaw [Grampian] Presumably 'Mint (*minte*, OE) mound (*hlaw*, OE)'.

Minto [Borders] Apparently a hybrid name: 'Mountain-land (*monadh*) haugh [i.e. an angle of land within the bend of a river] (*heuch*, ME)'. Ironically, after the village of Minto was so named, the uplands behind the village had to be renamed the Minto Hills.

mire adaptation of ON *myrr*: 'mire', 'swamp', 'bog'. The English word *mire* equally derives from the ON.

Mireland [Highland] 'Swamp (*myrr*, ON) land (ON)': the village is in a particularly low-lying fertile area in the valley of the Burn of Lyth.

mnà genitive form of *bean*, thus 'of the woman', 'of the wife'.

mnathan plural form of *bean*, thus 'women', 'wives'.

mòd 'council', 'court', 'trial', assembly'. The word is an adaptation of the ON *mót*, 'annual parish/county assembly' at which local legal decisions were made, young people were affianced, blood money was assessed and paid, and a good time was had by all. The English cognate is *meet[ing]*. The extended form of the ON word, *stad-mod*, 'meeting of state' (cf the parliamentary 'states' of the Isle of Man today), in Welsh became *eistedd-fod*.

Moffat [Dumfries & Galloway] 'Plain (*magh*), long (*fada*)': the 'long plain' is that of Annandale, also followed by a Roman road.

mòid genitive form of *mòd,* thus 'of thé council', 'of the court', 'of the trial', 'of the assembly'.

moid- adaptation of ON *moda*: 'mud[dy]'.

Moidart [Highland] 'Mud (*moda*, ON) fjord (-*art*, Gaelic adaptation of *fjordr*, ON)'.

moigh dative/locative form of *magh*, thus 'on the plain', 'in the field'.

moighe genitive form of *magh*, thus 'of the plain', 'of the field'.

202

M

mòine 'peat', 'peat-bed'.

mòinteach 'peat-bed', 'mossy ground', 'moorland'.

moire variant form of the name 'Mary'.

móire feminine genitive form of *mór*, thus 'of the big . . . '.

mol either 1) (also *mal, mul*) 'shingle beach', 'pebbly surface'. The
word derives from ON *möl*;
or 2) 'mass', 'lump'.

Mol-chlach [Soay] Probably 'Shingle beach (*mol*) stone (*chlach*)'. A large
rock on a shingle beach would stand out.

molt (also *mult*) 'wether'.

mon- elided form of either 1) *moine:* 'peat', 'peat-bed';
or 2) *monadh:* 'mountain-land', 'moorland'.

mòna genitive form of *mòine*, thus 'of peat', 'of the peat-bed'.

mònach variant genitive form of *mòine*, thus 'of peat', 'of the peat-bed'.

monadh (Welsh *mynydd*; Latin *mont-*; English *mount*) 'mountain',
'mountain-land', 'range of hills', 'moorland'.

Monadhliath Mountains [Highland] 'Mountain-land (*monadh*), grey
(*liath*), mountains (Eng)': the final element was evidently added much later
when the first two elements had become simply a name. The name
distinguishes the range from the Monadhruadh range (q.v.).

Monadh Mór [Highland/Grampian] 'Mountain (*monadh*), big (*mór*)'– and
it is, at 3,651 feet (1,112 m).

Monadhruadh Mountains [Grampian] 'Mountain-land (*monadh*), red
(*ruadh*), mountains (Eng)': the final element was evidently added much later
when the first two elements had become simply a name. The name
distinguishes the range from the Monadhliath range (q.v.).

Monamenach [Tayside] Probably 'Mountain (*monadh*) of the monk
(*manaich*)'.

Monawee [Tayside] Possibly 'Mountain (*monadh*), yellow (*bhuidhe*)'.

Monboddo [Grampian] Possibly 'Mountain (*monadh*), ghostly (derivative
of *bodach*, 'ghost', 'old man')'.

Moncrieff [Tayside] 'Mountain (*monadh*) of the tree (*craoibhe*)'.

Mondynes [Grampian] Apparently 'Moorland (*monadh*) slope (*eadain*)': the final -s would appear to be extraneous, perhaps because the place was once called Mondynes Bridge [over the Bervie Water], in which case 'Mondynes' might be a genitive form (Mondyne's).

Mongour [Grampian] Possibly 'Mountain (*monadh*) of the goat (*gobhair*)': the 1,232 foot (375 m) hillside has a TV booster on it.

Moniaive [Dumfries & Galloway] Possibly 'Mountain-land (*monadh*) with a path (*fhiaimh*, genitive form of *fiamh*)', although other commentators – very unconvincingly – suggest the meaning 'Peat-bed (*mòine*), peaceful (*suaimhneach*)', when the topography of the place is rather against it, and s- is generally pronounced in Goidelic. If a real alternative first element is demanded, how about *muine*, 'thicket'?

Monifieth [Tayside] 'Peat-bed (*mòine*) of the bog (*féithe*)'.

Monimail [Fife] Apparently 'Peat-bed (*mòine*) of the rounded hill (*mill*, genitive of *meall*)'.

Monkton [Strathclyde] 'Monk[s'] (ME) town (*toun*, ME)'.

Montgarrie [Grampian] Possibly 'Mountain-land (*monadh*) garden (*garradh*)'.

Montgreenan [Strathclyde] Probably 'Moorland (*monadh*) sunny hillock (*grianan*)'.

Montrose [Tayside] Probably 'Peat-bed (*mòine*) promontory (*ros*)', although until the 1970s the first element was said categorically to derive from *monadh*, 'mountain-land', 'moorland'. Early forms of the name, however, do not have the -t- .

Monymusk [Grampian] 'Peat-bed (*mòine*), muddy (*musgach*)'.

Mool [Shetland] 'Headland (*múli*, ON)'.

mór (Welsh *mawr*) 'big'; the word is evidently cognate with a whole host of Indo-European words all dealing with size and consequence.

mor   either   1) 'moor', 'fen' (OE);
          or   2) 'the sea' (proto-Goidelic).

móra plural form of *mór*: 'big [plural]'.

Morangie [Highland] Apparently '[At the] big (*mór*) water-meadow (*innse*, locative/dative of *innis*)'.

Morar [Highland] Possibly 'Big (*mór*) water (*dhobhar*, Goidelic loan-word from Brythonic Gaelic)'.

204

Moray [Highland/Grampian] 'Sea settlement (*mori*, proto-Goidelic)'.

more anglicised version of *mór*: 'big'.

Morebattle [Borders] Possibly 'Moor (*mor*, OE) house (*botl*, OE)'.

Morlich [Highland] 'Big (*mór*) hillock (*tulach*)'.

Morphie [Grampian] Apparently 'Seashore (*morfa*, Brythonic Gaelic)'.

Morsham [Borders] 'Moor's (OE) community (*ham*, OE)'.

Moruisk [Highland] Possibly '[The] Big (*mór*) water (*uisge*)', although it is the name of a mountain of 3,026 feet (922 m): with the name cf **Morar**.

Morven [Highland; Grampian] 'Big (*mór*) mountain (*bheinn*)' – and it is, at 2,861 feet (872 m).

Morvern [Strathclyde] '[The] Sea (*mor*, proto-Goidelic) gap (*bhearn*)': at least one commentator believes this a reference to the sea-loch Loch Sunart. But an alternative spelling is Morven, which suggests '[The] Big (*mór*) mountain (*bheinn*)' – although it must be said that this is hardly topographically accurate.

-mory elided form of *moire* or *muire*: 'of Mary'.

moss 'moss', 'peaty moorland' (Scots, from OE/ME).

Moss [Tiree] 'Moss [i.e. peaty moorland] (OE)'.

Mossburnford [Borders] 'Moss [i.e. peaty moorland] (OE) stream (*burna*, OE) ford (Eng)': the ford is through the Jed Water.

Mossdale [Dumfries & Galloway] Presumably 'Moss [i.e. peaty moorland] (ME) dale (ME)': the village overlooks the vale of the Black Water of Dee.

Mossend [Strathclyde] Presumably 'Moss [i.e. peaty moorland] (ME) end (ME)'.

motha 'bigger' (modern Gaelic).

Motherwell [Strathclyde] Apparently 'Mother['s] well (Eng)', in reference to the Virgin Mary – an example of a holy well presumably first named after a natural deity, then dedicated to St Mary, then when that seemed somewhat pagan, to 'the Mother'.

Moulin [Tayside] Apparently '[The] Small bare summit (diminutive of *maol*)', although one's immediate thought is toward *muileann*, '[the] mill'.

Mounth, the [Grampian/Highland/Tayside] 'Mountain-land (*monadh*)': this is an area name for the eastern Grampian Mountain range.

205

Mount Vernon [Strathclyde] Suburb named in around 1787 by a wealthy trader with the American colonies after George Washington's estate in Fairfax County, Virginia, which in turn had been named in 1740 by George's elder half-brother and guardian Lawrence after Admiral Edward Vernon under whom Lawrence had served.

Moy [Highland] 'On the plain (*moigh*, locative/dative of *magh*)'.

Moyness [Grampian] 'On the plain (*moigh*, locative/dative of *magh*), [the] water-meadow (*innis*)'.

mu 'around'.

muc 'pig'.

Muck [Inner Hebrides] 'Pig (*muc*) [island]', presumably because pigs were kept there rather than because of any topographical feature.

muckle Scots adaptation of either OE *mycel*, *micel* or ON *mikill*, all meaning 'large', 'great'.

Muckle Burn [Central/Tayside] 'Large (*mycel*, OE) stream (*burna*, OE)'.

Muckle Flugga [Shetland] 'Large (*mikill*, ON) cliffs (*flugga*, ON)'.

muice genitive form of *muc*, thus 'of the pig'.

Muick [Grampian] River name meaning 'of the pig (*muice*)'. The river flows from Loch Muick through Glen Muick to the Dee at Ballater.

Muie [Highland] 'On the plain (*moigh*, dative/locative of *magh*)'.

muighe variant genitive form of *magh*, thus 'of the plain', 'of the field'.

muileann (Welsh *melin*) 'mill'; the word has many cognates in European languages, most of them deriving from Latin *molina*, 'mill', itself a derivative of *mola*, 'millstone', 'grinder'.

muilinn genitive form of *muileann*, thus 'of the mill'.

muilne variant genitive form of *muileann*, thus 'of the mill'.

muilt genitive form of *mult* or *molt*, thus 'of the wether'.

muine 'thicket'.

muir either 1) 'moor': Scots version of the (ME) word;
2) 'the sea', present-day form of proto-Goidelic *mor(i)*;
or 3) 'big', corruption of *mór*.

M

Muir [Highland] Probably 'Moor (Scots)'.

Muirdrum [Tayside] Probably 'Moor (Scots) ridge (*druim*)', with the first element probably also referring to nearby Salmond's Muir. Both places are, however, within a couple of miles of the sea (*muir*).

Muirhead [Tayside; Strathclyde] Presumably 'Moor (Scots) head (Eng)'.

Muirhouses [Lothian] Presumably 'Moor (Scots) houses (Eng)' although the community is within a mile of the sea (*muir*).

Muirkirk [Strathclyde] 'Moor (Scots) church (*kirk*, Scots)'.

Muir of Ord [Highland] 'Moor (Scots) of (Eng) the rounded hill (*ord*)'.

Muirton [Highland; Tayside] Presumably 'Moor (Scots) town (*toun*, ME)'.

mul (also *mal, mol*) adaptation of ON *möl*: 'shingle beach', 'pebbly place'.

mull   adapted form of either   1) *múli* (ON): 'headland';

                                  2) *maol*: 'bare summit', 'bald top';

           or   3) *mul* (ON): 'shingle beach', 'pebbly place'.

Mull [Inner Hebrides] Probably 'Headland (*múli*, ON)'. Other commentators have plumped alternatively for 'Bare summit (*maol*)', in comparison with which 'Shingle beach (*mul*)' seems to me just as possible.

mullach 'summit', 'top'; the word is said to be an elided combination of *maol* 'bare summit' and *achadh* 'place'.

Mullach Clach a' Bhlàir [Highland] 'Summit (*mullach*), stony (*clach*), of the level clearing (genitive of *blàr*)'.

Mullach Fraoch-choire [Highland] 'Summit (*mullach*) [of] heather (*fraoch*) corrie (*choire*)'.

Mullach na Carn [Scalpay] 'Summit (*mullach*) of the (*na*) cairn (*carn*)', although the final element can also mean 'humped hill'.

Mullach nan Coirean [Highland] 'Summit (*mullach*) of the (*na-n*) little corrie (*coirean*)'.

Mullach na Reidheachd [Harris] Possibly 'Summit (*mullach*) of the (*na*) level (*réidhe*) place (*achadh*)'.

Mull of Kintyre [Strathclyde] 'Headland (*múli*, ON) of (Eng) [the area known as] Kintyre'. Ironically, Kintyre is *ceann-tìr:* 'head-land'.

mult (also *molt*) 'wether'.

múr 'wall', 'fortification'. The word is evidently cognate with – and may even derive from – Latin *murus*, 'wall'.

muran 'marsh-grass', 'sea-bent'.

-murchan possibly 'sea-otter (*muir-chu*, literally 'sea-dog')', but more probably 'sea-villainy [i.e. piracy] (*muir-chol*)'.

Murkle [Highland] Apparently 'Murky (*myrkr*, ON)'.

Murrayfield [Lothian] Suburb named after an early 18th-century landowner, one Archibald Murray.

-murrin elided form of *murain*, genitive of *muran*, thus 'of the marsh-grass'.

musgach 'muddy'.

-musk elided form of *musgach*: 'muddy'.

Musselburgh [Lothian] 'Mussel (*musle*, OE) town (*burh*, OE)'. Mussels are still gathered in the estuary of the River Esk.

Muthill [Tayside] Possibly 'Meeting (*[ge]mot*, OE) hill (*hyll*, OE)', where local assemblies convened; a number of roads also converge here.

Meall

The following are hill and mountain names that on the map are preceded by this word:

a' Bhata [Highland] 'of the boat (genitive of *bàta*)'.

a' Bhuachaille [Highland] 'of the shepherd (*bhuachaille*)'.

a' Chaorainn [Highland] 'of the rowan tree (genitive of *caorann*)'.

a' Choire Bhuidhe [Tayside] 'of the corrie (*choire*), yellow (*bhuidhe*)'.

a' Chrasgaidh [Highland] Possibly 'of the crossings (derivative of *crasg*)'.

a' Churain [Central] Possibly 'of the foam (genitive of *cúrán*)'.

a' Ghrianain [Highland] 'of the sunny hillock (genitive of *grianan*)'.

a' Mhadaidh [Central] 'of the fox (genitive of *madadh*)'.

a' Mhuic [Tayside] 'of the pig (*mhuice*, genitive of *muc*)'.

an Aonaich [Highland] 'of the moor (genitive of *aonach*)'.

an Damhain [Highland] Presumably 'of the stags (genitive plural of *damh*)'.

an Doirein [Highland] Possibly 'of the groves (derivative of *doire*)'.

an Fhuarain [Skye; Highland (2)] 'of the well (genitive of *fuaran*)'.

an Inbhire [Mull] 'of the river-mouth (genitive of *inbhir*)'.

an t-Sithe [Highland] 'of the fairy hill (*sith*)'.

an Tuirc [Highland] 'of the boar (genitive of *torc*)'.

a' Phiobaire [Highland] 'of the piper (genitive of *piobair*)'.

a' Phubuill [Highland] Possibly 'of the tents (genitive of *puball*, variant of *pebyll*)'.

Blàir [Highland] 'Of the plain (genitive of *blàr*)'.

Buidhe [Highland] 'Yellow (*buidhe*)': ironically, this mountain is some 3 miles north-east of Beinn Buidhe – which is 300 ft (90 m) shorter.

Buidhe [Tayside (2)] 'Yellow (*buidhe*)': the two mountains are within 5 miles of each other.

Cala [Central] Apparently 'Harbour (*cala*)', although there is no harbour for miles round; could it be an error for *call*, 'hazel tree'?

Cruinn [Tayside] 'Round (*cruinn*)'.

Dearg [Tayside] 'Red (*dearg*)'.

Dheirgidh [Highland] Possibly 'Reddish (derivative of *dearg*)'.

Dubh [Highland (2); Strathclyde] 'Black (*dubh*)'.

Fuar-mhonaidh [Highland] '[of the] Cold (*fuar*) mountain-land (*mhonaidh*)'.

Gainmheich [Central] Possibly 'Sandy (*gaineamhaich*)'.

Garbh [Tayside; Strathclyde] '[of] Rough [water] (*garbh*)'.

Ghaordaigh [Tayside/Central] Possibly 'Of the woods (*ghaorthaidh*)'.

Ghiubhais [Highland] 'Of the fir tree (genitive of *giubhas*)'.

Gorm [Highland (2); Grampian] 'Blue (*gorm*)'.

Leacachain [Highland] Possibly 'Flat stone (*leac*) places (derivative of *achadh*).

Liath Choire [Highland] '[of the] Grey (*liath*) corrie (*choire*)'.

Luaidhe [Tayside] '[of] Lead (*luaidhe*)'.

Meadhonach [Highland] 'In the middle (*meadhonach*)'.

Mhic Iomhair [Highland] 'of MacIvor' (literally: of the Son of Iomhar).

Mór [Western Isles; Highland (3)] 'Big (*mór*)'.

Moraig [Highland] 'Of Morag (Goidelic equivalent of Sarah)': this mountain is 2 miles south-west of Beinn Domhnaill ('Mountain of Donald').

na Caorach [Highland] 'of the (*na*) sheep (*caorach*)'.

na Drochaide [Highland] 'of the (*na*) bridge (genitive of *drochaid*)'.

na h-Aisre [Highland] 'of the (*na*) pass between rocks (*aisridh*)'.

na h-Eilrig [Highland] Possibly 'of the (*na*) deer-trap (genitive of *eileirg*)'.

na h-Uamha [Highland] 'of the (*na*) cave (genitive of *uamh*)'.

na Leitreach [Tayside] 'of the (*na*) steep hillside (*leitreach*, variant genitive form of *leitir*)'.

na Mèine [Highland] Presumably 'of the (*na*) ore (*mèinne*)'.

nam Fuaran [Tayside] 'of the (*na-m*) well (*fuaran*)'.

nan Caorach [Highland; Tayside] 'of the (*na-n*) sheep (*caorach*)'.

nan Con [Highland (2)] 'of the (*na-n*) dogs (genitive plural of *cù*)'.

Meall

nan Each [Highland] 'of the (*na-n*) horse (*each*)'.

nan Tarmachan [Tayside] 'of the (*na-n*) ptarmigan (*tarmachan*)'.

na Speireig [Highland] 'of the (*na*) sparrowhawk (genitive of *speireag*)'.

Odhar [Strathclyde; Central/Tayside] 'Dun-coloured (*odhar*)'.

Reamhar [Tayside (3)] 'Wide (*reamhar*)'.

Tarsuinn [Tayside] 'Lying crosswise (*tarsuinn*)'.

Uaine [Tayside] 'Green (*uaine*)'.

N

na 'of the', 'the'.

Nairn [Highland] The town is named after the river on which it stands, and the precise meaning of the ancient pre-Celtic river name is suspected to be 'penetrating' or 'submerging'.

namh 'holy one', 'saint'.

naoimh genitive plural form of *namh*, thus 'of the saints'.

nathair 'adder', 'snake': the word is cognate with the Latin *natrix*, 'adder', from which by elision the English *adder* is also derived ('a nadder' became 'an adder').

nathraichean genitive plural form of *nathair*, thus 'of adders'.

Navity [Highland; Fife] 'Holy place (from the ancient word *neimhidh*, related also to *namh* 'holy one')'.

nead 'nest': the word is cognate with the Latin *nidus*.

Neap [Shetland] 'Steep hill (*gnípr*, ON)'.

Neblonga [Orkney] Probably '[The] Bill (*nef*, ON), long (*longa*, ON)'.

Nedd [Highland] The village is possibly named after the stream on which it stands, or equally possibly after the loch on whose shore it is sited; this is because the name may represent an old Brythonic water name (found as Nedd and Neath in Wales, Nidd in England) meaning something like 'glistening'.

ness 'cape', 'promontory', 'point'; this element in Scottish place names most commonly derives either directly from ON *nes* or as a Gaelic adaptation from the ON; however, the OE equivalent was *naes* and is occasionally also attested in Scotland. All these are cognate with English *naze* and *nose*.

Ness [Highland] The loch is named after the river that flows from it to Inverness, as is attested by the river name's ultimate meaning, 'roaring' or 'rushing'. The name is ancient, pre-Gaelic; an earlier form is *nesta*, which makes it quite clear that it has nothing to do with most other *ness* elements in Scotland. Nevertheless, alternative fanciful derivations for the name abound. One nice story is that the name commemorates the hero Naoise, who eloped with Princess Deirdre-of-the-Sorrows, daughter of Conchobar, King of Ulster. However, it seems that variants on the name were fairly

212

common in those legendary days, for even Conchobar's mother was called Nessa.

nether elided ME and modern form of OE *neotherra* or *nitherra*: 'lower', 'nether'.

Netherbrae [Grampian] 'Lower (*nether*, ME) brae (*brai*, ME)'.

Netherburn [Strathclyde] 'Lower (*nether*, ME) stream (*burn*, ME)'.

Nether Kirkton [Strathclyde] 'Lower (*nether*, ME) church (*kirk*, Scots) farmstead (*toun*, ME)'.

Netherton [Tayside; Central] 'Lower (*nether*, ME) farmstead (*toun*, ME)': this was a standard part of a farming community, each of which might have a Mains (manor), an Overton (the big farm), a Netherton (a lesser farm) and perhaps a Kirkton (church farm).

Nethy Bridge [Highland] '[River] Nethy bridge': commentators have suggested that the river name might derive from *an eitghich*, 'the gullet' (as though the river ran through a *gorge*) or that there might be a connection with the Pictish King Nectan – but far more likely in an area called by the Brythonic name Abernethy is the Brythonic river name element *Nedd* (found in Wales as Nedd and Neath, in England as Nidd) probably meaning 'glistening'.

Neuk, The [Grampian] 'The nook (*neuk*, ME Northern dialect)'.

nev adapted form of ON *nef*: 'beak', 'bill' and thus 'point': the word is cognate with English *neb* and *nib*.

Nev, The [Shetland (3)] 'The bill (*nef*, ON)'.

Nevis [Highland] Virtually all commentators appear to regard this strictly as a water name, although to an impartial observer the Water of Nevis is the least likely aspect surrounding Ben Nevis after which to name the highest mountain in the entire country. The grand sea-loch Loch Nevis is cited as a clinching factor to their case. And yet the commentators have all to admit that there are many and various other interpretations – 'the venomous', 'the awesome', 'the sky-high' and so forth – which have little or nothing to do specifically with water. One pleasant and at least properly Celtic conceit is that Loch Nevis is 'the loch of heaven' (Welsh *nef*) as opposed to the neighbouring and spectacular Loch Hourn 'the loch of hell' (Welsh *uffern*), but this remains simply fanciful. There is (in my opinion) a far more likely explanation. Indo-European words for 'cloud' (such as Latin *nimbus, nebula*; German *Nebel*; Greek *nephele*; Welsh *nuddau*, cf Welsh *nef* 'heaven[s]') and for 'snow' (such as Latin *nivem*; Greek *niphos*; Welsh *nyf*; and even English *[s]now*) all have a common root that must originally have combined those meanings. And that double meaning is perfect for the place name Nevis – 'cloudy and snowy' – for both the often-shrouded mountain and the squall-beaten loch.

New Abbey [Dumfries & Galloway] The Cistercian abbey was founded in 1273 by a Lady Devorgilla, a noted patroness of architecture and education, who was buried in front of the high altar with the heart of her dead husband. Only ruins are left today. The New Abbey is thus not quite as old as the New Forest in Hampshire (late 11th century).

New Aberdour [Grampian] Village founded in 1798 and named in contrast to (Old) Aberdour in Fife. See also **Aberdour**.

Newark [Orkney] Probably 'New (*neowe*, OE) work[s] (*weorc*, OE)', either in building or in mining.

Newbattle [Lothian] 'New (*neowe*, OE) cottage (*botl*, OE)'.

Newbigging [Strathclyde; Tayside (3)] 'New (*newe*, ME) building (*bigging*, ME)'.

Newburgh [Grampian; Fife] 'New (*neowe*, OE) stronghold (*burh*, OE)'.

New Byth [Grampian] Village founded in 1764 and named in contrast to the nearby (Old) Byth.

Newcastleton [Borders] 'New Castleton (Eng)': village built in 1793 to replace the older village of Castleton in which Cromwell's troops a century earlier had razed the castle and done other damage.

New Elgin [Grampian] The district takes its name from a village set up in 1850 by the Incorporated Trades of Elgin about 1 mile south of that town. See also **Elgin**.

New Galloway [Dumfries & Galloway] The area was granted a Royal Charter in 1629 by Charles I, and then took the name of one of the other properties owned by the Gordon family. See also **Galloway**.

Newhaven [Lothian] 'New haven (Eng)': the little port was founded in around 1500 by James IV and populated by Dutchmen and Danes (in whose languages 'new haven' is instantly understandable). The old harbour was at Leith.

New Lanark [Strathclyde] Village set up in 1784 and named in contrast to the nearby (Old) Lanark, q.v.

Newmachar [Grampian] The name is a reference to Aberdeen, and its cathedral of (Old) Machar: St Machar was a 6th-century Irish bishop, the evangelist to the Picts around Aberdeen.

214

Newmains [Strathclyde] 'New (*newe*, ME) manor (*demesne*, ME)'.

Newmill [Grampian; Border] 'New mill (Eng)'.

Newmiln [Tayside] 'New (*newe*, ME) mill (*milne*, ME)'.

Newmilns [Strathclyde] 'New (*newe*, ME) mills (*milnes*, ME)': the village has for long specialised in the production of muslin.

New Pitsligo [Grampian] Village set up in around 1780 and named after one of the titles of the landowner, Sir William Forbes.

Newstead [Borders] 'New (*newe*, ME) farmstead (*stead*, ME)'.

Newton [Highland (3); Grampian; Strathclyde (2); Borders; Lothian; Western Isles] 'New (*newe*, ME) farmstead (*toun*, ME)'.

Newton Mearns [Strathclyde] 'New farmstead (ME)' in the parish of Mearns, a name which elsewhere represents *an mhaoirne*, 'the stewardship', an area administered by an official Steward, but which in this case is said by some – rather unconvincingly – to derive from ON *myrr*, 'moor'.

Newtonmore [Highland] 'New town [on the] moor (Eng)'.

Newton Stewart [Dumfries & Galloway] 'New town' established in the mid-17th century by William Stewart, son of the Earl of Galloway.

Newtown [Highland; Grampian; Central; Lothian] 'New town (Eng)'.

Niddrie [Lothian] 'New (*nuadh*, Brythonic Gaelic) settlement (*tref*, Brythonic Gaelic)'.

Nigg [Highland; Grampian] 'The bay (*an uig*, the latter an adaptation of ON *vík*)'.

nighean (also *inghean*, *inghinn*) 'young girl', 'daughter'.

nish elided form of 1) *innis*: 'island', 'haugh [piece of fertile land within the bend of a river]', and thus 'water-meadow';
or 2) (ON) *nes*: 'ness', 'cape', 'promontory'.

Nithsdale [Dumfries & Galloway] '[The River] Nith's dale (Eng)': the river name is probably the same as Nedd (Nedd and Neath in Wales, Nidd in England) and may mean 'glistening'.

Norriston [Central] A chapel-of-ease was established here in 1674 by one Gabriel Norrie: until the later 1800s the place was called Norriestown.

Northfield [Grampian; Borders] 'North field (Eng)'.

Northwall [Orkney] Probably 'North (ON) field (*völlr*)', although the second element might in fact be a corruption of *vágr*, 'bay'.

Norwick [Shetland] 'Northern (*norra*, ON) bay (*vík*, ON)': the bay on which the community is sited is called Nor Wick.

noup elided form of ON *gnúpr*: 'peak'.

Noup, The [Shetland] 'The peak (*gnúpr*, ON)'.

O

-oa elided form of either   1) *mhagh*: 'plain';
                         or   2) (ON) *vágr*: 'bay'.

òb 'bay': the word is an adaption of ON *hóp*, and is thus cognate with English *hoop*.

Oban [Strathclyde] 'Little bay (*òban*, diminutive of *òb*)'.

-och elided form of *achadh*: 'place', 'field', 'flat area'.

ochdamh 'one eighth'; this is very close in form to Latin *octava* (*pars*).

Ochil Hills [Central/Tayside] 'High (*uchel*, Brythonic Gaelic) hills (Eng)'.

Ochiltree [Strathclyde] 'High (*uchel*, Brythonic Gaelic) settlement (*tref*, Brythonic Gaelic)'.

ochter adapted form of *uachar*: 'top', 'upper (part)'.

Ochtermuthill [Tayside] 'Upper (*uachdar*) Muthill': Muthill is a town 3 miles east; its name, however, is probably English. See **Muthill.**

Ochtertyre [Tayside] 'Upper (*uachdar*) country (*tìr*)'.

Ochtomore [Strathclyde] Apparently '[An] Eighth [part] (*ochdamh*), big (*mór*)'.

-ock often a diminutive suffix.

odhar 'grey', 'dun-coloured'.

Ogilvie [Tayside] 'High (*uchel*, Brythonic Gaelic) plain (*fa*, Brythonic Gaelic)'.

oidhche 'night'.

oitir 'sandbank'.

Old Ladders [Grampian] 'Stream (*allt*) [on] the slope (*leitir*)'.

Old Maud [Grampian] 'Stream (*allt*) of the fox (*madaidh*)'.

Omoa [Strathclyde] The district takes its name from its former iron works, given the name by the landowner John Dalrymple who had fought at the Battle of Omoa, Honduras, in 1779.

Onich [Highland] Possibly 'Moor (*aonach*)'.

217

Dictionary of Scottish Place Names

-oon elided form of *obhainn*, variant of *abhainn*: 'river'.

Opinan [Highland (2)] 'Little bays (diminutive plural of *òb*)': the two villages are within 18 miles of each other as the crow flies.

òr 'gold': the word is evidently cognate with Latin *aurum*.

ord 'rounded hill', 'conical hill', also 'hammer'.

Ord [Skye] 'Rounded hill (*ord*)': from the hill there is a fine view across Loch Eishort to Strathaird and the Cuillin Hills.

Ordie [Grampian] Presumably 'Rounded hill (*ord*)'.

Ordiequish [Grampian] Possibly 'Rounded hill (*ord*) of the nooks (*cuise*)'.

Orknagable [Shetland] Possibly 'Seals' (*orkna*, ON) ridge (*gafl*, ON)'.

Orkney [Orkney] Probably 'Boar[-tribe's islands] (from an ancient pre-Celtic root mentioned in Latin texts in 320 BC)': the name was then apparently assimilated by the Norsemen to *Orkn-ey*, 'Seal island'.

Ormiscaig [Highland] Possibly 'Ormr's (personal name, ON) wood (*skógr*, ON)', although the area has few ON names.

Ormsaigmore [Highland] Possibly 'Ormr's (personal name, ON) bay (*-aig*, corruption of ON *vágr*), big (*mór*)': the bay is now, however, called Kilchoan Bay.

-ort elided adaptation of ON *fjordr*: 'fjord'. E.g. Sniz-ort.

Ose [Skye] Probably 'River-mouth (*ós*, ON)': the river that reaches the shore at Ose is now ironically called the River Ose.

Oskamull [Mull] Probably 'Åsgautr['s] (personal name, ON) promontory (*múli*, ON)': the personal name is well attested in place names in Lincolnshire and Yorkshire.

oss elided form of a word meaning 'of the elk'.

Otter Ferry [Strathclyde] 'Sandbank (*oitir*) ferry (Eng)': the village was formerly the site of a ferry across Loch Fyne to Port Ann on the mid-Argyll shore. The sandbank – actually a shingle bank – is exposed at low tide.

Otterswick [Shetland] Probably 'Otters' (ON) bay (*vík*, ON)': the bay overlooked by the village is now called Otters Wick – but Otr was also an ON personal name.

Otters Wick [Orkney] 'Otters (ON) bay (*vík*, ON)'.

Overbister [Orkney] 'Upper (*over*, ON) settlement-steading (*bol-stathr*, ON)'.

218

Overton [Grampian; Dumfries & Galloway] 'Upper (*ufer*, OE) farmstead (*tun*, OE)': this was a standard part of a farming community, each of which might have a Mains (manor), an Overton (the big farm), a Netherton (a lesser farm) and perhaps a Kirkton (church farm).

-oway   elided form of   1) *mhagh:* 'plain';
              or   2) (ON) *vágr:* 'bay'.

Oxna [Shetland] 'Oxen (*oxna*, ON)'.

Oxnam [Borders] 'Oxen (*oxna*, OE) meadow (*holm*, OE)'.

Oxton [Borders] Apparently 'Ulfkil's (personal name, OSwed) farmstead (*tun*, OE)'. The personal name, attested in many English place names, might mean 'wolf-hollow'. One commentator wants to identify the name with the Gaelic Gilfalyn (*gille Faolain*, 'servant of St Fillan') – but Ulfkil and Gilfalyn are much too far apart to be etymologically compatible.

Oykel [Highland] 'High [river] (*uchel*, Brythonic Gaelic)': it is possible, however, that the description is not of the river but of Glen Oykel or Strath Oykel.

Oyne [Grampian] Possibly 'Green (*uaine*)': the area is relatively fertile.

P

Pabay, Pabbay 'Priest (*pap*, ON) island (*ey*, ON)'. The Old Norse word for 'priest' derives from the late Latin for 'father', seen in English also in *papal* and *pope*.

Padanaram [Tayside] Apparently transferred from the Biblical village name in the mid-19th century by some Nonconformist community. The Hebrew name means 'Plain (*paddan*, Heb) of the Aramaeans (i.e. Syrians)'. Within the local Scottish vicinity are also Zoar and Jericho. Biblical transference occurs far more commonly in Wales.

Paisley [Strathclyde] Commentators have suggested variously a Brythonic derivation – 'Pasture (*pasgell*, Brythonic Gaelic) plain (*lledh*)', although the second element does not seem to be attested in modern Welsh – and a Church Latin derivation – 'Church (*basilica*, Latin [from Greek *basilikon* 'king's house'] eliding to Gaelic *paislig*)'. There are indeed some Brythonic names quite close (e.g. Renfrew); the place presumably was a religious centre; but there are even more Old English place names round about, so 'Pælli's (OE) pasture (*leah*, OE)' – where Pælli is an attested OE personal name in place names in England – seems just as reasonable.

pait 'rise', thus 'ford', 'stepping-stones' and also 'hump'.

paitean plural and diminutive of *pait*, thus 'fords' and also 'humps'.

Papa Stour [Shetland] 'Priest (*pap*, ON) island (*ey*, ON), great (*storr*, ON)'. This appellation distinguishes the island from all other 'Priest islands', of which there are quite a few.

partan (also *portan*) 'crab'.

Patna [Strathclyde] The name was transferred from the city in Bihar, India, on its foundation as a mining community in the early 1800s by Provost William Faulkner – who had been born in the Indian Patna.

Peebles [Borders] 'Mobile homes', 'Tents', 'Temporary huts' (*pebyll*).

-peffer elided form of an element (? Brythonic) that corresponds with Welsh *pefr*: 'radiant', 'bright' and generally refers to water.

peighinn 'land valued at one penny per year', an ancient valuation that derives from ON taxation customs (ON *penningr*).

peit modern Gaelic version of Pictish *pet[t]*: 'portion', 'share (of land)', and therefore 'place'. The word is cognate with French *petit* (from Vulgar Latin), Cornish *peth*, but also Gaelic *beag* 'little' and English *piece* and (probably) *patch*. Cf also Eng *bit* (usually derived from 'bite').

Pencaitland [Lothian] 'Head (*pen*, Brythonic Gaelic) of the wood (*coed*, Brythonic Gaelic), field (*lann*, Brythonic Gaelic)'.

Penicuik [Lothian] 'Head (*pen*, Brythonic Gaelic) [of] the (*y*, Brythonic Gaelic) cuckoo (*cog*, Brythonic Gaelic)'.

Pennan [Grampian] 'Head (*pen*, Brythonic Gaelic), water (*-an*, Brythonic Gaelic)'. The village is not at the head of a stream; instead it is near a headland on the coast where a stream flows into the North Sea. That headland is now, ironically, called Pennan Head.

Penpont [Dumfries & Galloway] 'Head (*pen*, Brythonic Gaelic), bridge (*pont*, Brythonic Gaelic)'. The bridge is over the Scar Water.

Pentland [Highland/Orkney] 'The Picts' (*Pettr*, ON) land (ON)'. Evidently named by the Vikings before the Scots came to Scotland.

pert elided form of Brythonic Gaelic *perth*: 'wood', 'thicket'.

Perth [Tayside] 'Thicket (*perth*, Brythonic Gaelic)'. It is strange that the city has reverted to its ancient name having for hundreds of years from the Middle Ages been known as St Johnstoun, after the building of the cathedral of St John (hence the football team's name, St Johnston).

Peterhead [Grampian] '[St] Peter['s] (personal name) head[land] (Eng)'. Named after the large church (St Peter's Kirk) established here in 1132, although the town was founded only around 1593.

petty- elided form of Pictish (Brythonic Gaelic) *pet[t]*: 'portion', 'share (of land)', and therefore 'place'. The word is cognate with French *petit* (from Vulgar Latin), Cornish *peth*, but also Gaelic *beag* 'little' and English *piece* and (probably) *patch*. Cf also Eng *bit* (usually derived from 'bite').

Pettymuick [Grampian] 'Place (*pet[t]*, Brythonic Gaelic) of the pig (*muice*)'.

-phanan elided form of the genitive of the personal name [St] Finnan.

-pheder (also *phedir*) elided forms of the genitive of the personal name [St] Peter.

-phedir See *-pheder*.

-phichen elided form of *phigheainn*: 'of the magpie'.

phigheainn mutated genitive form of *pigheann*, thus 'of the magpie'.

phiobair mutated form of *piobair*: 'piper'.

phluic mutated genitive form of *ploc*, thus 'of a rough promontory'.

phris mutated genitive form of *preas*, thus 'of the thicket', 'of the bush'.

phuill mutated genitive form of *poll*, thus 'of the pool', 'of the slough', 'of the pit'.

phùir mutated genitive form of *pòr*, thus 'of the pasture'.

phuirt mutated genitive form of *port*, thus 'of the harbour', 'of the ferry'.

pigheann 'magpie'; it is tempting to relate this word to Eng *pigeon*, which in turn derives from Late Latin *pipion-*, '[the] piping [bird]'.

piobair 'piper'.

pirc 'field': the word is cognate with Eng *park*.

pit- (also *pitte[n]*) elided forms of Pictish (Brythonic Gaelic) *pet[t]*: 'portion', 'share (of land)', and therefore 'place'. Cognate with French *petit* (from Vulgar Latin), Cornish *peth*, but also Gaelic *beag* 'little' and English *piece* and (probably) *patch*. Cf also Eng *bit* (usually derived from 'bite').

Pitcairngreen [Tayside] 'Place (*pet[t]*, Brythonic Gaelic) of the cairn (genitive of *carn*), green (Eng)'. The last element is likely to be English, rather than *gréine*, 'sunny', because on some maps it occurs as a separate word.

Pitcaple [Grampian] 'Place (*pet[t]*, Brythonic Gaelic) of the horse (*capuill*)'.

Pitfour [Tayside] 'Place (*pet[t]*, Brythonic Gaelic) of the grass (*feòir*)'.

Pitlochry [Tayside] 'Place (*pet[t]*, Brythonic Gaelic), stony (*cloichreach*)'.

Pitmedden [Tayside] 'Place (*pet[t]*, Brythonic Gaelic) in the middle (*meadhoin*)'.

Pittenweem [Fife] 'Place (*pet[t]*, Brythonic Gaelic) of the (*na*) cave (*h-uamha*)'. The cave is that of St Fillan, near the harbour.

ploc 'rough promontory', 'headland-mound'.

plock anglicised form of *ploc*: 'rough promontory', 'headland-mound'.

Plock of Kyle [Highland] Anglicised name: 'Rough promontory (*ploc*) of (Eng) Kyle [of Lochalsh] (*caol*)'. A 'kyle' is a narrows or strait.

Plockton [Highland] Hybrid name: 'Rough promontory (*ploc*) farmstead (*tun*, OE)'. The village is on a lowish headland projecting into the mouth of Loch Carron.

222

Pluscarden [Grampian] Apparently 'Estate (element in Brythonic Gaelic equivalent to modern Welsh *plas*), wooded (*cardden*, Brythonic Gaelic)'.

poite genitive form of *pot*, thus 'of the pot'.

pol elided form of *poll*: 'pool', 'slough'.

Polbain [Highland] Possibly 'Pool (*poll*), white (*bàn*)'. Perhaps in contrast to Polglass some 3½ miles south-east (q.v.). Both villages overlook a channel between the mainland and one of the Summer Isles.

Polglass [Highland] Possibly 'Pool (*poll*), blue-green (*glas*)'. Perhaps in contrast to Polbain some 3½ miles north-west (q.v.). Both villages overlook a channel between the mainland and one of the Summer Isles.

poll (Welsh *pwll*) 'pool', 'slough', and also 'pit'.

pollaidh '(area) of pools', thus 'bog', 'marshy area'.

polly anglicised version of *pollaidh*, '(area) of pools', 'marshy area'.

Polmaddie Hill [Strathclyde] 'Pool (*poll*) of the fox (*madaidh*), hill (Eng)'.

pool   either   1) an anglicised form of *pol*, 'pool', 'slough', 'pit';
         or   2) elided form of ON *bol*: 'settlement'. E.g. Ulla-pool.

pòr 'pasture'.

port 'harbour', but also 'ferry'.

Port a' Bhàta [Colonsay; Ulva] 'Harbour (*port*) of the boat (*bhàta*, genitive of *bàta*, itself a loan-word from ON *bàtr*)'.

Port a' Gharaidh [Highland] Presumably 'Harbour (*port*) of the den (*gharaidh*)'.

Port Allt a' Mhuilinn [Highland] 'Harbour (*port*), stream (*allt*) of the mill (*mhuilinn*, genitive of *muileann*)'.

Port a' Mhadaidh [Strathclyde] 'Harbour (*port*) of the fox (*mhadaidh*, genitive of *madadh*)'. The village on its shore has the same name but is spelled in English transliteration: Portavadie, q.v.

Port a' Mhurain [Coll] 'Harbour (*port*) of the marsh-grass (*mhurain*, genitive of *muran*)'.

portan (also *partan*) 'crab'.

Port an Eas [Islay] 'Harbour (*port*) of the waterfall (*an eas*)'.

Port-an-eorna [Highland] 'Harbour (*port*) of the barley (*an eòrna*)'.

223

Port Appin [Strathclyde] Presumably 'Harbour (*port*), abbey grounds (*apuinn*)'. The grounds are presumably those of St Maluag's foundation (cathedral) on Lismore Island across the Lynn of Lorn.

Portavadie [Strathclyde] 'Harbour (*port*) of the fox (*mhadaidh*, genitive of *madadh*)'. The bay beneath the village is called, more properly, Port a' Mhadaidh (q.v.).

Port Bàn [Highland] 'Harbour (*port*), fair (*bàn*)'. The second element can alternatively mean 'white'.

Port Cam [Highland] 'Harbour (*port*), crooked (*cam*)'.

Port Ceann a' Ghàrraidh [Colonsay] Presumably 'Harbour (*port*), head [land] (*ceann*) of the garden (*ghàrraidh*, genitive of *garradh*, itself a loan-word from ON *garthr*)'. In Gaelic, the final element can alternatively mean 'dyke' or 'wall'.

Port Charlotte [Islay] Named by the Gaelic scholar W. F. Campbell after his mother Lady Charlotte Campbell in 1828.

Port Cill Maluag [Strathclyde] 'Harbour (*port*), church[yard] (*cill*) [of] [St] Maluag'. It was Maluag – or Moluag – who in 562 founded the religious community on Lismore Island some 40 miles north.

Port Ellen [Islay] Named by the Gaelic scholar W. F. Campbell after his wife Lady Ellenor Campbell in 1821.

Port Gleann na Gaoidh [Islay] Presumably 'Harbour (*port*), glen (*gleann*) of the (*na*) winds (*gaoidh*)'. The final element may alternatively mean 'marshes', and there is a river down the glen to the 'harbour'.

Portincaple [Strathclyde] 'Harbour (*port*) of the horse (*an capuill*)'.

Portknockie [Grampian] 'Harbour (*port*), little hill (diminutive of *cnoc*)'.

Port Leathan [Strathclyde] 'Harbour (*port*), broad (*leathan[n]*)'.

Port Mean [Strathclyde] Possibly 'Harbour (*port*) in the middle (*meadhoin*)'.

Port Mine [Coll] 'Harbour (*port*), smooth (*mìn*)'.

Port Mór [Strathclyde; Tiree; Gigha] 'Harbour (*port*), big (*mór*)'.

Port Mór na Carraig [Islay] Presumably 'Harbour (*port*), big (*mór*), of the rock (*carraig*, from Brythonic Gaelic *careg*, 'rock')'.

Portnacroish [Strathclyde] 'Harbour (*port*) of the (*na*) cross (*crois*)'. This is likely to refer to a religious cross rather than a crossroads: like nearby

224

Port Appin (q.v.) it seems to have been part of the territory of the cathedral on Lismore Island across the Lynn of Lorn.

Port na Cuilce [Colonsay] Presumably 'Harbour (*port*) of the (*na*) reeds (*cuilce*)'.

Port na Feannaiche [Arran] Possibly 'Harbour (*port*) of the (*na*) crows (*feannag*)'.

Port nam Partan [Mull] 'Harbour (*port*) of the (*na-m*) crab (*partan*)'.

Port na Muice Duibhe [Mull] 'Harbour (*port*) of the (*na*) pigs (*muice*), black (*duibhe*, genitive of *dubh*)'.

Portnancon [Highland] 'Harbour (*port*) of the (*na-n*) dogs (genitive plural of *cù*)'.

Port nan Laogh [Jura] 'Harbour (*port*) of the (*na-n*) calf (*laogh*)'.

Portobello [Lothian] Originally the name of a house here, built by a sailor who had seen action at a battle of Puerto Bello in Panama in 1739. The name thus derives from the Spanish for 'Fine harbour', entirely suitable for the sailor's purpose.

Portpatrick [Dumfries & Galloway] 'Harbour (*port*) of [St] Patrick'. Named from an old local chapel (and not, as locals may aver, after any mythical crossing to or from Ireland to or from there by St Patrick himself). The saint's name derives from Latin *patricius*: 'nobleman'.

Portree [Skye] 'Harbour (*port*) of the slope (*ruigheadh*)'. Mistranslated for years in guide-books as 'Harbour of the king (*rìgh*)'.

Portsoy [Grampian] 'Harbour (*port*) of the warrior (*saoi*)'.

pot 'pot': why isn't all translation this easy?

preas 'thicket', 'bush', 'clump'.

Prestonpans [Lothian] 'Priest's (*preost*, OE) farmstead *(tun*, OE), [salt] pans (ME)'. The monks of Newbattle Abbey panned salt here from the 13th century.

Prestwick [Strathclyde] 'Priest['s] (*preost*, OE) settlement (*wic*, OE)'.

225

Q

Quarrelton [Strathclyde] Apparently 'Quarry (*quarrere*, ME) farmstead (*tun*, OE)'. The word 'quarry' itself derives from Latin *quadri-* '[stone] squared off'.

Queensferry [Lothian/Fife] 'Queen [Margaret]'s (*quenes*, ME) ferry (*ferien*, ME)'. Apparently named after Margaret, wife of Malcolm Canmore, son of [Macbeth's] Duncan, in the 11th century. Roughly the same elements appear also in Old English, but the meaning of 'queen' rather than 'quean' had at that time not really been distinguished.

Queich [Tayside] A river name that may mean 'of the cup-shaped hollow (*cuaich*)'.

-quhart a very corrupt Gaelic form of Brythonic Gaelic *cardden*: 'wood', 'thicket'. (See **Urquhart**.)

-quhidder a very corrupt Gaelic form of ON *fothr* or OE *fodor*: 'fodder'.

Quinag [Highland] Said to mean '[The] Water-stoup [i.e. pail, basin or goblet]', although the element(s) involved is/are obscure.

Quiraing [Highland] Apparently a hybrid name: 'Cattle-shelter (*kwei*, ON) shieling (*àirigh*)'. The first element, if truly Old Norse, has at least some etymological connection with English *cow* (see **-quoy** below).

Quoich [Highland] 'Cup-shaped hollow (*cuach*)'. The River Quoich flows through Glen Quoich and meets Loch Quoich at a narrow fjord-like arm that comes to a rounded end.

-quoy in Orkney and Shetland, elided form of ON *kwei* or *kví*: 'cattle-shelter'. It probably includes an element that is the equivalent of English *cow*; cf Quy (in Cambridgeshire) which is derived as OE *cu-eg* 'cow-island'.

Quoy Ness [Orkney] 'Cattle-shelter (*kwei*, ON) cape (*nes*, ON)'.

R

Raasay [Inner Hebrides] Probably 'Roe[-deer]'s (*raa-s*, ON) island (*ey*, ON)'.

ràimh genitive form of *ràmh*, thus 'of the oar'.

-rainy elided form of *raineach*: 'fern[y]'.

rait sometimes an elided form of *ràth*: 'fort', 'fortified dwelling', 'broch'.

Rait [Tayside] Possibly 'Fort (*ràth*)'.

ràmh 'oar': the word has Germanic cognates.

rann (also *roinn*) 'division', 'boundary'.

Rannoch [Strathclyde/Highland/Tayside] 'Fern[y] (*raineach*)'. There are ferns on Rannoch Moor – but there is far more heather and water-sedges. The name may have applied initially only to the area around Loch Rannoch.

raon 'field'.

ras 'shrubland', 'heath'.

rath anglicised form of *ràth*: 'fort', 'fortified dwelling', 'house with ramparts', 'broch'.

ràth 'fort', 'fortified dwelling', 'house with ramparts', 'broch'.

rathad 'road', 'way'.

rathaid (also *rothaid*) genitive form of *rathad*, thus 'of the road', 'of the way'.

Rattray [Tayside] Peculiar hybrid name: 'Fort (*ràth*) settlement (*tref*, Brythonic Gaelic). Should one assume that the name was originally just 'Tref' and that the Goidelic incomers took it simply as a name?

Ravenstruther [Strathclyde] Possibly a hybrid name: 'Hraefn's (personal name, OE) rivulet (*sruthair*)'. The personal name is well established in English place names, and means 'raven'. But note that in Ravenglass, Cumbria, the first element is a corruption of Gaelic *rann*: 'division', 'boundary'.

reamhar 'wide', 'thick', 'fat'.

Reamhar [Arran] 'Wide (*reamhar*)'. Presumably in reference to the width of the hill that it names.

227

reanna plural form of *rinn/roinn*, thus 'points', 'capes', 'promontories'

Reaster [Highland] Possibly 'Hrörekr's (personal name, ON) house (*setr*, ON)'. The personal name means something like 'agile', and may also be apparent in the place name Reasby, in Lincolnshire.

Reawick [Shetland] Possibly 'Roe [deer] (*rá*, ON) settlement (*wic*, OE)'. The first element would seem to have been corrupted from the Old Norse by incoming English-speakers: the village is definitely a settlement and not an ON *vík* 'bay' but it stands on Roe Ness (q.v.).

Reay [Highland] Possibly 'Fort (*ràth*)' – Dounreay Castle is only 2 miles away. But possibly alternatively '[Animal-]Pen (*rett*, said to be ON)'; it is a fertile coastal area.

Redcastle [Highland] Purely English name of the estate that was the home of the Mackenzie family. The present stately mansion on the shore of the Beauly Firth incorporates some 16th-century masonry.

-ree elided form of   1) *ruighe[adh]*, genitive of *ruighe*: 'slope', 'cattle-run';
   or   2) *rìgh*: 'king', 'royal';
   or   3) Brythonic form of Gaelic *rubha*: 'cape', 'headland'.

rèidh 'level', 'flat', 'plain'.

Rèidh Eilean [Inner Hebrides] 'Flat (*rèidh*) island (*eilean*)'.

reilig (also *roilig*) 'cemetery': the word derives from Latin *reliquiae*, 'remains', 'relics'.

réisg genitive form of *riasg*, thus 'of the moor', 'of the fen', 'of the marsh'.

Renfrew [Strathclyde] 'Headland (*rhyn*, Brythonic Gaelic), torrent (*frwd*, Brythonic Gaelic, Modern Welsh *ffrwd*)'.

Renton [Strathclyde] Named after Cecilia Renton by her mother-in-law Jean Telfer-Smollett (sister of Tobias Smollett), the founder of the industrial community, in 1782. Dr Johnson wrote a Latin epitaph for the monument to Tobias Smollett in the village.

-reoch elided form of *riabhach*: 'grey', 'brindled'.

-res sometimes an adaptation of *ras*: 'shrubland', 'heath'.

Rest And Be Thankful [Strathclyde] Summit of the pass between Glen Croe and Glen Kinglas, and at 900 feet (274 m), a place any footsore traveller would be pleased to reach. The poet Wordsworth described the seat erected there by the soldiers of General ('Wee') Johnnie Cope in the 1740s, as they built a military road from Dumbarton to Inveraray.

228

-rhea elided form of 1) *Rheithainn:* 'of R[h]eithann (personal name)';
or 2) *riabhach:* 'grey', 'brindled'.

Rhiconich [Highland] Apparently 'Headland (*rubha*), mossy (*coinnich*)', although this is strange because the area has been described as a 'lunar landscape'. The name may well derive from that of a hotel once famous here.

Rhifail [Highland] Possibly 'Split (*rifa*, ON) watercourse (*gil*, ON)': Beinn Rifa-gil overlooks the tiny community.

Rhiroy [Highland] Possibly 'Headland (*rubha*), red (*ruaidhe*)'. It is on the shore of Loch Broom, but there is little by way of a headland there.

rhu elided form of *rubha* or *rudha*: 'headland', 'cape', 'point'. Cf Welsh *rhiw*.

Rhu [Strathclyde] 'Headland (*rubha*)'. At Rhu there is quite a significant cape jutting into the Gare Loch, opposite another, Rosneath.

Rhue [Highland] Probably 'Headland (*rubha*)'. The village is on a headland at the end of Loch Broom.

Rhum [Inner Hebrides] Probably an elided form of ON *röm-ey:* 'Roomy island'; the -h- was inserted into the name only at the beginning of the 20th century by its contemporary owner Sir George Bullough, a wealthy Lancashire textile magnate.

Rhynd [Tayside] 'Headland (*rhyn*, Brythonic Gaelic)'. The village is at the highest part of the bank overlooking the Tay estuary.

riabhach 'grey', 'brindled'.

-riach elided form of *riabhach*: 'grey', 'brindled'.

riasg 'moor', 'fen', 'marsh'.

-rie sometimes an elided form of *ruighe*: 'slope', 'cattle-run'.

rig(g) either 1) 'field (*rig*, Scots)';
or 2) 'ridge (*hrycg*, OE)'.

Rigg [Dumfries & Galloway] Presumably 'Field (*rig*, Scots)': it is less likely to be 'Ridge (*hrycg*, OE)' for there is not much evidence of any height in the flatlands around Gretna.

Riggend [Strathclyde] Presumably 'Ridge (*hrycg*, OE) end (OE)'. Looking from the north, the village is at the end of a line of low hills that stretch from Falkirk to Airdrie.

righ 'king', or as an adjective 'royal'. The word has a host of Indo-European cognates.

Dictionary of Scottish Place Names

Rigside [Strathclyde] 'Ridge (*hrycg*, OE) side (Eng)': the village is along a contour line above the Douglas Water, amid a host of villages also with English names (such as Bankend).

Ringorm [Grampian] Probably 'Point (*rinn*), blue (*gorm*)'. The village is situated above where the River Spey flows from the foothills of the Cairngorms into the flatter coastal valley. Near by is a radio-TV booster.

Rinmore [Grampian] 'Point (*rinn*), big (*mór*)'. The village lies under quite a significant peak.

rinn (also *roinn*) 'point', 'cape'.

-rioch elided form of *riabhach*: 'grey', 'brindled'.

Rireavach [Highland] Possibly 'Headland (*rubha*), grey (*riabhach*)'. The tiny village is at the end of an escarpment on the shore of Loch Broom.

Risay [Lewis] 'Brushwood (*hrís*, ON) island (*ey*, ON)'.

-rishaig mutated form of the doublet *dris-aig*: 'briars-bay', 'thorns-bay'.

Roe Ness [Shetland] Presumably 'Roe [deer] (ON) headland (*nes*, ON)'. Cf **Rubha Bhocaig**.

Rogie [Highland] River and waterfall name deriving from two ON elements meaning 'rough water'.

roid 'bog myrtle'.

roilig (also *reilig*) 'cemetery': the word derives from Latin *reliquiae*, 'remains', 'relics'.

ròin genitive form of *ròn*, thus 'of the seal'.

roinn either 1) (also *rinn*) 'point', 'cape';
or 2) (also *rann*) 'division', 'boundary'.

Roinn a' Bhuic [Lewis] Point (*roinn*) of the buck (*buic*, genitive of *boc*)'.

rois genitive form of *ros*, thus 'of the headland', 'of the cape', 'of the wood'.

Rois-Bheinn [Highland] 'Headland's (*rois*, genitive of *ros*) mountain (*beinn*)'. The mountain – 2,895 feet (882 m), with at least four major peaks – forms an impressive barrier to the sea and on one shore of Loch Ailort. The village at the mouth of Loch Ailort is also called by its name, but anglicised to Roshven (q.v.).

Romannobridge [Borders] 'Fort (*ràth*) of the monk (*manaich*), bridge (Eng)'. The place may have been named after the rampart-like terraces representing mediaeval cultivation lychets near Newlands Church. The bridge is over the Lyne Water.

230

ròn 'seal'.

Ronaldsay, North [Orkney] Reputed to be a corruption of 'Ringan's (personal name) island (*ey*, ON)'. Moreover, 'Ringan' is said to be equivalent to '[St] Ninian' although the saint is known never to have travelled so far north, the island has no such ecclesiastical history, and etymologically the mutation is so unlikely as to be unbelievable. (Indeed, the Scottish name Ninian is already a corruption of the Latin *Vivianus* 'lively'.) Don't believe a word of it; see below.

Ronaldsay, South [Orkney] 'Rögnvaldr's (personal name, ON) island (*ey*, ON)'. The Old Norse Rögnvaldr is the equivalent of Scottish Ronald or Ranald, itself an adaptation of Old English *Regen-weald* 'reign-wield', i.e. power-exerting. Why this etymology should not be that also of North Ronaldsay perhaps only the inhabitants can say.

-ronich elided form of *raineach*: 'fern[y]', '[of] bracken'.

Rora [Grampian] Possibly 'Agile (*rör*, ODan) river (*å*, ODan)'. The village stands close to a river and at one end of the Rora Moss; there are some other Scandinavian village names around (such as Crimonmogate).

ros   either 1) 'promontory', 'headland', 'cape', but also 'wood';
       or 2) much less commonly, an elided form of *riasg*: 'moor', 'fen', 'marsh'.

rose adapted form of *ros*: 'headland', 'cape' or 'wood'.

Rosehearty [Grampian] Possibly '[On the] Headland (*ros*), high (*ard* plus dative/locative)'. The headland forms quite a cove beneath the town, although it is indeed not particularly high.

Roseisle [Grampian] Possibly 'Headland (*ros*) isle (Eng)'. The village lies to the immediate west of the only significant rise within many square miles of coastal plain between Nairn and Buckie, on top of which (286 feet/87 m) is a radio-TV booster. There are many English village names around (such as Newtown).

Rosemarkie [Highland] 'Headland (*ros*) of the horse (*marc*)'. The village is at the foot of the long peninsula now known as Chanonry Point, which juts into the Moray Firth; the town beneath the same peninsula is thus Fortrose (q.v.).

Roshven [Highland] Anglicised form of *Rois-Bheinn*: 'Headland's (*rois*, genitive of *ros*) mountain (*beinn*)', the name of the mountain immediately to the east of the village at the mouth of Loch Ailort. See **Rois-Bheinn**.

231

Dictionary of Scottish Place Names

Roslin [Lothian] 'Marsh (*riasg*) pool (*linn*)'.

Rosneath [Strathclyde] Possibly 'Headland (*ros*) of Neath (probably a Brythonic Gaelic water name)'. With -neath cf the Welsh Neath, Irish Lough Neagh, and Scottish River Nidd, all from an ancient root that seems to mean 'shining', cognate with Latin *nidens*. At Rosneath there is an appreciable headland jutting into the Gare Loch, opposite another, Rhu. Two miles south-east is Rosneath Point, the final element evidently added considerably later when the meaning of Ros- was not remembered.

ross adapted form of *ros*: 'headland', 'cape' or 'wood'.

ross in Shetland, elided form of *hross*: 'horse'.

-rossan adapted form of the diminutive of *ros*: 'headland', 'cape' or 'wood'.

Rosyth [Fife] 'Headland (*ros*) of arrows (*saighead*)'.

roth adapted form of *ràth*: 'fort', 'fortified dwelling', 'broch'.

rothaid variant genitive form of *rathad*, thus 'of the road', 'of the way'.

Rothesay [Bute] Probably 'Rudri [MacDonald]'s (personal name) island (*ey*, ON)'. The island was given to Rudri (or Ruari or Roderick) MacDonald as a franchise for his fast-food chain by Haakon, 13th-century King of Norway (see **Kyleakin**). The name Ruari(dh) originally meant 'red' but was early confused with the Germanic Roderick (*hrodi-ricja* 'renown-domain').

rothie- adapted form of the doublet *ràth a*': 'fort of [the] . . . '.

Rothiemay [Grampian] 'Fort (*ràth*) of the plain (*a' maigh*)'.

Rousay [Orkney] 'Hrolfr's (personal name) island (*ey*, ON)'. The personal name is an adaptation of Old German Hrodulf ('renown-wolf').

row rare elided form of *rubha* or *rudha*: 'headland', 'cape', 'point'.

Rowardennan [Central] 'Headland (*rubha*), high (*ard*), of [St] Adamnan'. Adamnan (or Adomnan) was the late 7th-century Abbot of Iona and biographer of his predecessor, St Columba. It was in Rowardennan that he is supposed to have halted the spread of plague by striking the soil with his crozier. The headland projects into Loch Lomond.

Roxburgh [Borders] 'Hroc's (personal name, OE) fortified dwelling (*burh*, OE)'. This was once a great royal town but is now merely an out-of-the-way village with a mound where the castle used to be. The personal name means 'Rook'.

Roybridge [Highland] '[River] Roy bridge (Eng)'. The River Roy – the river name means 'red' – rises up in the Corrieyairack Forest and flows

232

down Glen Roy – between the 'parallel roads' – to join the River Spean at Roybridge, surprisingly not at Inverroy a mile or so west.

ruadh 'red', 'brownish-red'. Common Indo-European, attested to in Germanic, Celtic and Sanskrit-based languages; thus cognate with English *ruddy* and *red*.

Ruadh Sgeir [Sound of Jura] 'Red (*ruadh*) skerry (*sgeir*, adaptation of ON *sker*)'.

Ruaig [Tiree] Probably 'Headland (*rubha*) bay (*-aig*, adaptation of ON *vágr*)'. The tiny village overlooks a long spit of a headland enclosing a fine cove.

rubha 'headland', 'cape', 'point'. Cf Welsh *rhiw*: 'hill'.

Rubha an Aird [Mull] 'Headland (*rubha*) of the height (*ard*)'.

Rubha an Daraich [Highland] 'Headland (*rubha*) of the oak (*darach*)'.

Rubha an Dùine [Uist] 'Headland (*rubha*) of the strongholds (*dùine*, genitive of *dùn*)'. The final element can alternatively mean 'mounds', which may be more appropriate here.

Rubha Bàn [Highland] 'Headland (*rubha*), white (*bàn*)'.

Rubh' a' Bhaid Bheithe [Highland] 'Headland (*rubha*) of the copse (*bhaid*, genitive of *bad*), birch (*beithe*)'.

Rubh' a' Bhàigh Uaine [Lewis] 'Headland (*rubha*) of the bay (*bàgh*, adaptation of ON or OE), green (*uaine*)'.

Rubh a' Bhaird [Lewis] 'Headland (*rubha*) of the poet (*baird*, genitive of *bard*)'. In later times the word *bard* came instead to mean 'enclosed meadow'.

Rubha Bhocaig [Harris] Presumably 'Headland (*rubha*), buck (*b[h]oc*), bay (*-aig*, corruption of ON *vágr*)'. Whether deer were common there, or whether the geography of the area recalls the shape of a stag, is not known.

Rubha Buidhe [Highland] 'Headland (*rubha*), yellow (*buidhe*)'.

Rubha Cam nan Gall [Outer Hebrides] 'Headland (*rubha*), crooked (*cam*), of the (*na-n*) foreigner (*gael*)'. The headland is indeed hooked round, although whether the foreigner is Viking (a *fionn gael* – Fingal – 'fair [-haired] foreigner) or Saxon/Danish (a *dubh gael* – Dougal – 'dark[-haired] foreigner') is known only to local folklore.

Rubha Caol [Lewis] 'Headland (*rubha*), narrows (*caol*)'.

233

Rubha Caolard [Strathclyde] Presumably 'Headland (*rubha*), narrows (*caol*) crag (*ard*)'.

Rubh' a' Chàirn Bhàin [Gigha] 'Headland (*rubha*) of the cairn (genitive of *carn*), white (*bhàin*, genitive of *bàn*)'.

Rubh' a' Chamais [Jura] 'Headland (*rubha*) of the bay (genitive of *camas*)'.

Rubha Charn nan Cearc [Skye] 'Headland (*rubha*), cairn (*carn*) of the (*na-n*) hen (*cearc*)'.

Rubha Chlachan [Strathclyde] 'Headland (*rubha*), stony (*clachan*)'.

Rubh' a' Choin [Highland] 'Headland (*rubha*) of moss (*coin*)'.

Rubha Dubh [Mull; Tiree] 'Headland (*rubha*), dark (*dubh*)'.

Rubha Dubh Tigharry [Uist] Presumably 'Headland (*rubha*), dark (*dubh*), house (*tigh*), boundary (*airbhe*)'. The final element might instead be *àirigh*: 'shieling'.

Rubha Garbh-à[i]rd [Strathclyde] 'Headland (*rubha*), rough[-water] (*garbh*), height (*ard*)'.

Rubha Iosal [Lewis] 'Headland (*rubha*), low (*ìosal*)'.

Rubh' Aird an Fheidh [Highland] 'Headland (*rubha*), height (*ard*) of the deer (*fhéidh*, genitive of *fiadh*)'.

Rubh' Aird an t-Sionnaich [Highland] 'Headland (*rubha*), height (*ard*) of the fox (*sionnaich*, genitive of *sionnach*)'.

Rubha Langanes [Inner Hebrides] Hybrid name: 'Headland (*rubha*), long (*langr*, ON) headland (*nes*, ON)'. Once the Old Norse had become nothing but a name, the Gaelic descriptive was added.

Rubha Leacach [Harris] 'Headland (*rubha*), stony slope (*leacach*)'.

Rubha Leathan [Strathclyde] 'Headland (*rubha*), broad (*leathann*)'.

Rubha Leathann [Lewis] 'Headland (*rubha*), broad (*leathann*)'.

Rubha Leumair [Highland] 'Headland (*rubha*) of leaps (*leumair*)'.

Rubha Màs a' Chnuic [Harris] 'Headland (*rubha*), bottom (*màs*) of the rounded hill (*chnuic*, genitive of *cnoc*)'. The word *màs* literally means 'buttock'.

Rubh' a' Mhill Dearg [Highland] 'Headland (*rubha*) of the round hill (*mhill*, genitive of *meall*), red-brown (*dearg*)'.

234

R

Rubh' a' Mhucard [Highland] 'Headland (*rubha*) of the pig (*mhuc*), height (*ard*)'.

Rubha Mór [Highland; Mull; Coll; Islay; Barra] 'Headland (*rubha*), big (*mór*)'.

Rubha na Brèige [Highland] 'Headland (*rubha*) of (*na*) falsehood (*brèige*, genitive of *breug*)'. This means that the headland is deceptive in appearance: there are dangerous rocks hidden in the waters in front of it.

Rubha na Faing Móire [Highland] 'Headland (*rubha*) of the (*na*) sheep-pen (*faing*, genitive of *fang*), big (*mór*)'.

Rubha na Fearn [Highland] 'Headland (*rubha*) of the (*na*) alder tree (*fearn*)'.

Rubha na Greine [Lewis] 'Headland (*rubha*) of the (*na*) sun (*greine*, genitive of *grian*)'.

Rubha na h-Airde [Strathclyde] 'Headland (*rubha*) of the (*na*) height (*ard*)'.

Rubha na h-Aird Glaise [Skye] 'Headland (*rubha*) of the (*na*) height (*ard*), stream (*glais*)'.

Rubha na h-Aiseag [Skye] 'Headland (*rubha*) of the (*na*) ferry (*aiseag*)'. No regular ferry has run from this northerly tip of Skye for many decades.

Rubha na h-Easgainne [Skye] 'Headland (*rubha*) of the (*na*) swamp (*easgainn*)'.

Rubha na h-Uamha [Mull] 'Headland (*rubha*) of the (*na*) cave (*uamh*)'.

Rubha na' Leac [Raasay] 'Headland (*rubha*) of the (*na*) stone (*leac*)'.

Rubha na Leacaig [Highland] 'Headland (*rubha*) of the (*na*) stony (*leac*) bay (*-aig*, corruption of ON *vágr*)'.

Rubha nam Bàrr [Strathclyde] 'Headland (*rubha*) of the (*na-m*) summit (*barr*)'. Behind the headland is one rather meagre height within an area of lowland.

Rubha nam Maol Móra [Mull] 'Headland (*rubha*) of the (*na-m*) bare hill (*maol*), big (*mór*)'.

Rubha nan Cearc [Mull] 'Headland (*rubha*) of the (*na-n*) hen (*cearc*)'.

Rubha nan Clach [Skye] 'Headland (*rubha*) of the (*na-n*) stone (*clach*)'.

Rubha nan Còsan [Highland] 'Headland (*rubha*) of the nooks (plural of *còs*)'.

Rubha nan Eun [Outer Hebrides] 'Headland (*rubha*) of the (*na-n*) bird (*eun*)'.

Rubha nan Gall [Mull; Ulva] 'Headland (*rubha*) of the (*na-n*) foreigner (*gael*)'. Whether the foreigner is Viking (a *fionn gael* – Fingal – 'fair[-haired] foreigner) or Saxon/Danish (a *dubh gael* – Dougal – 'dark [-haired] foreigner') is known only to local folklore.

Rubha nan Leacan [Islay] 'Headland (*rubha*) of the (*na-n*) stones (plural of *leac*)'.

Rubha nan Sgarbh [Highland; Strathclyde] 'Headland (*rubha*) of the (*na*) cormorant (*sgarbh*)'.

Rubha nan Tri Chlach [Eigg] 'Headland (*rubha*) of the (*na-n*) three (*tri*) stones (*clach*)'.

Rubha na Roinne [Rhum] 'Headland (*rubha*) of the (*na*) seal (*ròin*)'.

Rubha na Sròine [Inner Hebrides] 'Headland (*rubha*) of the (*na*) naze (*sròine*, genitive of *sròn* 'nose', 'point')'.

Rubh' an Dùnain [Skye] 'Headland (*rubha*) [of] the (*an*) strongholds (plural of *dùn*)'. There is both an ancient rampart and a cairn on the headland.

Rubha Nead a' Gheòidh [Tiree] 'Headland (*rubha*), nest (*nead*) of the goose (*gheòidh*, genitive of *gèadh*)'.

Rubh' an Fhir Léithe [Highland] 'Headland (*rubha*) of the man (*fir*), grey[-headed] (*léithe*)'.

Rubh' an Teampuill [Harris] 'Headland (*rubha*) of the church (*teampuill*)'.

Rubh' an Tòrra Mhóir [Skye] 'Headland (*rubha*) of the hill (*torr*), big (*mór*)'.

Rubh' an t-Suibhein [Mull] Presumably 'Headland (*rubha*) [of] the seat [-like] (*suidhe*) mountain (*bheinn*)'. The headland lies just in front of a round flat hill.

Rubh' Aoineadh Mhéinis [Mull] Possibly 'Headland (*rubha*), rocky and precipitous (*aoineadh*), ore-bearing (*mhèin-*)'.

Rubh' Ard na Bà [Highland] 'Headland (*rubha*), height (*ard*) of the (*na*) cow (*bà*, genitive of *bó*)'.

Rubha Ruadh [Highland] 'Headland (*rubha*), red (*ruadh*)'.

Rubha Seanach [Strathclyde] Presumably 'Headland (*rubha*), [the] old (*sean*) place (*ach*)'.

Rubha Thormaid [Highland] Possibly 'Headland (*rubha*) of Thormóthr (personal name, ON)'; cf the Irish name Dermot (Diormaid), meaning perhaps 'free man'.

Rubha Tràigh an Dùin [Tiree] 'Headland (*rubha*), beach (*tràigh*, Brythonic Gaelic) of the stronghold (*dùin*)'.

Rubh' Dubh [Lewis] 'Headland (*rubha*), dark (*dubh*)'.

rudha rarer version of *rubha*: 'headland', 'cape', 'point'.

Rueval [Benbecula] Said to be 'Miracles' (*rueidh*) fell (*mheall*)'.

Ruel [Strathclyde] River name that apparently means 'of blood', in reference to a local battle between Norsemen and Celtic warriors fought in the year 1160, in which the Norsemen were all eventually slain and the river ran red with their gore. Nice, eh.

ruidh variant of *ruighe*: 'fore-arm', 'slope', 'cattle-run', 'shieling'.

ruighe 'fore-arm', thus also 'slope', 'cattle-run', 'shieling'.

ruigheadh genitive form of *ruighe*, thus 'of the fore-arm', 'of the slope', 'of the cattle-run', 'of the shieling'.

Rum [Inner Hebrides] See **Rhum**.

ruth elided form of *ruadh*: 'red', 'brownish-red'.

ruther   adapted form of either   1) OE *hryther*: 'cattle';
                          or   2) *ruadh*: 'red'.

Rutherford [Borders] Probably 'Cattle (*hryther*, OE) ford (ME)'; the town is in an area of Anglo-Saxon names between Kelso and St Boswells. The first element is then identical with that of many English place names beginning Rother-.

Rutherglen [Strathclyde] 'Red (*ruadh*) glen (*gleann*)'.

Ruthven [Grampian; Highland; Tayside] Probably 'Red (*ruadh*) mountain (*bheinn*)'. All these villages are at some height on a mountainside, straddling a mountain stream.

Ruthwell [Dumfries & Galloway] 'Cross (*rod*, OE) well (OE)'. The well is some way away from the 8th-century 'preaching cross', with its runic inscription in Northumbrian Old English, now incorporated into the parish church.

-ry elided form of *ruidh*, variant of *ruighe*: 'slope', 'cattle-run', 'shieling'.

S

Saasaig [Skye] Possibly 'Sheep's (*sauthr-s*, ON) bay (*vágr*, ON)', although the first element might instead be a nickname meaning the same.

sabhal (also *sobhal* and *sodhal*) 'barn'.

Sabhal Beag [Highland] '[The] Barn (*sabhal*), small (*beag*)': small or not, the mountain reaches 2,393 feet (730 m).

sac 'as much as a horse can carry', 'horse-pack'.

Saddell [Strathclyde] Probably 'Priest (*sagart*) dale (*dail*)': there are slight remains of an old Cistercian monastery said to have been founded here by Somerled, first Lord of the Isles, progenitor of Clan Donald. Some commentators therefore alternatively suggest derivation of the place name from ON: 'Somerled's (*Somerlithi-s*, personal name, ON) dale (*dalr*, ON)', in which the personal name means 'summer warrior'.

sagart 'priest'; the word derives from Latin *sacerdos*, 'priest'.

saic genitive form of *sac*, thus 'of a horse-pack'.

saidh 'bitch'.

saighdear 'soldier', 'archer'; the word derives from Latin *sagittarius*, 'archer'.

saighead 'of arrows'.

sàil either 1) 'heel';
       or 2) (also *sàl*) 'the sea'.

Sail Gharbh [Highland] '[The] Heel (*sàil*) [of] rough [water] (*gharbh*)'.

Sail Gorm [Highland] '[The] Heel (*sàil*), blue (*gorm*)'.

Saint Abb's [Borders] Village named after Saint Ebbe (or Aebbe), the daughter of King Ethelfrith of Northumbria who fled to Scotland on her father's death in 616 and founded Coldingham Priory, becoming its first abbess.

Saint Andrews [Fife] City named after its cathedral, built in 1160, previously called Kilrule ('the church of [St] Regulus'). It was St Regulus (or Rule) who by legend brought the relics of the Apostle Andrew from Greece to Scotland in the 4th century, so causing St Andrew to become the patron saint of Scotland. Andrew means 'manly'.

238

Saint Baldred's [Lothian] Coastal and offshore rock formations named after the 8th-century hermit who lived on the Bass Rock out to sea northwards and is held miraculously to have removed them from between that rock and the mainland.

Saint Boswells [Borders] Town named after St Boisil, 7th-century abbot of Melrose and friend of St Cuthbert.

Saint Fergus [Grampian] Village named after St Fergus, Irish apostle to several large areas of north-eastern Scotland in the early 8th century.

Saint Fillan's [Tayside] Village named after St Fillan, nephew of St Congan, whose relics were regarded to have considerable powers: Robert the Bruce attributed his victory at Bannockburn to the presence of Fillan's arm.

Saint Fort [Fife] Apparently 'Sand (Eng) ford (Eng)'.

Saint Kilda [Western Isles] There are various accounts to explain this name, for there certainly was no saint so called. My favourite story is that it derives from a misreading of the name on Old Norse maps: *Skildar*, 'Shields', a perfectly presentable description of the rocky island group, encompassing both forcefulness and shelter. The alternative suggestion that it derives somehow from ON *kelda*, 'spring', 'well' ignores the initial S- and the fact that the name applies to the whole island group and not just the largest.

Saint Margaret's Hope [Orkney] Village that takes its name from the bay on which it stands – ON *hóp*, 'bay' – and is also named after Queen Margaret, daughter of the English Edward the Atheling and wife to the Scottish King Malcolm III; a great patron of ecclesiastical buildings and learning, she died in 1093 and was canonised in 1250. Margaret means 'child of light'.

Saint Monance [Fife] Village (occasionally spelled St Monans) said to be named after a 6th-century Irish bishop (possibly called Moinnen) – but there is no such name in official hagiographies.

Saint Ninians [Central] Village named after the 5th-century British bishop who is regarded as an apostle to the Picts and who established a famous religious centre at Whithorn where, later, a shrine was dedicated to him. His name is a form of Vivianus, 'lively'.

Saint Vigeans [Tayside] Village named after St Fechin, a 7th-century Irish abbot who never actually came to Scotland although many influential disciples did. See also **Ecclefechan**.

sàl (also *sàil*) 'the sea'; literally 'the briny' and cognate with Eng *salt*.

salach 'dirty', 'foul'.

sàlan diminutive of *sàl*, thus 'little sea', 'bay', 'pool'.

Salen [Highland; Mull] 'Bay (*sàlan*, diminutive of *sàl*, 'the sea')': these two places are within 16 miles of each other, both at the head of a bay.

Sallachy [Highland] Probably 'Sea (*sàl*) place (*achadh*)': the village lies at the head of Loch Long (a name with maritime significance, 'loch of the ship'), a sea-inlet from Loch Alsh. On the other hand, the tidal mud may instead have made the area *salach*, 'dirty' . . .

Salsburgh [Strathclyde] Village apparently named after one Sally Young, wife of the landowner, in the late 1700s.

Saltburn [Highland] 'Salt (OE) stream (*burna*, OE)': the stream was used to hide smuggled containers of salt in order to evade the salt tax.

Saltcoats [Strathclyde] 'Salt[-pan workers'] (Eng) cottages (*cotes*, ME)': salt has been obtained here from the 16th century, and the first cottages were constructed by James V.

samh 'sorrel'.

samhradh 'summer'.

Sand [Shetland; Highland] 'Sand (ON)'.

Sandaig [Highland] 'Sand (ON) bay (*vágr*, ON)'.

Sandford [Strathclyde] 'Sand ford (Eng)': the ford, now bridged, was through the Kype Water.

Sandhaven [Grampian] 'Sand haven (Eng)'; the village was a planned settlement of about 1840.

Sandness [Shetland] 'Sand (ON) cape (*nes*, ON)'.

Sandsound [Shetland] Village that takes its name from the inlet it overlooks: 'Sand (ON) creek (*sund*, OScand)'; the inlet is now called Sandsound Voe.

Sandwick [Shetland; Orkney; Western Isles (2)] Probably all ON: 'Sand (ON) bay (*vík*, ON)', but if any are in fact OE, then 'Sand (OE) farm (*wic*, OE)'.

Sand Wick [Shetland; Orkney] 'Sand (ON) bay (*vík*, ON)'.

Sanquhar [Dumfries & Galloway] 'Old (*sean*) fortress (*chathair*)'; there are both a ruined castle and a prehistoric earthwork near by.

240

saobhaidh 'fox-earth'.

saoir genitive form of *saor*, thus 'of the carpenter', 'of the wright'.

saor 'carpenter', 'wright'.

Sarclet [Highland] Possibly 'Sheep (*sauthr*, ON) rock (*klettr*, ON)': the foreland on which the village stands is now called Sarclet Head.

sauchie elided form of *socach*: 'snout', 'projecting ground', 'patch between forking streams'.

Sauchieburn [Grampian] Presumably 'Projecting ground (*socach*) stream (*burna*, OE)'.

Sauchrie [Strathclyde] Possibly 'Projecting ground (*socach*) [of the] cattle-run (*ruighe*)'.

-*scadden* elided form of *sgadain*, genitive of *sgadan*, thus 'of herring'.

Scalasaig [Colonsay] Probably 'Skalli's (personal name, ON) bay (*vágr*, ON)', with the personal name meaning 'skull', as attested in Yorkshire place names; but the first element might possibly instead be ON *skáli-s*, 'huts', 'shielings'.

Scalloway [Shetland] 'Shieling (*skáli*, ON) bay (*vágr*, ON)'.

Scalpay [Western Isles] 'Boat[-shaped] (*skalpr*, ON) island (*ey*, ON)'.

Scapa Flow [Orkney] Probably 'Shellfish-bed (from ON, elided in present-day Scots to *scaup*) isthmus (*eith*, ON) flat surface (*flo*, ON)': the bay is almost totally surrounded by the islands of Orkney, and is less likely therefore to be described as a 'channel (ON equivalent of Eng *flue*)'. There were indeed productive oyster-beds in the area, which would have needed calm tidal seas.

Scarba [Inner Hebrides] Probably 'Sharp (*skarpr*, ON) island (*ey*, ON)': the island is surrounded on three sides by rocky cliffs – but those same cliffs lead to a different possibility: 'Cormorant (*skarfr*, ON) island (*ey*, ON)'.

scarf elided form of either   1)   ON *skarfr*: 'cormorant';
　　　　　　　　　　　　or   2)   the Gaelic loan-word from it, *sgarbh*:
　　　　　　　　　　　　　　　　　'cormorant'.

Scarfskerry [Highland] The village takes its name from the rocky headland on which it stands: 'Cormorant (*skarfr*, ON) skerry (*sker*, ON)'.

scarth elided form of ON *skarthr*: 'cleft', 'mountain-pass'.

Scavaig [Highland] 'Claw (*ská*, ON) bay (*vágr*, ON)'.

241

Schiehallion [Tayside] 'Fairy hill (*sìdh*) of the Caledonians (*chaillean*)': the mountain, at 3,554 feet (1,083 m), is rather larger than most 'fairy hills' in Scotland.

-sco elided form of ON *skógr*, 'wood', 'forest'. The OE equivalent/cognate was *scaga* (which ordinarily elided to *-shaw*).

Scolpaig [Uist] Possibly 'Boat[-shaped] (*skalpr*, ON) bay (*vágr*, ON)'.

Scone [Tayside] Possibly 'Mound (*sgonn*)', referring perhaps to the mote-hill, an ancient meeting-place used for assemblies, royal and otherwise, from the 8th century.

Scoraig [Highland] Possibly 'Long ridge (*sgorr*) bay (*-aig*, adaptation of ON *vágr*)': the tiny village lies along the long, low peninsula north of Little Loch Broom.

Scotasay [Harris] Possibly 'Scots' (ON) island (*ey*, ON)'.

Scotsburn [Highland] Presumably 'Scots' (OE) stream (*burna*, OE)'.

Scottas [Highland] Probably '[Place of] Scots (ON)': the area is otherwise marked by ON names.

scour anglicised form of *sgorr* or *sgurr*: 'peak', 'mountain'.

Scourie [Highland] Possibly 'Rocky (*sgoreach*)'.

Scrabster [Highland] Probably 'Skari['s] (personal name, ON) settlement-steading (*bol-stathr*)', although the first element is sometimes suggested instead to be ON *sker*, 'skerry' – but Scrabster is at the head of a low-lying bay.

Screapadal [Raasay] Probably 'Skrápi['s] (personal name, ON) dale (*dalr*, ON)'. The personal name is also attested in a Leicestershire place name.

seabhag 'hawk'; the word is an adaptation of OE *heafoc*.

seachd 'seven'; the word is cognate with its English translation.

Seaforth Head [Lewis] 'Sea (*saer*, ON) fjord (*fjordr*, ON), head (Eng translation of ON *höfuth*)': the village stands at the head of the longest sea-inlet in the Western Isles, about 14 miles long.

seagal 'rye'.

sealg 'hunting', 'the hunt'.

seamrag 'shamrock', 'trefoil'.

sean (Welsh *hen*) 'old'; the word is cognate with Latin *senis*.

seangan 'ant'.

searrach 'foal', 'colt'.

seileach 'willow tree'; the word is cognate with the Latin *salix* (and thus with English *sallow*).

Seilebost [Harris] Possibly 'Shallows (*selia*, ON) settlement-steading (*bol-stathr*)': the village overlooks the tidal mud-flats of the very shallow sea-inlet out to the Sound of Taransay.

seilge genitive form of *sealg*, thus 'of hunting', 'of the hunt'.

seilich genitive form of *seileach*, thus 'of the willow tree'.

seipeil 'chapel'; the word is a corruption of English *chapel*.

Selkirk [Borders] 'Hall (*sele*, OE) church (*cirice*, OE)'.

Setter [Shetland] Probably 'Shieling (*setr*, ON)', for the village lies to the east of a ridge that protects it from prevailing westerly winds; the alternative meaning, 'house', is not impossible, however.

Settiscarth [Orkney] Probably 'Shieling (*setr*, ON) mountain-pass (*skarthr*, ON)': the village lies on the protected east side of a cleft in the ridge that is used by a minor road.

sgadan 'herring'.

sgairneach 'stony hill'.

Sgairneach Mor [Tayside] 'Stony hill (*sgairneach*), big (*mór*)'.

sgarbh 'cormorant'; the word is an adaptation of ON *skarfr*.

Sgarbh Breac [Islay] Apparently 'Cormorant (*sgarbh*), speckled (*breac*)', but as in the neighbouring Sgarbh Dubh the first element may instead be a bad corruption of *sgorr*, 'peak', for both of them are names of hills. And there are not many speckled cormorants.

Sgarbh Dubh [Islay] Apparently 'Cormorant (*sgarbh*), black (*dubh*)', but as in the neighbouring Sgarbh Breac the first element may instead be a bad corruption of *sgorr*, 'peak', for both of them are names of hills.

sgairbh genitive form of *sgarbh*, thus 'of the cormorant'.

sgeir 'skerry', 'sharp rock projecting from the sea'; the word is an adaptation of the ON *sker*.

Sgeir Dhearg [Scalpay] 'Skerry (*sgeir*), red-brown (*dhearg*)'.

Sgeir Dhoirbh [Inner Hebrides] 'Skerry (*sgeir*), grim (*dhoirbh*)': a hazard to shipping that is the isolated southernmost of the Torran Rocks, 4 miles south of the Ross of Mull.

Sgeir Ghlas [Highland] 'Skerry (*sgeir*), blue-green (*ghlas*)'.

Sgeir Liath [Barra] 'Skerry (*sgeir*), grey (*liath*)'.

Sgeir Mhór [Highland] 'Skerry (*sgeir*), big (*mhór*). This combination is sometimes spelled *Skerryvore*.

Sgeir na Faoilinn [Mull] 'Skerry (*sgeir*) of the (*na*) beach (*faoilinn*)'.

Sgeir nam Biast [Skye] 'Skerry (*sgeir*) of the (*na-m*) monster (*biast*)'.

Sgeir nan Gabhar [Scarba] 'Skerry (*sgeir*) of the (*na-n*) goat (*gabhar*)'.

Sgeir nan Gall [Highland] 'Skerry (*sgeir*) of the (*na-n*) foreigner (*gall*)'.

Sgeir Thraid [Scalpay] Possibly 'Skerry (*sgeir*) of the beach (*thràghad*, genitive of *tràigh*)'.

sgiath 'wing', 'arm', 'shield'.

Sgiath Bhuidhe [Tayside/Central] '[The] Shield (*sgiath*), yellow (*bhuidhe*)'.

sgìre (also *sgìreachd*) 'parish'; the word is an adaptation of the English *shire*.

sgitheach 'hawthorn'.

sgithich genitive form of *sgitheach*, thus 'of the hawthorn'.

sgoil (Welsh *ysgol*) 'school'; the word is cognate with its English translation.

sgoilt (also *sgoilte*) 'split'.

sgonn 'lump', 'mass', therefore 'mound'.

sgoran diminutive form of *sgorr*, thus 'little peak', 'sharp hill'.

Sgoran Dubh Mór [Highland] 'Sharp hill (*sgoran*), black (*dubh*), big (*mór*)'.

sgorr (also *sgurr*; Welsh *esgair*) 'peak', 'sharp rock', 'mountain', but also 'long escarpment', 'steep ridge'. See separate list of mountain and hill names beginning with this element.

sgurr (also *sgorr*; Welsh *esgair*) 'peak', 'sharp rock', 'mountain', but also 'long escarpment', 'steep ridge'. See separate list of mountain and hill names beginning with this element. This is the more common form in place names.

Shader [Lewis] Probably '[The] House (*setr*, ON)'; the alternative meaning, 'shieling' is geographically less likely.

-shalloch anglicised form of *seileach*: 'willow tree'.

Shanquhar [Grampian] Probably 'Old (*sean*) fortress (*chathair*)'.

-shaw   elided form of either 1) '(personal name)'s haugh [i.e. angle of land enclosed by a river] (*halh*, OE)';
                       or 2) OE *scaga* or ON *skógr*: 'wood', 'thicket', 'grove'.

Shawbost [Lewis] Apparently 'Sea (*saer*, ON) settlement-steading (*bol-stathr*, ON)'.

Shawhead [Dumfries & Galloway] 'Copse (*scaga*, OE) head (Eng)'.

-shealach adapted form of *seileach*: 'willow tree'.

shee elided form of *sìdh* or *sìth*: 'fairy hill', 'place of fairies', but the word also means 'peace'.

-sheen anglicised form of *sìan* or *sìon*: 'storm'.

-shellach anglicised form of *seileach*: 'willow tree'.

-sherrie anglicised form of *searraich*: 'young horses', 'foals'.

Shetland [Shetland] Apparently a corruption of 'Hjalti['s] (personal name, ON) land (ON)' in which an inverted-Swedish-style mutation replaced Hj- by Sh- and the first -l- was lost through the proximity of the second. In some areas, the initial Hj- was instead replaced by Z- (a Gaelic form of mutation; cf pronunciation of the surname Menzies), yielding the dialectal variant Zetland.

Shiel Bridge [Highland] The village is sited where a bridge crosses the River Shiel, which flows down Glen Shiel to the sea at Loch Duich. The meaning of the river name is uncertain.

Shieldaig [Highland (2)] 'Shelter (*skjöldr*, ON) bay (*vágr*, ON)'; both villages are picturesquely sited on their respective bays. One commentator alternatively translates the first element as 'Herring' – although no derivation is evinced.

Shieldhill [Strathclyde] Probably 'Shield (Eng) hill (Eng)': the village is aligned along the side of a ridge.

shotts elided form of OE *sceots*: 'steep slopes'; see **Kirk o' Shotts**.

245

Shotts [Strathclyde] 'Steep slopes (*sceots*, OE)'.

sian (also *sion*) 'storm'.

sidh (also *sith*) 'fairy hill', 'place of fairies', but the word also means 'peace'.

sidhean (also *sithean*) diminutive form of *sidh* (or *sith*), thus 'little fairy hill', 'fairy knoll'.

Sidhean Achadh nan Eun [Highland] 'Fairy knoll (*sidhean*) [of] the place (*achadh*) of the (*na-n*) bird (*eun*)'.

Sidhean Mór [Highland] 'Fairy knoll (*sidhean*), big (*mór*)'.

Sidh Mór [Strathclyde] 'Fairy hill (*sidh*), big (*mór*)': for a fairy hill it is a positive giant, at 1,339 feet (408 m) high.

-sinane elided form of *sineachan*: 'breast'.

Sinclairtown [Fife] District named after the St Clair family, the Earls of Rosslyn, who had their family seat near by at Dysart.

sine genitive form of *sian* or *sion*, thus 'of the storm'.

sineachan 'breast'.

sion (also *sian*) 'storm'.

sionnach 'fox'.

sith (also *sidh*) 'fairy hill', 'place of fairies', but the word also means 'peace'.

sithean (also *sidhean*) diminutive form of *sidh* (or *sith*), thus 'little fairy hill', 'fairy knoll'.

Skail [Highland] 'Shieling (*skáli*, ON)' by the River Naver.

-skaill elided form of ON *skáli*: 'shelter', thus both 'hut' and 'shieling'.

Skaill [Orkney] 'Hut (*skáli*, ON)'.

Skaw [Shetland] Presumably 'Claw (*ská*, ON)', referring to the headland at the foot of which the village stands.

Skeabost [Skye] Said to mean 'Beach (ON) settlement-steading (*bol-stathr*, ON)', but there are several ON personal names that could substitute as convincingly for the first element (e.g. Skeggi and Skyti, both leading to place names in Yorkshire beginning Ske-).

Skelbo [Highland] 'Shell (*skel*, ON) community (*bo*, OScand)': the tiny village is on the shores of a vast tidal bay, Loch Fleet.

Skellister [Shetland] Possibly 'Skalle's (personal name, ON) house (*setr*, ON)'; the first element must be a personal name, even if not this one.

246

Skelpick [Highland] Possibly 'Roaring (*skiallr*, ON) brook (*bekkr*, ON)': the village lies close beside the fast-flowing River Naver as, on the other side, the Skelpick Burn comes down the hillside to meet it.

Skelwick [Orkney] The village takes its name from the bay on which it stands, now called Skel Wick: 'Shell (*skel*, ON) bay (*vík*, ON)'.

sker ON for 'skerry', 'sharp rock projecting from the sea'; the word is cognate with English *skerry*, *scar*, and was adapted in Goidelic Gaelic as *sgeir* and the slightly different-meaning *sgorr* and *sgurr*.

skerry anglicised form of ON *sker*: 'sharp rock projecting from the sea'; the Gaelic adaptation is ordinarily *sgeir*.

Skerryvore See **Sgeir Mhór**.

Skervuile [lighthouse, Sound of Jura] Probably 'Skerry (*sker*, ON) [with a] shingle beach (*mhuil*, Gaelic mutation of ON *möl*)'.

Skibo [Highland] Apparently 'Ship[ping] (*skip*, ON) community (*bo*, OScand)': the village stands on a useful inlet on the Dornoch Firth.

Skipness [Strathclyde] Probably 'Ship[ping] (*skip*, ON) cape (*nes*, ON)'; ironically, the headland (at the northern end of the Kilbrannan Sound) on which the village lies at the foot is now called Skipness Point.

Skirling [Borders] Difficult name: one commentator has suggested 'Rocky (*sker* ON) land (*lann*)', but this is to ignore the fact that the ON element, a noun not an adjective, is used virtually only of rocks at sea; that the second (Gaelic) element refers to enclosed land, land suitable for farming, which is not really the case here; and that there should be no need for a hybrid name in an area mostly filled with English names. If the ON element was replaced by the Gaelic *sgorr*, 'rocky peak', it does not help matters, for there are no rocky peaks here, although the area is one of considerable ups and downs. So perhaps the answer is an all-Scandinavian one, possibly 'Mountain-pass (*skarthr*, ON) land (*land*, ON)', as the A72 finds its way through the village across the mountains. An English name beginning Ski- is distinctly unlikely.

Skye [Skye] Thought to be 'Winged [island] (*sgiathach*)', a description that certainly fits the great peninsulas that stem from the relatively straight and small interior.

slack elided form of ON *slakki*, 'shallow valley', 'depression between two hills'.

Slamannan [Central] The meaning is obscure – perhaps 'Terraces (*slámannan*, literally 'slices')' – but it is certainly not, as one commentator would have us believe, 'Moor (*sliabh*) of Manau', relating to the Stone of Manau (or Manu) that stands in Clackmannan, attractive as that idea may be. For one thing, *sliabh* does not mean 'moor' (which would reasonably fit the geography of the site of the village) but 'mountain' (whereas the village is in a valley between hillsides), and for another Slamannan is way out of sight of the head of the Firth of Forth (supposedly the territory of the highly mythological Manau) 14 miles south of Clackmannan and not convincingly in the same geographical region at all.

-slat elided form of ON *slétta*: 'plain', 'flat field'.

sleac 'place of flat stones'; the word is connected with *clach* and *leac*.

sleamhainn 'slippery'; the word is cognate with English *slimy*.

-sleat elided form of ON *slétta*: 'plain', 'flat field'.

Sleat [Skye] '[The] Plain (*slétta*)': in comparison with much of the rest of the island, this peninsula is definitely a plain.

sléibhe genitive form of *sliabh*, thus 'of the mountain'.

sliabh 'mountain', 'hill-face'; the element is common in Irish place names (generally in the form Slieve) and may be cognate with the word *alp*.

Sliabh Gaoil [Strathclyde] Possibly 'Mountain (*sliabh*) of the foreigners (genitive plural of *gall*)'.

slic genitive form of *sleac*, thus 'of the place of flat stones'.

Sligachan [Skye] 'Shell (*slige*) place (*achadh*)'.

sligeach 'of shells'.

-sligo elided form of *sligeach*: 'of shells'.

slios 'side', 'slope'.

Slios Garbh [Highland] 'Slope (*slios*) of the rough [water] (*garbh*)': the slope overlooks Loch Beoraid.

sloc (also *slochd*) 'deep hollow', 'pit'.

Slochd [Highland] 'Deep hollow (*slochd*)'.

Slockavullin [Strathclyde] Presumably 'Deep hollow (*sloc*) of the mill (*a' mhuilinn*)'.

Sloc nam Ferna [Strathclyde] 'Deep hollow (*sloc*) of the (*na-m*) alder tree (*fearna*)'.

248

sluic genitive form of *sloc*, thus 'of the deep hollow', 'of the pit'.

Sma' Glen [Tayside] 'Small glen (Eng)', named strictly for the tourists who might never go farther north yet wish to say they've been to a glen.

Smailholm [Borders] 'Small (*smael*, OE) community (*ham*, OE)'; the pseudo-Scandinavian corruption of *ham* into *holm* is unusual.

Smallburn [Strathclyde; Grampian] 'Small (*smael*, OE) stream (*burna*, OE)'.

Smoo Cave [Highland] Said, though not very authoritatively, to be a possible corruption of an ON name: 'Rock (*smjuga*, ON) cave (Eng)'.

snàimh genitive form of *snàmh*, thus 'of swimming', 'for swimming in'.

snàimh 'swimming'.

sneachd (also *sneachda*) 'snow'; the word is cognate with its English translation.

Snizort [Skye] 'Sni's (personal name, ON) fjord (*-ort*, corruption of ON *fjordr*)'; the personal name is sometimes quoted as Snei. The name of the village was at one stage corrupted into Sneisport.

Soa [Coll; Tiree; St Kilda] 'Sheep (*sauthr*, ON) island (*ey*, ON)'.

Soay [Inner Hebrides; Harris] 'Sheep (*sauthr*, ON) island (*ey*, ON)'.

sobhal (also *sabhal* and *sodhal*) 'barn'.

soc 'snout'.

socach 'snout', therefore 'projecting land', 'mossy patch between the fork of streams'.

Society [Lothian] Said, though not very authoritatively, to be a possible corruption of 'Sea city (Eng)', because it lies on the shores of the Firth of Forth.

sodhal (also *sabhal* and *sobhal*) 'barn'.

solas 'light' (modern Gaelic).

Solway Firth [Dumfries & Galloway] Probably 'Pillar (*súl*, ON) ford (*vath*, ON), fjord (*fjordr*, ON)'. The ford that marked the border between Scotland and England was once apparently marked on the Scottish side with a pillar-like granite boulder called the Lochmaben Stone. Nonetheless, an acceptable alternative suggestion for the first element is ON *súla*, 'Solan goose', a bird that is common in the area.

Dictionary of Scottish Place Names

Sorbie [Dumfries & Galloway] Apparently 'Muddy ground (*saurr*, ON) community (*byr*, ON)', although the first element might instead be ON *sauthr*, 'sheep'.

Sordale [Highland] Possibly 'Muddy ground (*saurr*, ON) dale (*dalr*, ON)': the village lies close to the River Thurso; the first element might instead be ON *sauthr*, 'sheep'.

sorn 'kiln'.

Sorn [Strathclyde] 'Kiln (*sorn*)'.

soul (also *toul*) elided form of *sobhal*: 'barn'.

Sound [Shetland (2)] 'Channel (*sund*, OScand)': both of these villages lie on the shore of extensive creek-like bays.

Sourhope [Borders] Possibly 'Neck [i.e. col] (*swira*, OE) enclosed valley (*hop*, OE)': this would be an apt description of the terrain.

souter Scots word for '[place of the] shoemaker'.

Southdean [Borders] Apparently a revised (refined) version of 'Souden', for Souden Kirk is close by, as is Souden Law on which stands a hill-fort amid further prehistoric remains. It would seem that the second element is thus the Brythonic equivalent of Goidelic *dùn*, 'hill-fort'; the first element remains obscure. 'Kirk' is 'church' (OE) and 'Law' is 'mound' (OE).

Southend [Strathclyde] '[The] South end (Eng) [of the Mull of Kintyre]'.

Soutra Mains [Lothian] Brythonic name: 'Viewpoint (*sulw*, Brythonic Gaelic) house (*tref*, Brythonic Gaelic), manor (*mains*, Scots)'. There is a tremendous view from the small village, which lies on an ancient Pilgrims' Way.

spardan 'roost'.

Spean Bridge [Highland] '[River] Spean bridge (Eng)': the River Spean flows through Glen Spean to the Great Glen at Loch Lochy. The meaning of the river name is unknown but, if the name is Brythonic Gaelic in origin, may be to do with 'brambles' (cf 'Old Welsh *spian* or the like' quoted by Ekwall as a possible derivation for the place name Speen in Berkshire).

speireag 'sparrowhawk'; the word is a regrettable corruption of the ME *sparhauk*, the forerunner of the present-day English word.

Spey Bay [Grampian] '[River-mouth of the] Spey bay (Eng)': the meaning of the river name is unknown.

250

Speybridge [Highland] '[River] Spey bridge (Eng)': the meaning of the river name is unknown.

spidean strengthened form of *bidean:* 'peak', 'pinnacle', 'jagged tooth'.

spionnaidh 'thorny', 'prickly': the word is cognate with Eng *spiny*.

spittal 'hostelry'; the word represents a Gaelic adaptation of medieval Latin *hospitale*. The Welsh equivalent is *ysbyty*, although this is strictly cognate with English *hospice* (Latin *hospitium*) rather than *hospital*, but in all cases the theme is the hospitality and hospitability of the host. Most places of this name were once remote though on a major cross-country route, very suitable spots for overnight accommodation for travellers.

Spittal [Highland; Lothian] 'Hostelry (Gaelic form of medieval Latin *hospitale*)'.

Spittal of Glenmuick [Grampian] 'Hostelry (Gaelic form of medieval Latin *hospitale*) of Glen Muick': the glen name means 'of the pigs', and the name of the river that flows through it is probably back-formed from it.

Spittal of Glenshee [Tayside] 'Hostelry (Gaelic form of medieval Latin *hospitale*) of Glen Shee': the glen name means 'of the fairy-hill', and the name of the river that flows through it is probably back-formed from it.

spréidh 'cattle'; the word is cognate with, if not adapted from, Latin *praeda*, 'something captured'.

spring OE word that still today means what it meant then: the season, to leap up, and – especially in place names – a source of ground-water. In all cases the root meaning is 'rising up'.

Springfield [Dumfries & Galloway] Village founded in 1791 by a group of weavers, and named in straightforward English, possibly also with passing reference to the name of Sir William Maxwell the landowner's residence 7 miles north-west: it was called Springkell.

Sprouston [Borders] Possibly 'Sprow's (personal name, OE) farmstead (*tun*, OE)': the personal name is attested in other place names in East Anglia.

sràid 'road', 'street'; the word derives ultimately from the Latin *strata*, 'flatly-layered'.

srath 'strath', 'wide, straight valley'; the word is probably cognate with the previous element. The Welsh equivalent is *ystrad*.

Srath na Seilge [Highland] 'Wide valley (*srath*) of the (*na*) hunt (*seilge*)'.

251

Dictionary of Scottish Place Names

sròine genitive form of *sròn*, thus 'of the nose', 'of the point'.

sròn 'nose', thus also 'cape', 'point'.

Sròn a' Chleirich [Tayside] 'Point (*sròn*) of the cleric (genitive of *cleireach*)'; literally, of course, the 'parson's nose'.

Sròn a' Choire Ghairbh [Highland] 'Point (*sròn*) of the corrie (*choire*) of rough [water] (genitive of *garbh*)'.

Sròn a' Geodha Dhuibh [Highland] 'Point (*sròn*) of the ravine (*geodha*), dark (*dhuibh*)'

Sròn Bheag [Highland; Tayside] 'Point (*sròn*), small (*bheag*)'.

Sròn Mhór [Tayside] 'Point (*sròn*), big (*mhór*)'.

Sròn na Carra [Highland] 'Point (*sròn*) of the (*na*) rough ground (*carr*)'.

Sròn na Cleite [Highland] 'Point (*sròn*) of the (*na*) cliffs (*cleite*)'.

sruth 'stream', 'current'.

sruthair diminutive of *sruth*, thus 'little stream', 'streamlet'.

sruthan diminutive of *sruth*, thus 'little stream', 'rivulet', 'rill'.

-sta elided form of ON *stathr*: 'steading', 'farmstead'.

stac 'steep-sided conical hill'; the word is an adapted form of ON *stakkr*.

Staca Leathann [Lewis] 'Conical hill (*stac*), broad (*leathann*)'.

Stac an Aoineidh [Iona] 'Conical hill (*stac*) of the rocky moraine (genitive of *aoineadh*)'.

stack anglicised version of *stac*, itself an adaptation from ON *stakkr*: 'steep-sided conical hill'.

Stack Polly See **Stac Pollaidh.**

Stac Pollaidh [Highland] 'Steep-sided conical hill (*stac*) [of the River] Polly': the river name means 'of pools (*pollaidh*)'. On some maps the name is spelled Stack Polly.

Staffa [Inner Hebrides] 'Staff (*stafr*, ON) island (*ey*, ON)'. The 'staff' is thought to refer collectively to the perpendicular columns of basaltic rock peculiar to Staffa and to the Giant's Causeway in Northern Ireland.

Staffin [Skye] Presumably 'Tree-trunk (*stafn*, ON)', although the element can also mean 'stem of a ship', because the stem of a ship was indeed generally a massive tree-trunk.

252

stain elided form either of   1) ON *steinn*: 'stone';
                or of   2) OE *stan*: 'stone'.

Stane [Strathclyde] Probably 'Stone (*stan*, OE)'.

Stanhope [Border] Presumably 'Stone (*stan*, OE) valley (*hop*, OE)'.

Stanley [Tayside] Village named after Amelia Stanley, fourth daughter of the Earl of Derby, who married the Marquis of Atholl, the local landowner.

Staxigoe [Highland] Probably 'Staki's (personal name, ON) ravine (*gjá*, ON)'; another personal name, Stakkr (ON), is also attested in English place names.

sten elided form either of   1) ON *steinn*: 'stone';
               or of   2) OE *stan*: 'stone'.

Stenhousemuir [Central] 'Stone (OE) house (Eng) moor (Eng)': that is, 'the moor with the stone house' as opposed to 'the stone house on the moor'. The final element was added later than the beginning of the 17th century.

Stenness [Orkney] 'Stone (*steinn*, ON) cape (*nes*, ON)'.

Stenton [Lothian] Presumably 'Stone (*stan*, OE) community (*tun*, OE)': the stone referred to may be the medieval Wool Stone, standing on the village green, once used to weigh the wool at the annual Stenton Fair.

-ster elided form of ON *setr*: 'house', 'residence' or *stathr*: 'steading'.

Stevenston [Strathclyde] 'Steven's (personal name, ME) farmstead (*toun*, ME)': the name is recorded in 1246. 'Steven' means 'wreathed', 'crowned'.

Stewartry [Dumfries & Galloway] District name recording the former juridical stewardship by the Earls of Douglas over the 'stewartry' – not county – of Kirkcudbright.

Stirling [Central] Said by some to mean 'Stream (*sruth*), enclosed land (*lann*)': that is, 'enclosed land by a stream'. This would be quite an apt description, for the city began as a village within a loop of the River Forth.

stob 'point', 'headland', 'mountain'; see separate list of mountain names beginning with this element.

Stonehaven [Grampian] Said by some to be 'Stone (*steinn*, ON) harbour (*höfn*, ON)'; others state definitively that this derivation is quite out of the question because of documented evidence of the name (e.g. Steanhyve, 1629) that 'proves' the name is not ON nor the second element 'haven'. Moreover, locals put the main stress of the word on the second syllable, so the first element may well not even be 'stone'.

Stonehouse [Strathclyde] 'Stone (ME) house (ME)'.

Stoneygate [Grampian] Presumably 'Stony (ME) road (*gate*, ME)'.

Stoneykirk [Dumfries & Galloway] Presumably 'Stony (ME) church (*kirk*, ME)'.

Stonganess [Shetland] Apparently 'Poles (*stonga*, ON) cape (*nes*, ON)'.

stor elided form of ON *stórr*: 'big', 'great', 'dominant'.

Storholm [Shetland] 'Big (*stórr*, ON) island (*holmr*, ON)'.

Stornoway [Lewis] 'Steerage (*stjörn*, ON) bay (*vágr*, ON)'; the first element may, however, be the former name of the river that runs through the town to the sea (the meaning would be the same anyway).

Storr [Skye] 'Dominant (*stórr*, ON)': the wild crags of this 2,360-foot (719 m) mountain easily dominate the scenery for miles round.

stour elided form of ON *stórr*: 'big', 'great', 'dominant'.

Straad [Bute] Possibly 'Wide valley (*srath*)': the village lies on a stream close to its confluence with the sea at the Sound of Bute.

Strachan [Grampian] Apparently 'Little valley (*srathan*, diminutive of *srath*)': the village lies on the shore of the Water of Feugh.

Strachur [Strathclyde] Possibly 'Little valley (*srathair*, diminutive of *srath*)'.

Stranraer [Dumfries & Galloway] 'Point (*sròn*), thick (*reamhar*)': there is no point at Stranraer itself, so perhaps the name refers to the fact that the town lies at the foot of the thicker of the two long peninsulas running northwards and southwards, known as The Rhins.

strath anglicised form of *srath*: 'wide, straight valley'; the Welsh equivalent is *ystrad*. See separate list of valley names beginning with this element.

Strath [Highland] 'Wide valley (*srath*)', although in this case the valley is rather small to be so described.

Strathan [Highland (2)] Presumably 'Little wide valley (diminutive of *srath*)', although in both cases the geography would also suit *sruthan*, 'streamlet'.

Strathaven [Strathclyde] 'Wide valley (*srath*) [of] the Avon [Water]': the river name itself means simply 'river'. The pronunciation is generally cited as 'strayvn' although even this, as pronounced by Scots, sounds like 'streevn' to southerners; moreover, the logical pronunciation – remembering that -th- need not be pronounced at all – would be 'strahvn'.

Strathblane [Strathclyde] 'Wide valley (*srath*) [of] the Blane [Water]': the Blane Water flows through Strath Blane beneath the Strathblane Hills to the villages of Blanefield and Strathblane. The meaning of the river name is, however, obscure.

Strathcarron [Highland] 'Wide valley (*srath*) [of the River] Carron': the River Carron flows from Glen Carron down to the village of Strathcarron and on to the sea-loch Loch Carron. The river name probably derives from the name of the glen or of the sea-loch, and means 'of the cairn'.

Strathdon [Grampian] 'Wide valley (*srath*) [of the River] Don': this is the Don that finally flows to the sea at Aberdeen (q.v.). The river name means simply 'water'.

Strath Kanaird [Highland] Presumably 'Wide valley (*srath*) [of the] head[land] (*ceann*), high (variant of *ard*)'. The River Kanaird flows through Strath Kanaird to the sea at Loch Kanaird, but it is the strath that probably gives its name to both river and loch. What high headland is referred to in the name is unclear.

Strathkinness [Fife] 'Wide valley (*srath*) [of the] Kinness [Burn]': the Kinness Burn flows from minor uplands in the centre of Fife to the sea at St Andrews. The stream name means 'at the head of the cape'.

Strathmiglo [Fife] Said to be 'Wide valley (*srath*) [of the] marsh (*mig*), loch', although that introduces an element not otherwise attested in Scottish place names and presupposes the existence of a loch where none is at present. Cf (as merely an interesting thought) Irish *míchlú*: '[of] evil repute'.

Strathpeffer [Highland] Possibly 'Wide valley (*srath*) [of] bright [water] (a Brythonic element corresponding to modern Welsh *pefr*, which is generally used in connection with water)'. There is no stream or river with the name, but there are chalybeate springs here, and signs of occupation from very ancient times.

Strathrannoch [Highland] Probably 'Wide valley (*srath*), ferny (*raineach*)': the name of the river associated with the valley is likely to have been back-formed from the valley name.

Strathtay [Tayside] 'Wide valley (*srath*) [of the River] Tay': the River Tay flows from Loch Tay through the village of Strathtay all the way down to the sea at the Firth of Tay just east of Perth. The river name means something like 'dark'.

Stroma [Highland] 'Current (*straumr*, ON) island (*ey*, ON)': the island is situated in the strong currents of the Pentland Firth north of John o' Groats.

255

Stromeferry [Highland] '[To] Strome, [the] ferry [landing] (Eng)': from this side of Loch Carron a car-ferry used to run across the loch to Stromemore (q.v.).

Stromemore [Highland] 'Promontory (*sròn*), big (*mór*)': in fact, this is the only side of Loch Carron on which there is any promontory at all at this point. It was from the promontory (formerly called just Strome) that a car-ferry used until the later 1960s to ply back and forth across the loch, the landing on the southern shore being called Stromeferry.

Stromness [Orkney] 'Current (*straumr*, ON) cape (*nes*, ON)'.

Strom Ness [Shetland (2)] 'Current (*straumr*, ON) cape (*nes*, ON)'.

Stronachlachar [Central] 'Promontory (*sròn*) of the stonecutter (*a' chlachar*)'.

Strond [Harris] Probably 'Beach (*strand*, OScand)'.

Strone [Highland (2); Strathclyde] 'Promontory (*sròn*)': the word means literally 'nose', and some of these are more nose-like than others.

Strontian [Highland] 'Promontory (*sròn*) [of] the beacon (*teine*)'. It was after this village, where it was first discovered in 1790, that the mineral strontium was named.

Struan [Highland; Tayside] 'Streamlet (*sruthan*, diminutive of *sruth*)'.

-struther elided form of *sruthair*: 'rill', 'rivulet'.

Struie [Highland] 'At the stream (dative/locative of *sruth*)': from the top of this 1,218 foot (371 m) mountain there is a tremendous view over the Dornoch Firth.

Struy [Highland] 'At the stream (dative/locative of *sruth*)': the village lies close to where the River Farrar meets the River Glass, both thereafter together called the Beauly River.

Stuartfield [Grampian] Village set up in around 1772 by the local landowner, John Burnett, for a weaving community, and named after Burnett's grandfather, Captain John Stuart.

stùc (also *stuchd*) 'peak', 'sharp crag'.

Stuchd an Lochain [Tayside] 'Peak (*stùc*) of the lochs (plural of *loch*)': Loch an Daimh lies to the north, Stronnich Reservoir and Loch Lyon to the south.

Stuckgowan [Strathclyde] Probably 'Sharp crag (*stùc*) of the blacksmith (*gobhainn*)'.

256

subh 'raspberry'.

Succoth [Grampian; Strathclyde] Villages named after one of two places called this in the Bible: the Hebrew meaning is 'thatch huts' (it is a plural).

Sugarloaf [Highland] English name for the distinctive mountain properly called Suilven (q.v.). A sugarloaf was a hard, conical lump of refined sugar from which chunks were broken off to use as necessary for domestic purposes; nobody makes them any more, although they were standard for two centuries before this one. The mountain is whiter in colour than any near it, and in certain lights its pallor emphasizes a relative isolation.

suibhean plural form of *subh*, thus 'raspberries'.

suidhe literally 'seat', thus both 'resting-place' and 'ledge on a hillside'.

suie elided form of *suidhe*: 'seat', 'resting-place', 'ledge'.

Suie Hill [Grampian] Hybrid name: 'Ledge (*suidhe*) hill (Eng)'.

suil 'pillar'.

sùil 'eye'.

Suilven [Highland] Generally rendered 'Pillar (*suil*) mountain (*bheinn*)', although the mountain is also known universally as The Sugarloaf and apparently called by the locals Caisteal Liath (q.v.).

sùla genitive form of *sùil*, thus 'of the eye'.

Sullom [Shetland] Village that takes its name from the sound on which it stands, Sullom Voe: 'Gannets' (*súlan*, ON) bay (*vágr*)'. The first element may alternatively mean 'Solan geese'.

Sunart [Highland] 'Sven['s] (personal name, OScand) fjord (-*art*, corrupt form of ON *fjordr*)'.

sutor (also *souter*) Scots word for '[place of the] shoemaker'.

Swainbost [Lewis] Possibly 'Sven['s] (personal name, OScand) settlement-steading (*bol-stathr*)'.

Swanbister [Orkney] 'Sven['s] (personal name, OScand) settlement-steading (*bol-stathr*)'.

Swarister [Shetland] 'Svarri's (personal name, ON) steading (*stathr*)': the name is attested also in a Lincolnshire place name.

Symington [Strathclyde (2)] 'Simon['s] (personal name, OE) farmstead (*tun*, OE)'.

-syth elided form of *saighead*: 'of arrows'.

Sgorr

Sgorr

The following are mountain names that on the map are preceded by this word:

an Tarmachain [Highland] 'of the ptarmigan (genitive of *tarmachan*)': the final element is thought to derive from a verb meaning 'to settle', and it may be that this is instead the mountain 'of the settler'.

Craobh a' Chaorainn [Highland] Presumably 'Tree (*craobh*), of the rowan (genitive of *caorann*)'.

Gaoithe [Highland] 'Of the winds (genitive plural of *gaoth*)'; the element can alternatively mean 'of the marshes'.

Mór [Grampian (2)] 'Big (*mór*)'.

na Dollaid [Highland] 'of the (*na*) saddle (*dollaid*)'.

na h-Ulaidh [Highland] 'of the (*na*) treasure (*ulaidh*)': the final element is a possible variant of an earlier word meaning 'of the tomb'.

Ruadh [Highland] 'Red-brown (*ruadh*)'.

Sgurr

Sgurr

The following are mountain names that on the map are preceded by this word:

a' Bhealaich Dheirg [Highland] 'of the pass (*bhealaich*), brown (*dheirg*)'.

a' Chaorachain [Highland] Presumably 'of the sheep (*chaorach*)'.

a' Choire-beithe [Highland] Presumably 'of the corrie-birch (*choire-beithe*)'.

a' Choire Ghlais [Highland] 'of the corrie (*choire*), blue-green (*ghlais*)'.

a' Gharaidh [Highland] 'of the hideaway (*gharaidh*)'.

a' Ghlas Leathaid [Highland] 'of the blue-green (*ghlas*) slope (*leathaid*)'.

Alasdair [Skye] Presumably from the personal forename Alasdair, a Scottish version of the original Greek *Alexander*, 'protector of men'.

a' Mhàim [Highland] 'of the mountain pass (genitive of *màm*)': the mountain lies to the south of the long Glen Nevis and to the north of the Lairig Mór, both of which are mountain passes.

an Eilean Ghiubhais [Highland] 'of the island (*eilean*) of the fir tree (*ghiubhais*)'.

an Lochain [Highland] 'of the little loch (diminutive of *loch*)'.

Breac [Highland] 'Speckled (*breac*)'.

Coire Choinnichean [Highland] Possibly '[Of the] Corrie (*coire*), mossy (*choinnich-*)'.

Coire nan Gobhar [Highland] '[Of the] Corrie (*coire*) of the (*na-n*) goat (*gobhar*)'.

Dearg [Mull] 'Red-brown (*dearg*)'.

Dubh [Highland] 'Black (*dubh*)'.

Fhuaran [Highland] 'Of the spring [i.e. source of water] (*fhuarain*)'.

Fuar-thuill [Highland] 'Cold (*fuar*), of the hollow (genitive of *toll*)'.

Ghiubhsachain [Highland] Presumably 'Of the fir tree place (*ghiubhasachadh*)'.

Mór [Highland (3)] 'Big (*mór*)'.

na Bana Mhoraire [Highland] Possibly 'of the (*na*) women (*bana*, plural of *bean*)' of Morar'; some commentators alternatively translate the final element as 'the lord' – though they do not explain how.

na Ciche [Highland] 'of the (*na*) nipple (*cìche*, genitive of *cìoch*)'.

na Coinnich [Skye] Possibly 'of the (*na*) moss (*còinneach*)'.

na h-Iolaire [Skye] 'of the (*na*) eagle (*h-iolaire*)'.

na Lapaich [Highland] 'of the (*na*) bog (genitive of *lapach*)'.

nan Caorach [Skye] 'of the (*na-n*) sheep (*caorach*)'.

nan Eag [Skye] 'of the (*na-n*) notch (*eag*)'.

nan Gillean [Skye; Rhum] 'of the (*na-n*) young men (*gille-an*)'.

na Ruaidhe [Highland] Presumably 'of the (*na*) red-brown [colours] (plural of *ruadh*)'.

Thuilm [Highland] 'Of the island (genitive of *tolm*)': the inference is that there is a distinctive island in one of the rivers leading away from the mountain.

Stob

Stob

The following are mountain names that on the map are preceded by this word:

a' Choin [Central] 'of the dog (genitive of *cù*)'.

a' Ghrianan [Highland] 'of the sunny hillock (*ghrianan*)'.

an Aonaich Mhóir [Tayside] 'of the moor (*aonaich*), big (*mhóir*)'.

an Eas [Strathclyde] 'of the waterfall (*eas*)'.

an t-Sluichd [Grampian] 'of the hollow (genitive of *sloc[hd]*)'.

Binnein [Central] 'of the small peaked crag (genitive of *binnean*)'.

Coir' an Albannaich [Highland/Strathclyde] Possibly 'Corrie (*coire*) of [the people of] Albion': the mountain has long formed a boundary between administrative areas.

Coire a' Chearcaill [Highland] 'Corrie (*coire*) of the circle (genitive of *cearcall*)'.

Coire Easain [Highland (2)] 'Corrie (*coire*) of the waterfalls (genitive plural of *eas*)'.

Dubh [Highland] 'Black (*dubh*)'.

Ghabhar [Highland/Strathclyde] Presumably '[The] Goat (*ghabhar*)'.

Law [Borders] Probably a hybrid name, the second element a translation of the first: 'Hill (*hlaw*, OE)' following the equivalent Gaelic, much like the nearby Dun Rig.

na Cruaiche [Highland/Tayside] 'of the prominent hills (genitive plural of *cruach*)': the prominent hills of A' Chruach here form the border between two Regions.

Strath

Strath

The following are valley names that on the map are preceded by this word:

a' Chràisg [Highland] Presumably 'of the crossing (*chraisg*)'.

Allan [Tayside/Central] '[Of the] Allan [Water]': the river name is pre-Goidelic and found also in England (as Aln and Alne); it is thought to mean 'very white'.

Ardle [Tayside] '[Of the River] Ardle': the meaning of the river name is unclear.

Avon [Grampian] '[Of the River] Avon': the river name itself means 'river'.

Beag [Highland] 'Small (*beag*)': a northern equivalent of 'Sma' Glen'.

Blane [Strathclyde] '[Of the] Blane [Water]': the meaning of the river name is unclear.

Bogie [Grampian] '[of the River] Bogie', although in fact the river name may be back-formed, for the meaning seems to be 'boggy' – which would be appropriate to the Strath.

Cuileannach [Highland] 'Of holly (*cuileannach*)': the name of the river associated with the valley is back-formed from that of the strath.

Carron [Highland (2)] '[Of the River] Carron', although the river in each case might just be named after an associated dale or inhabited area, for the river name means 'of the cairn'.

Glass [Highland] '[Of the River] Glass': the river name is itself a proto-Gaelic word for 'stream'.

Halladale [Highland] '[Of the River] Halladale': the river name means 'holy dale' in ON.

Kanaird [Highland] Presumably '[Of the] Headland (*ceann*), high (*aird*)'. The River Kanaird flows through Strath Kanaird to the sea at Loch Kanaird, but it is the strath that probably gives its name to both river and loch. What high headland is referred to in the name is unclear.

More [Highland] 'Big (*mór*)'.

Nairn [Highland] '[Of the River] Nairn': the river name is an ancient pre-Celtic word suspected to mean 'penetrating' or 'submerging'.

nan Lòn [Highland] 'of the (*na-n*) marsh (*lòn*)'.

262

nan Lùb [Strathclyde] 'of the (*na-n*) bend (*lùb*)'.

of Kildonan [Highland] 'of [the area of] Kildonan': the area name means 'the church of [St] Donan'. See **Kildonan**.

Rannoch [Highland] 'Ferny (*raineach*)': the name of the river associated with the valley is likely to be back-formed from the name of the strath.

Sgitheach [Highland] 'Hawthorn (*sgitheach*)': the name of the river associated with the valley is likely to be back-formed from the name of the strath.

T

taigh 'house' (modern Gaelic): see *tigh*.

Tain [Highland] Ancient Celtic river name, identical with Tyne (of which there are examples in both Scotland and northern England). Like most such names it appears to mean either 'river' or 'water'. The name may also be related to the Old British river name now spelled Teign (modern Welsh *taen*, 'sprinkling'). In Irish, *táin* means 'cattle-drive' – and this may be significant for, despite all the foregoing, there is no major river at Tain.

taing in Shetland, an adapted form of ON *tunga*: 'tongue (of land)'.

tairbeart 'isthmus', 'portage crossing', 'pass used as a short cut over which boats could be carried'.

tairbh genitive form of *tarbh*, thus 'of the bull'.

talamh 'land'.

tallen (also *tallon*) rare anglicised forms of *sàilan*, genitive diminutive of *sàl*, thus 'of the little sea'.

tallon See *tallen*.

Talmine [Highland] Possibly 'Land (*talamh*), smooth (*mìn*)'.

Taransay [Western Isles] Apparently 'Taran's (personal name, ON) island (*ey*, ON)'. But who Taran was is a mystery.

Tarbat Ness [Highland] Presumably a translation doublet: 'Isthmus' (*tairbeart*) ness (*nes*, ON)'. As such, the isthmus is one of the largest in the British Isles, between the Dornoch and Moray Firths.

Tarbert [Strathclyde; Gigha] 'Portage-crossing (*tairbeart*)'. Portage across the Mull of Kintyre at Tarbert would have cut off some 65 miles of sailing. Likewise, portage at Tarbert on Gigha would have saved 6 miles of sailing.

Tarbet [Highland; Strathclyde] 'Portage-crossing (elided form of *tairbeart*)'. There is a very fine, useful portage point at Tarbet [Strathclyde] between Loch Lomond and Loch Long (Arrochar); and another at Tarbet [Highland] between Loch Nevis and Loch Morar.

tarbh 'bull'. The modern Welsh is *tarw*, and both forms of Celtic show an obvious relation to Latin *taurus*. But also cognate are Lithuanian *tauras* 'aurochs', Persian *tauris* 'buffalo' and English *steer* (which has the Germanic forceful s- prefix). See also **Thurso**.

264

tarmachan 'ptarmigan': the English word derives from the Gaelic, its p- is totally intrusive. The Gaelic element seems in turn to relate to a verb meaning 'to settle', and may thus have some connection with Latin *termen*, 'temporary occupation', 'pause', and Greek *terma*, 'limit', 'boundary'.

tarsuinn 'across', 'transverse', 'athwart', 'lying crosswise'.

tartar 'roaring', 'loud noise'.

Tay [Tayside] River name that most commentators liken to the English *Thames*, which derives from an Old British root itself relating to a Sanskrit word meaning 'dark'. Others suggest an ancient Celtic root used as the name of a goddess and meaning 'silent'.

tay rare adapted form of *tigh*: 'house'.

Taynuilt [Strathclyde] 'House (*tigh*) on the stream (*an uillt*)'. The village lies just above where the Nant Water runs into Airds Bay (Loch Etive).

Tayvallich [Strathclyde] 'House (*tigh*) of the pass (*bhealaich*, genitive of *bealach*)'. The village is sited at an excellent portage point between Loch Sween and the Sound of Jura.

teallach 'forge', 'anvil'.

teampull 'church'; the word is evidently cognate with Latin *templum*, 'area within a holy place marked out for auguries', thus 'temple'.

Teanamachar [Western Isles] Possibly 'House (*tigh*) of the (*na*) plain (*machaire*)'.

teanga Gaelic version of ON *tunga*: 'tongue (of land)'.

Teangue [Skye] Presumably 'Tongue [of land] (*teanga*, Gaelic version of ON *tunga*)'.

tearmad (also *tearmann*) 'limit of sanctuary', 'boundary', 'girth'; the word derives from the Latin *termen*, Greek *terma*, both meaning 'occupation within limits'. See also *tarmachan*.

tearmann See *tearmad*.

teine (Welsh *tân*) 'fire', therefore 'beacon'. The word has religious connotations – the Celtic fire god was Tina, a name found, for instance, in the Mayday festival Beltane, on which fires were lit. (Interestingly, the Etruscan god of fire was also Tina.) The English word 'tinder' is possibly – but only possibly – cognate.

Temple [Lothian] 'Temple' because it was the headquarters of the Knights Templar in Scotland until the order was banned there in 1312.

-ter, -ster   elided forms of either   1)   ON *setr*: 'house', 'dwelling';
            or   2)   ON *stathr*: 'steading', 'farmstead'.

Terregles [Dumfries & Galloway] 'House (*tref*, Brythonic Gaelic) of the (*yr*, Brythonic Gaelic) church (*eglwys*, Brythonic Gaelic)'.

Teviot [Borders] River name that is very ancient, related to a Sanskrit root (*tavás*) that means 'to surge'. It would seem to be identical with the river name Tweed – which of course the Teviot joins at Kelso.

Teviothead [Borders] '[River] Teviot (pre-Celtic) head (OE)'. The river name probably means 'surging'.

thairbeart, thairbheart mutated forms of *tairbeart*: 'isthmus', 'portage-crossing'.

Thaneston [Grampian] Presumably 'Thane's (OE) enclosure (*tun*, OE)'. The village is in an area with a number of OE names, although of course 'thane' was also a Scottish title.

thirl elided form of OE *thyrel*: '[with a] hole through [it]'. The hole each side of the nose is thus a nose-thirl – or 'nostril'.

Thirlestane [Borders] 'Hole[d] (*thyrel*, OE) stone (*stan*, OE)'.

thorn 'thorn[y] (OE)'.

thorr mutated form of *torr*: 'small hill'.

Thrumster [Highland] Possibly 'Thormóthr's (personal name, ON) house (*setr*, ON)'. For the personal name cf Thrumpton, Nottinghamshire, and see also **Tormsdale** and **Rubha Thormaid**.

Thundergay [Arran] Apparently 'Hill (*torr*) of the (*na*) wind (*gaoth*)'.

Thurso 'Bull's (*thjor-s*, ON) river (å, ON)'. Many earlier etymologists have ascribed the river on which the city stands to the god Thor, but wrongly. With ON *thjor* 'bull', cf Latin *taur-* and note that English *steer* is also cognate. See *tarbh* above.

tibber elided form of *t[i]obar*: 'well'.

Tibbermore [Tayside] 'Well (*t[i]obar*) of [the Virgin] Mary (*Moire*)'. The spring is in the ancient churchyard.

tiber elided form of *t[i]obar*: 'well'.

tigh 'house'. The word would seem to relate with the Greek *tekt-* 'to make', 'to build' (as in English 'architect'), Latin *tectus* 'covered', *tectum* 'roof', in turn related to English *thatch* (through OE) and even *tile* (through French).

A very basic word, it may in fact derive ultimately from the utterly fundamental root represented in English by 'do', but originally meaning 'to use the hand to do' (as in Latin -*dex*). Cf even Finnish *tehdä* 'to do', 'to make'.

Tigharry [Uist] Probably 'House (*tigh*) [on the] boundary (*airbhe*)', although the second element might alternatively be *àirigh*, 'shieling'.

Tigh-na-Blair [Tayside] 'House (*tigh*) on the (*na*) level clearing (*blàir*)'.

Tighnabruaich [Strathclyde] 'House (*tigh*) of the (*na*) bank (*bruaich*)'. The 'bank' is the shore of the western Kyle of Bute overlooking that island.

Tighvein [Arran] 'House (*tigh*) mountain (*bheinn*)'.

tilla-, *tilli(e)-* elided forms of *tulach*: 'hillock', 'mound'.

Tillicoultry [Central] 'Hillock (*tulach*) [in the] back (*cul*) land (*tir*)'. The town is on the edge of the Ochil Hills, the beginning of the uplands north of the main inhabited areas around the Firth of Forth.

-tilloch elided form of *tulach*: 'hillock'.

tilly- elided form of *tulach*: 'hillock'

Tillyfourie [Grampian] Possibly 'Hillock (*tulach*), grassy (*feòir*, genitive of *feur*)'. The village is in the middle of a lowland area between hills.

Tillygreig [Grampian] Probably 'Hillock (*tulach*) of the rock (*creige*, genitive of *creag*)'.

Tingwall [Shetland] 'Parliament (*thing*, ON) open space (*völlr*, ON)'. The site of the annual *stad-mot* or 'estate-meet' (later corrupted in Welsh to *eisteddfod*) at which laws were promulgated, outlaws banned, and crimes paid for in cash or kind to the victims. And of course the scene afterwards for much merry-making and amorous dalliance.

-tinny elided form of either 1) *teine*: 'fire' and thus 'beacon';
or 2) *t-sionnaich*: 'of the fox'.

Tinwald [Dumfries & Galloway] 'Parliament (*thing*, ON) open space (*völlr*, ON)'. The site of the annual *stad-mot* or 'estate-meet' (later corrupted in Welsh to *eisteddfod*) at which laws were promulgated, outlaws banned, and crimes paid for in cash or kind to the victims. And of course the scene afterwards for much merry-making and amorous dalliance.

tiobar (also *tobar*) 'well'; occasionally – but seldom – 'spring'. The word would seem really to be a version of the almost identical *dobhar* 'water', found more in Brythonic place names (like Dover, Kent).

tioram 'dry'.

tipper- elided form of *t[i]obar*: 'well', 'spring'.

Tipperty [Grampian] 'At the well (*t[i]obar* + dative/locative case-ending)', although the second element might alternatively be 'house (*tigh*)'. The village is close to the Tarty Burn.

tìr 'land', 'country', 'terrain'. Evidently cognate with Latin *terra*, the word nevertheless has few cognates in other Indo-European tongues, but is identical in Welsh.

Tiree [Inner Hebrides] Probably 'Land (*tìr*) [of] corn (*eadha*)', although the second element may be a personal name otherwise unattested. The island was apparently once famous for its grain crops.

tòb in Lewis, a version of ON *òb*: 'bay'; the initial t- probably represents a definite article, thus 'the bay'.

tobar (also *tiobar*) 'well'; occasionally – but seldom – 'spring'. The word would seem really to be a version of the almost identical *dobhar* 'water', found more in Brythonic place names (like Wendover, Buckinghamshire).

tober- adapted form of *t[i]obar*: 'well'.

Tobermory [Mull] 'Well (*t[i]obar*) of [the Virgin] Mary (*Moire*)'.

tobhta 'ruins'. The word is an adaptation of ON *topt*, 'site'.

todhar 'manure', 'dung'.

Tofts Ness [Orkney] Building site's (*topt-s*, ON) ness (*nes*, ON)': the ON second element makes the meaning of the first element 'site' rather than the ON-derived Gaelic meaning 'ruins'.

tòin genitive form of *tòn*, thus 'of the haunch', 'of the buttock'.

toll 'hole', 'hollow'.

Toll Creagach [Highland] 'Hollow (*toll*), craggy (*creagach*)'.

tolm a version of ON *holmr*: 'island'; the initial t- probably represents a definite article, thus 'the island'.

tom- 'mound', 'hump'. This is evidently cognate with Latin *tumu(lu)s* and *tumor*, the basic idea being 'swelling up [and covering]', and thus also cognate with Greek *tumbos* '[burial] mound' and English *tomb*.

Tom a' Chòinich [Highland] 'Mound (*tom*) of the moss (*a' chòin[n]ich*)'.

Tom an t-Saighdear [Strathclyde] 'Mound (*tom*) of the archer ([genitive of] *an t-saighdear*)'.

Tom an t-Suidhe Mhóir [Highland] 'Mound (*tom*) of the shelf (*an suidhe*), big (*mór*)'. The 'mound', rather flattened like a shelf, is actually 1,742 feet (531 m) high – but smaller than all surrounding mountains (near Tomintoul).

Tomatin [Highland] 'Mound (*tom*) [of the] juniper (*aitionn*)'.

Tombreck [Highland] Presumably 'Mound (*tom*), speckled (*breac*)'.

Tomchrasky [Highland] Presumably 'Mound (*tom*) of the crossing (*chraisg*)'. Possibly a crossing of the nearby River Moriston is referred to: the area is one of the few along the river with hard ground on both sides.

Tomintoul [Grampian] 'Mound (*tom*) of the barn (*an t-sabhail*)'.

Tom na Gruagaich [Highland] 'Mound (*tom*) of the (*na*) fairy-woman (genitive of *gruagach*)'.

Tomnahurich [Highland] 'Mound (*tom*) of the (*na*) yew-tree (*h-iubhraich*)'.

Tomnaven [Grampian] 'Mound (*tom*) of the (*na*) mountain (*bheinn*)'.

Tomnavoulin [Grampian] 'Mound (*tom*) of the (*na*) mill (*mhuilinn*)'. The mill would have been a water-mill close to or on the River Livet, perhaps the one used by the nearby whisky distilleries of Glen Livet.

Tomsléibhe [Mull] 'Mound (*tom*) of the mountain (genitive of *sliabh*)'.

tòn 'buttock', 'haunch'.

-ton elided form of OE *tun*: 'enclosure', or ME *toun*: 'farm' therefore 'house' or even 'community'. The origin of the modern English word *town*.

Tonga [Shetland] 'Tongue [of land] (*tunga*, ON)'.

Tongue [Highland] 'Tongue [of land] (*tunga*, ON)'. The actual tongue, projecting into the Kyle of Tongue, has been thoroughly taken over by the road bridge that now spans the Kyle, cutting off what used to be 9 miles of hard road around the shore.

Tòn Mhór [Islay] 'Haunch (*tòn*), big (*mór*)'.

tor- elided form of *torr*: 'small hill'.

Torboll [Highland] 'Thor['s] (personal name, ON) settlement (*bol*, ON)'.

Torbeg [Arran] 'Hill (*torr*), small (*beag*)'. This to distinguish it from Tormore 2½ miles north.

torc 'boar'.

Tore [Highland] 'At the hill (locative of *torr*)'.

Torfichen Hill [Lothian] 'Hill (*torr*) of the magpie (*phigeainn*), hill (OE)'. The final element was evidently added when the meaning of the first two had been forgotten. See also **Torphichen.**

Tormore [Skye; Arran] 'Hill (*torr*), big (*mór*)'. On Arran, this is to distinguish it from Torbeg 2½ miles south.

Tormsdale [Highland] Possibly 'Tormóthr's (personal name, ON) dale (ON)'. Thrumster (q.v.) is about 12 miles east.

Tornagrain [Highland] Possibly 'Hill (*torr*) of the (*na*) sun (*gréine*)'.

Tornahaish [Grampian] Possibly 'Hill (*torr*) of the (*na*) waterfall (*h-easa*)'.

Tornapress [Highland] Probably 'Hill (*torr*) of the (*na*) thicket (*pris*)'.

Torness [Highland] 'Hill (*torr*) of [Loch] Ness', although the village is some 2 miles east of the loch, on the River Farigaig as it descends to the loch.

Tor Ness [Orkney] Probably 'Thor['s] (personal name, ON) ness (ON)'.

Torosay [Inner Hebrides] 'Thor's (personal name, ON) island (*ey*, ON)'.

Torphichen [Lothian] 'Hill (*torr*) of the magpie (*phigheainn*)'.

Torphins [Grampian] Probably 'Hill (*torr*), white (*fionn*)', but the final -s seems to lend some credence to the local story that the place was named after Macbeth's Norse half-brother Thorfinn the Raven-feeder.

torr 'small hill', but also 'castle'. The word really derives from Brythonic Gaelic (as particularly evidenced in Cornwall) but is commonly found in Scotland with Goidelic descriptives.

Torran [Strathclyde; Raasay] Presumably 'Little hill (diminutive of *torr*)'.

Torridon [Highland] A problematical name for which no one has found a satisfactory explanation. Some commentators prefer to think that the element *tairbeart* 'isthmus', 'portage-crossing' is somehow involved – not impossible if the -b- is mutated while both the t's are not. But, there is no isthmus of any significance there, nor any short-cut to justify the effort of a portage. Might I in turn suggest that the derivation could be 'Hill (*torr*) [of] Aidan (personal name)' or some similar personal ascription. Aidan was a 7th-century Irish saint – a one-time abbot of Lindisfarne and the hero of [St] Columba of Lismore – whose name was common in Celtic lands for centuries thereafter: his name means 'flame' or 'spark'.

270

Torrisdale [Highland; Strathclyde] 'Thor's (personal name, ON) dale (ON)'.

Torr Meadhonach [Arran] 'Hill (*torr*) in the middle (*meadhonach*)'. The 'hill' is a major height in the ridge along the centre of the north-eastern tip of Arran.

Torry [Grampian] 'At the hill (locative of *torr*)'.

Torrylinn [Arran] 'At the hill (locative of *torr*), the pool (*linn*)'.

Torsa [Luing] Presumably 'Thor's (personal name, ON) island (*ey*, ON)'.

Torvaig [Skye] 'Hill (*torr*) bay (*bhaig*, loan-word from ME)' – very much an equivalent of the Torbay in Devon, only not so full of schools-of-English pupils.

tot- rare elided form of   1) *tuatha*: '[the] people [of]';
                or   2) *tuath*: 'north'.

Tough [Grampian] 'Hillock (*tulach*)'. What a horrible corruption!

-toul elided form of *t-sabhail*: 'of the barn'.

-toun adapted form of OE *tun*: 'enclosure', or ME *toun*: 'farm', therefore 'house' and even 'community'. The origin of the English word *town*.

tra- elided form of the Brythonic Gaelic *tref*: 'settlement', 'house'.

-trae adapted form of *tràigh*: 'sands', especially on the sea-shore.

tràghad variant genitive form of *tràigh*, thus 'of the sands', 'of the beach'.

tràigh 'sands', particularly on the sea-shore and so tidal. The word is cognate with the Welsh *traeth*.

Tràigh Mhór [Barra] 'Sands (*tràigh*), big (*mhór*)'. So wide is the beach here that it is used as the airport.

-traive adapted form of *tràigh*: 'sands', especially on the sea-shore.

Tranent [Lothian] Apparently 'Settlement (*tref*, Brythonic Gaelic) [on] the (*yr*, Brythonic Gaelic) streams (*neint*, Brythonic Gaelic, plural of *nant*)'.

Traprain [Lothian] Apparently 'Settlement (*tref*, Brythonic Gaelic), tree (*pren*, Brythonic Gaelic)'.

trì 'three'. A common Indo-European word.

trian 'third'.

Trilleachan Presumably 'Three (*trì*) stones (plural of *leac*)'.

Triuirebheinn [Uist] Presumably 'Three (*tri*) [arms] of the grey (*uidhre*, genitive of *odhar*) mountain (*bheinn*)'. The mountain has an overall V-shape, thus presenting three points.

Troon [Strathclyde] 'Cape (*trwyn*, Brythonic Gaelic)'. And indeed there is a fine cape at Troon, a lighthouse at its tip. However, some commentators arrive at the same meaning via a Goidelic derivation: *an t-sròn*, 'the nose'.

Trossachs, The [Central] Apparently 'The (*na*) cross-hills (*troiseachan*)', although in previous decades some commentators used to derive the name from an adjective meaning 'bristly'. But the name is of late derivation anyway (1790s), and may even be a direct transference (and translation) of the Welsh place-name *Trawsfynydd* [Gwynedd].

-try elided form of *tràigh*: 'sands', especially on the sea-shore.

tuath 'north'.

tuatha 'people', 'nation'; also 'laity'.

tuill genitive form of *toll*, thus 'of the hole', 'of the hollow'.

tuilm genitive form of *tolm*, thus 'of the island'.

tuim genitive form of *tom*, thus 'of the mound', 'of the hump'.

tuirc genitive form of *torc*, thus 'of the boar'.

tulach 'hillock', 'knoll', 'hard ground amid marshy area'.

tulla-, tulli- elided forms of *tulach*: 'hillock'.

Tullibody [Central] 'Hillock (*tulach*) hut (*both*)'.

Tullich [Strathclyde] 'Hillock (*tulach*)'.

tulloch adapted form of *tulach*: 'hillock'.

Tulloch [Grampian; Highland, near Dingwall] 'Hillock (*tulach*)'.

Tulloch [Highland, in Glen Spean] Probably 'Hard ground amid marshy area (*tulach*)'.

Tullochgorum [Highland] 'Hillock (*tulach*), blue (*gorm*)'.

tully elided form of *tulach*: 'hillock'.

Tullybothy Craigs [Fife] 'Hillock (*tulach*) hut (*both*) stacks (*creag-s*, English ending on a primarily Brythonic Gaelic word)'. The stacks are sea-girt rocks off Fife Ness. Cf **Tullibody**.

Tunga [Lewis] 'Tongue (of land)' from ON *tunga*.

272

tunnag 'duck'.

Turk [Central] River name that actually means 'boar' but is commonly applied to rivers that are deep and may become subterranean. Another example is found in Gloucestershire. In any case, the river here is now known more commonly as the Finglas Water – although it still flows under the Brig o' Turk.

-turk elided form of *tuirc*, genitive of *torc*, thus 'of the boar'.

Turnberry [Strathclyde] Hybrid name: 'Tower (*turn*, ON) fort (*burh*, OE)'. The name presumably refers to the ruins of an ancient castle that stand here, a castle in which Robert the Bruce is said to have been born. True or not, he is historically associated with the area.

Tweed [Borders] It seems very probable that this river name is identical with *Teviot*, a name that is very ancient and is related to a Sanskrit root (*tavás*) that means 'to surge'. The Tweed actually is joined by the Teviot at Kelso.

Tweeddale [Borders] '[River] Tweed (pre-Celtic) dale (ON/OE)'.

-ty either 1) a dative/locative case-ending, thus 'at the . . . ';
or 2) an elided form of *tigh*: 'house'.

Tyndrum [Central] 'House (*tigh*) on the ridge (*an druim*)'.

Tynehead '[Water of] Tyne (ancient Celtic) head (OE)'. The river name is one of the old British ones, identical with Tain (of which there is more than one in Scotland). Like most such names it appears to mean either 'river' or 'water'. The name may also be related to the Old British river name now spelled Teign (modern Welsh *taen*, 'sprinkling').

Tynron [Dumfries & Galloway] Presumably 'House (*tigh*) of the (*na*) point (*sròn*)'.

tyr-, -tyre adapted forms of *tìr*: 'land', 'country'.

U

uabhais genitive form of *uabhas*, thus 'of terror'.

uabhas 'terror'.

uabhasach 'terrible'; as adverb 'awfully' (modern Gaelic).

uachdar 'upper [part]', 'top'. This element is frequently elided in place names to *auchter-* or *ochter*. The opposite is *ìochdar*, q.v.

uachtar adapted form of *uachdar*: 'upper [part]', 'top'.

uaighe rare adapted form of *uamh*: 'cave'.

uaime rare adapted form of *uaine*: 'green'.

uaine 'green'.

uamh 'cave'.

Uamh an Tartair [Highland] 'Cave (*uamh*) of the roaring (genitive of *tartar*)': roaring water, that is, across an 80-foot (25-m) chasm.

Uamh Beag [Central/Tayside] 'Cave (*uamh*), small (*beag*)' – but it is the name of a mountain 2,181 feet (665 m) high!

uchd 'breast', thus 'rounded slope'.

Uchd a' Chlarsair [Tayside] 'Rounded slope (*uchd*) of the harpist (genitive of *clarsar*)'.

uchdan diminutive of *uchd*, thus 'little breast', thus 'short, steep bank'.

Uddingston [Strathclyde] 'Oda's people's (*Od-ingas*, OE) farmstead (*tun*, OE)'. An early form (of 1296) is *Odistoun*, just 'Oda's farmstead' – take your pick.

udlamain 'gloomy'.

uidh 'isthmus', 'ford', 'tidal movement of water'. The word is an adaptation of the ON *eith* and thus cognate with English *ait*, *eyot*, alternatives that refer to tidal islands. Cf also ON *vath*, English *wade*.

uidhir, *uidhre* genitive forms of *odhar*: 'grey', 'dun-coloured'.

uidhre See *uidhir*.

ùig 'bay', 'shelter', 'creek'; also 'hollow'. The word is an adaptation of the ON *vík*, and is cognate with English *bight*, whereas *bay* corresponds to the identically-meaning ON *vágr*.

274

Uig [Highland; Skye; Lewis] 'Bay (*vík*, ON)'.

Uigshader [Skye] 'Bay (*vík*, ON) house (*setr*, ON)', although the little community is actually some distance from the sea.

uinneag 'window'.

uinneige genitive form of *uinneag*, thus 'of the window'.

uinseann 'ash tree'.

uird genitive form of *ord*: 'rounded hill' (originally 'hammer').

uisge 'water' (cf *easg* 'marsh', 'swamp'). This word, as the first half of the expression 'water of life', is the derivation of the word 'whisk(e)y'. It is probably cognate also with the Eng *water* and thus the Russian *vod(k)a*, and is found as a river name in England (Usk, Isca, etc.) and in other European countries.

Uisgnaval Mór [Harris] Presumably 'Water (*uisge*) of the (*na*) bare summit (*mhaol*), big (*mór*)'.

uisk(e) elided form of *uisge*, 'water'.

uladh early Goidelic variant of *ealadh*: 'tombs', 'graves'.

ulaidh 'treasure', possibly because – as in form a genitive of *uladh* – treasure is something 'of the tomb', 'of the grave' (cf grave goods and burial treasures of Viking communities).

Ulbster [Highland] 'Olaf's (personal name, ON) settlement-steading (*bol-stathr*, ON)'. For the meaning of 'Olaf' see **Ullapool** below.

Ullapool [Highland] 'Olaf's (personal name, ON) settlement (*bol*, ON; present Swedish -*böle*)'. Most commentators want to make this 'Olaf's settlement-steading (*bol-stathr*)' but this double element most often appears in corrupt form as '-bster', showing that the first element in that case is pretty well elided altogether. Moreover there is an Ulbster in Caithness [see above] (and cf Ulster in Viking Ireland). For the element 'bol' in English, cf Bolton 'Dwelling (*bol[d]*, OE) enclosure (*tun*, OE)'. 'Olaf' is a corrupt form of *An-leifr:* 'Forefathers' inheritance', which is the origin of the English *Oliver*; it is not the same as *Ulf* 'Wolf', although in Viking times pronounced almost identically.

Ulva [Western Isles] 'Wolf (*ulf[r]*, ON) island (*ey*, ON)': the first element may well be a personal name of identical meaning.

Unapool [Highland] 'Uni's (personal name, ON) settlement (*bol*, ON; present Swedish *böle*)'.

ùr 'new' (modern Gaelic).

-urie elided form of *uidhre*, the genitive of *odhar*: 'grey', 'dun-coloured'.

Urquhart [Highland; Grampian] 'Near (*ar*, Brythonic Gaelic) the thicket (*cardden*, Brythonic Gaelic)'. The slopes above Loch Ness behind Urquhart Castle are still thickly wooded. The second element is indeed related to the English words 'garden', 'court', 'yard' and 'earth' – all ultimately deriving from one root – but for one commentator to suggest that this Brythonic two-element form is the origin of the English *orchard* is misguided: that derives instead from a tautological coupling of two ancestors of the above four English forms.

ùruisg 'goblin', 'leprechaun', 'monster'.

V

-vachar mutated form of the genitive of *m(h)achair*, thus 'of the plain'.

vagh mutated form of *bàgh*, itself an adaptation of the Eng *bay* or the ON *vágr*: 'bay'.

vaich mutated and elided form of *bàthaich*: literally 'cow-house', thus 'byre'.

-vaig mutated form of the genitive of *bágh* 'bay', itself deriving from the Eng *bay* or ON *vágr*: 'bay'.

-val mutated form of *m(h)eall*: 'rounded hill'. Cognate with Eng *fell*.

-van(n)ich mutated form of *m(h)anach:* 'monk'. Ultimately derived from late Greek *monachos* 'solitary', 'recluse', thus Lat *monachus* 'monk'.

-vannie mutated form of *m(h)eannidh*, related to *monadh*: 'mountain'. Cf perhaps *beinn*. Cognate with Lat *mont-* 'mountain'.

-vat in Harris and Lewis, elided form of ON *vatn*: 'water'.

Vatersay [Western Isles] 'Glove's (*vottr-s*, ON) island (*ey*, ON)': in view of the rather strange first element, perhaps 'Glove' was a nickname for someone who always wore them.

Vatten [Skye] Possibly 'Water (*vatn*, ON)'. It is on the coast and has a very tidal bay.

veag mutated feminine form of *beag*: 'little'.

ven either 1) mutated and elided form of *beinn*: 'mount(ain)';
    or 2) less commonly, elided form of *fionn*: 'white', thus 'fair', 'clear', thus 'holy', 'sacred'.

-vern anglicised form of *bhearn*: 'gap'.

voe elided form of ON *vágr*: 'bay'.

Voe [Shetland] 'Bay (*vágr*, ON)'.

voulin mutated form of *m(h)uilinn*, genitive of *muileann*, thus 'of the mill'.

vrackie anglicised form of either 1) *bhràghad*: 'of the upper part';
    or 2) *bhreac*: 'speckled', thus, as a noun, 'trout'.

277

-vreckan   mutated form of either   1) the personal name Brecon or Brychan (for further information, see **Brechin**);

or   2) *bhrocain*, genitive form of *brochan*, thus 'of the rough ground'.

-vruaich mutated form of *b(h)ruaich*, genitive of *bruthach*, thus 'of the bank', 'of the brink'.

vuilinn mutated form of *m(h)uilinn*, genitive of *muileann*, thus 'of the mill'.

vullin mut(il)ated form of *m(h)uilinn*, genitive of *muileann*, thus 'of the mill'.

-wald (also **-wall**) elided form of ON *völlr*: 'plain', 'open space'. E.g. Tin-wald [Dumfries & Galloway].

Walkerburn [Borders] 'Wauker['s] (Scots) stream (*burn*, ME)'. A *wauker* is lowland Scots for a fuller of cloth: there was a wool mill here from the 1850s. The 'burn' is the River Tweed, on which the village stands.

-wall elided form of 1) ON *völlr*: 'plain', 'open space'. E.g. Ding-wall [Highland];

or 2) ON *vágr*: 'bay', 'shelter'. E.g. Kirk-wall [Orkney].

Wallacetown [Strathclyde] 'Town' (actually a village) laid out around 1760 by Sir Thomas Wallace of Craigie.

Wanlockhead [Dumfries & Galloway] 'White (*gwyn*, Brythonic Gaelic) flat stone (*llech*, Brythonic Gaelic) head (ME)'. High up in the Lowther Hills, the village is at the head of a stream that runs into a tributary of the River Nith. The third element of the place name was evidently added much later.

Waterloo [Strathclyde; Tayside; Skye] These places were named in the euphoria that followed Napoleon's defeat, especially by returning soldiers. (More than 1,500 men from Skye fought in the battle.) Examples also exist in England – in Norfolk, Dorset and Merseyside. (The name actually is Dutch for 'watery place'.)

-wath 'ford' in OScand; cognate with ON *eith*, English *wade*.

Watten [Highland] 'Water (*vatn*, ON)'. Watten is in a very fertile area of Caithness, on Loch Watten, surrounded by ON names and (thus) connected to Wick by the Wick River.

-way either 1) (also **-wall**) on Viking coasts, elided form of ON *vágr*: 'bay', 'shelter'. E.g. Storno-way [Lewis];

2) elided/mutated form of *mhaigh*: 'plain'. E.g. Allo-way;

or 3) very corrupt form of *achadh*: 'field', 'place'. E.g. Kenn-oway.

weem rare elided form of *uaine*: 'green'.

-weem elided form of *uamh*: 'cave'.

Dictionary of Scottish Place Names

Weem [Tayside] 'Cave (*uamh*)'.

Wemyss [Fife] 'Caves (*uamh*-s)'. There are indeed many coastal caves here. The pronunciation is 'weems'.

Westerdale [Highland] 'West (*vestr*, ON) dale (*dalr*, ON)'. This is a fertile area, more westerly than most in Caithness, around the River Thurso.

Westerkirk [Dumfries & Galloway] 'West (*vestr*, ON) church (*kirkja*, ON)'.

Westerwick [Shetland] 'West (*vestr*, ON) bay (*vík*, ON)'. The tiny village overlooks an enclosed bay west of Skelda Ness. The name of the bay is now spelled Wester Wick.

Westray [Orkney] 'West (*vestr*, ON) island (*ey*, ON)'. Not by any means the most westerly island of the Orkney group – in fact the most north-westerly – but that is because the Viking convention regarding the points of the compass was at a 45-degree difference from the present bearings.

Wethersta [Shetland] Presumably 'Ram (*vethr*, ON) farmstead (*stathr*, ON)'.

Whalsay [Shetland] 'Whale's (*hval*-s, ON) island (*ey*, ON)'.

whaup 'curlew'.

Whitburn [Lothian] 'White (*hwit*, OE) stream (*burna*, OE)'. Whitburn is three miles west of Blackburn and four miles north of Greenburn.

Whitekirk [Lothian] 'White (*hwit*, OE) church (*kirk*, ME)'. The church itself was first built in the 15th century.

Whithorn [Dumfries & Galloway] 'White (*hwit*, OE) house (*erne*, OE)'. Called Candida Casa ('White House' in Latin) from its foundation in 397 by St Ninian, this was a leading Scottish theological centre for centuries.

Wick [Highland] 'Bay (*vík*, ON)'.

Wig, The [Dumfries & Galloway] 'The Bay (*uig*, adaptation of ON *vík*)'.

Wigtown [Dumfries & Galloway] Probably 'Farm (*wic*, OE) enclosure (*tun*, OE)'.

Wormit [Fife] 'Snake (*[w]orm*, ON), the (-*et*, ON)'.

Wrath 'Turning[-point]', deriving from the ON verb *hverfa* 'to turn'. It was round this westerly cape that the Viking sailors turned to go south, down to the Western Isles. Sailing ships still *warp* round in modern English.

wyvis anglicized form of *uabhais*, genitive of *uabhas*, thus 'of terror'.

Yarrow [Borders] 'Rough (a corruption of *garbh*)'. As a river name it is found also in England (Yar, Yare) and France (Garonne).

Yell [Shetland] 'Barren (*geldr*, ON)'.

yet(t) phonetically spelled form of OE *geat*: 'gate', but equally 'path', 'going', and thus 'pass'.

Yetholm [Borders] 'Pass (*geat*, OE) village (*ham*, OE [not *holm* 'island'])'.

Yetts o' Muckart [Tayside] Muckart – 'Pig's (*muice*) height (*ard*)' – is the area name to which the Yetts ('gates') provide an entrance. The Pool of Muckart is near by.

Yoker [Strathclyde] 'Lower [ground] (*iochdar*)'.

Z

Zetland [Shetland] Dialectal variant of the name Shetland, deriving ultimately from 'Hjalti['s] (personal name, ON) land (ON)'. See **Shetland**.

Zoar [Tayside] Apparently transferred from the Biblical village name in the 19th century by some Nonconformist community. The Hebrew name means 'small (*zo'ar*, Heb)' and relates to a settlement not far from Sodom and Gomorrah.